Warm Hands in Cold Age

Gender and Aging

Edited by
Nancy Folbre, Lois B. Shaw, and
Agneta Stark

Routledge
Taylor & Francis Group

LONDON AND NEW YORK

First published 2007 by Routledge
2 Park Square, Milton Park, Abingdon, Oxon OX14 4RN

Simultaneously published in the USA and Canada
by Routledge
270 Madison Ave, New York, NY 10016

Routledge is an imprint of the Taylor & Francis Group, an informa business

© 2007 IAFFE

Typeset in Times by KnowledgeWorks Global Limited, Southampton, Hampshire, UK
Printed and bound in Great Britain by MPG Books Ltd, Bodmin, Cornwall.

British Library Cataloguing in Publication Data
A catalogue record for this book is available from the British Library

Library of Congress Cataloging in Publication Data
A catalogue record for this book has been requested

ISBN 10: 0-415-39676-x (hbk)
ISBN 10: 0-415-41559-4 (pbk)
ISBN 13: 978-0-415-39676-9 (hbk)
ISBN 13: 978-0-415-41559-0 (pbk)

CONTENTS

EXPLORATIONS

Warm Hands in Cold Age

Public discussion of population aging usually focuses on the financial
͡ ͡ ͡ n that increasingly elderly populations will impose on younger
͡ ͡ ͡ tions. Scholars give much less attention to who does the actual work
͡ ͡ day-to-day care for those no longer able to care for themselves, and
although women are the majority among the elderly, little is heard about
gender differences in economic resources or the need for care. This volume
is dedicated to giving gender — and a full range of social and cultural
differences — their rightful place in these discussions. The authors in the
following pages address, among other issues:

* the worldwide dilemmas of eldercare;
* the structure of income and care provisions for older populations;
* the role of family, marital status, and class in these provisions;
* the impact of polices affecting retirement age;
* and the role of social insurance in preventing poverty among elderly
  women.

The essays included address these topics in a myriad of geographical
contexts, including South Africa, the US, Palestine, Australia, South Korea,
Spain, Germany, and Sweden. The concerns highlighted here also remind us
that whether through individual families or social insurance, through family
caregivers or paid help, the oldest generation will continue to depend on
working age adults for its well-being.

This book was previously published as a special issue of *Feminist Economics*.

Nancy Folbre is Professor of Economics at the University of Massachusetts
at Amherst and an Associate Editor of *Feminist Economics*. Her research
focuses on non-market and care work.

Lois B. Shaw is Senior Consulting Economist at the Institute for Women's
Policy Research in Washington, DC, where she advises on social insurance,
pensions, and other issues of concern to women.

Agneta Stark has been President of Dalarna University in Sweden since
2004. Her research interests focus on the concept of work and international
comparisons of paid and unpaid work. She is an Associate Editor of *Feminist
Economics*.

This book was previously published as a special issue of *Feminist Economics,* the official journal of the International Association for Feminist Economics (IAFFE). All contributions have been subjected to the journal's rigorous peer review process and comply with the journal's editorial policies, as overseen by the editor, Diana Strassmann, and the journal's editorial team, including the associate editors, the editorial board, numerous volunteer reviewers, and the journal's in-house editorial staff and freelance style editors. The special issue and book have been made possible by the generous financial support of Rice University and the Swedish International Development Agency.

SUSAN C. EATON
1957–2003

In Memoriam

Susan Eaton's long fight with leukemia ended on December 30, 2003, about six months after submitting her article "Eldercare in the United States: Inadequate, Inequitable, but Not a Lost Cause" to *Feminist Economics*. With the encouragement of her friends and colleagues and the agreement of her husband, Marshall Ganz, the editorial team decided to include this article in the volume on gender and aging, making only minor editorial revisions.

Susan's life and work deserve recognition here. Before becoming Assistant Professor of Public Policy at the John F. Kennedy School of Government at Harvard University, she spent twelve years working for the Service Employees International Union as an international representative, organizer, negotiator, researcher, and eventually a senior manager.

Susan's activist concerns inspired her research showing the benefits of improved working conditions for caregivers, which enjoyed considerable scholarly recognition. In the summer of 2003 she received a Robert Woods Johnson Award to study the links between the quality of work and the quality of care in the nursing home industry. Her article "Beyond Unloving Care: Linking Nursing Home Quality and Working Conditions" was a co-winner of the 1996 Margaret Clark award of the Institute of Gerontology.

As David Ellwood, Dean of the Kennedy School, put it, "She demonstrated that nursing homes and hospitals could both do better by their workers and improve the quality of care simply with better management practices. Much of her work spoke to the dignity that both caregivers and patients seek and deserve. This generalizable lesson seems so terribly important in this increasingly marketized era."

Her committed voice will be missed, but the spirit of her scholarship and activism will continue to inspire those working to improve the lives of children, women, and men.

INTRODUCTION:
GENDER AND AGING

Nancy Folbre, Lois B. Shaw, and Agneta Stark

Public discussion of population aging is usually focused on the financial burden that increasingly elderly populations will impose on younger generations. In the developed world, arguments arise over the role of private saving for retirement versus public social insurance systems. Scholars give much less attention to who does the actual work of day-to-day care for those no longer able to care for themselves. Although women are the majority among the elderly, little is heard about gender differences in economic resources or the need for care. This volume is dedicated to giving gender its rightful place in these discussions.

Feminist economists have been in the forefront of research on caring work. Since public discussions of aging tend to neglect this aspect, it is fitting that this volume of *Feminist Economics* begins with Agneta Stark's overview of the worldwide dilemmas of eldercare today. As Stark shows, the actual work of caring is still done primarily by women, even though a larger portion of care than before is paid rather than unpaid. The role of the state in supporting caregiving varies widely, as examples from three European countries show. Susan Eaton describes the inadequacy of eldercare provision in the United States, where most government funding goes to privately run nursing homes, and the quality of care is often not adequately monitored. Both Stark and Eaton advocate new ways of organizing care and an increased role in caregiving by men.

One approach to this issue is the structure of income provision for older populations. Outside the developed world, economic resources for the elderly are provided primarily by families. Jennifer Olmsted describes the case of Palestine where, as in most of the Arab world, a strong patriarchal contract gives older women a claim on family resources through their sons or sometimes brothers. Women who do not have children are vulnerable to poverty in old age. This system is tending to weaken as families become smaller and high rates of unemployment make support less certain.

South Africa, as described by Justine Burns, Malcolm Keswell, and Murray Leibbrandt, is unusual for the developing world in having a generous means-tested social pension in which about three-quarters of the participants are women. Although the system has reduced poverty among the elderly, the pensions appear to be widely shared among other family members, and unemployed children often move in with elderly parents or send their children to live with grandparents in order to benefit from the pension. This is an aspect of social insurance systems that has not received much attention. Might social insurance for the elderly also contribute to the well-being of younger family members in wealthy countries as well, especially countries like the US that have inadequate safety nets for young families and children?

In rich countries, public attention has been focusing on shifting more responsibility for economic support of the elderly from social insurance to private investment. Some countries with well-established public and private pension systems have recently shifted toward privatization. Therese Jefferson and Alison Preston describe the disadvantages for women when such a change was made in Australia. Women should regard greater dependence on markets for retirement income with skepticism because women tend to live longer, while earning less than men.

The US is currently debating changes in its Social Security system. One proposal to put the system on a firmer financial basis is to increase the age of eligibility for benefits, which would in effect be a benefit reduction. Carole Greene argues that this proposal would have an especially adverse effect on African Americans and other minorities because they tend to hold physically demanding jobs that make them less able to work at older ages. Madonna Harrington Meyer, Douglas A. Wolf, and Christine L. Himes show that the majority of women in the US currently receive Social Security benefits based on marital status rather than their own earnings. However, far fewer minority women qualify for spousal or survivor benefits, and the system thus favors women in stable marriages – predominantly white women. Unfortunately, in the present political climate, the most likely change will be toward privatization, which is likely to be harmful for both minorities and all but the wealthiest women.

A concluding report section offers cross-national contrasts of different kinds of support systems for the elderly. Timothy Smeeding and Susanna

Sandström show that a social insurance system with an adequate minimum benefit does the best job of avoiding poverty among elderly women. Lois Shaw and Sunhwa Lee demonstrate that elderly women in the US depend heavily on the Social Security system, which nevertheless leaves all too many of them in poverty. Finally, Kyunghee Chung considers the problems in a rapidly developing country with a newly instituted public pension system that covers few of the elderly at present. In South Korea, families provide most of the support for elderly members, including both financial support and daily care when needed.

This final report brings all the strands of aging together: economic resources, health and care needs, and actual care provision. This kind of inventory of resources and needs can serve to remind us that whether through individual families or social insurance, through family caregivers or paid help, the oldest generation will continue to depend on adults of working age for its well-being.

Nancy Folbre, Department of Economics, University of Massachusetts,
Amherst, MA 01003, USA
e-mail: folbre@econs.umass.edu

Lois B. Shaw, Institute for Women's Policy Research,
403 Russell Avenue, Suite 804, Gaithersburg, MD 20877, USA
e-mail: lbshaw@his.com

Agneta Stark, Dalarna University, SE-791 88 Falun, Sweden
e-mail: Agneta.Stark@du.se

ACKNOWLEDGMENTS

This volume has been a collaborative effort by the editors, the journal *Feminist Economics*, and the International Association for Feminist Economics. The journal's rigorous reviewing process, aided by the thoughtful and unpaid work of many reviewers, has greatly contributed to the quality of this volume. Diana Strassmann, the journal's editor, assembled the editorial team, helped write the funding proposal, and provided superb managerial oversight. The editorial staff of *Feminist Economics*, particularly Raj Mankad, Cheryl Morehead, Mónica Parle, and Eva Chan, and the journal's graduate fellows, Anne Dayton, Jill Delsigne, and Victoria Ford, assisted with a myriad of important tasks, including checking that each article conformed to the journal's editorial policies and was clear to the journal's diverse and interdisciplinary audience. Special thanks also to the journal's style editors, Polly Koch and Polly Morrice. Finally, we thank Rice University and the Swedish International Development Agency for their financial support.

WARM HANDS IN COLD AGE – ON THE NEED OF A NEW WORLD ORDER OF CARE

Agneta Stark

The world is aging. More people grow old than ever before, and the old form a greater proportion of the population in almost all countries. Care for the elderly must be expanded quickly to cope with increasing needs. However, suggestions and policy debates regarding care for old and very old people often focus on financial issues. The organization and distribution of the practical work of caring for the elderly are rarely seen as central themes. This article focuses on practical care activities.

Today, care for the elderly is deeply gendered, both in terms of the care that aging women and men receive and regarding those who perform care work and their working conditions. Women provide both unpaid and paid care work, often with great skill and creativity, and often with much satisfaction to the care worker herself and to the person needing care. But unacceptable situations also exist: overworked carers who receive little emotional or financial support, carers who lack skill and motivation, and old people whose care needs are largely unmet.

For many women, the unpaid care they provide for aging husbands and other relatives may actually decrease the amount or quality of care that they can expect in their old age. This is especially true in countries with pension systems that closely connect benefits to years in paid work. The ability of these women – who may have given up years of salaried employment to tend to a spouse or relative – to pay for their own care needs in old age will be small, and they will need to depend on the existence and willingness of relatives to perform or pay for their care. In a sense, these retired caregivers will be competing for caregivers with the majority of men, who depend on women for both unpaid and paid elderly care, both for their own parents and for themselves.

There are countries in which a large public sector organizes care, countries in which family care is supported by public general insurance, comparatively affluent countries in which families are left to care for the elderly with almost no outside support, and, finally, there are many countries in which poverty is widespread and many care needs – not only for the elderly – go largely unmet. In all countries, women provide the great majority of practical care work, and the need for care is growing fast. A new world order of care is needed.

I question the sustainability of today's gendered order of care for the elderly for several reasons. Changing demographics is one of the most important: people are having fewer children and living longer. As a result, more people will grow old without adult children to care for them, and more individual children will face great care burdens.[1] Another factor that threatens the current, gendered order of care is migration, which puts greater distances between family members. That more women now engage in paid work increases the demands on their time and makes it difficult for them to provide unpaid, family-based care for elderly relatives. Contributing to the squeeze, countries in economic transition have cut back on services they earlier provided to the elderly, who now must rely even more heavily on their families. Affluent countries, facing their own financing difficulties, have cut back as well, or not increased services as the elderly grow in numbers.

These trends could – in principle – be balanced by other factors: in the future, people might remain in good health as they age, so that they need less care; or partners in marriage could provide more care for each other as they live longer; or paid care could be expanded, whether organized by the market or by the state; or voluntary organizations could provide more care work. These factors are important, but also problematic, and their impact may not be enough to meet the demand for care.

Today's gendered order of care is based on women's paid and unpaid work, and there are few signs that this situation will change. I question the sustainability of this order not because women seem to be refusing to provide care for husbands, parents, other relatives, clients, customers, or patients. Instead, the problems are that the need for care of the elderly is rapidly increasing, the structures organizing that care have adapted badly to the new demands, efforts to combine the institutions that provide care work have proved difficult, economic resources are inadequate, and the economic conditions of those who provide care are poor. In the debates about aging populations and their corresponding care needs, women's care contributions are often taken for granted, and the problem is sometimes defined as women not doing enough or shrinking from taking their proper responsibilities. This conception is based on a gendered concept of social obligation that is inconsistent and unfair.

AN AGING WORLD

Two declines have led to the aging of the world's population: one in fertility and the other in mortality.

During the last half of the twentieth century, the world fertility rate decreased from 5.0 children per woman to just 2.7. In the more-developed regions, the fertility rate fell from 2.8 to 1.5 children per woman, which is well under the so-called zero-growth rate of 2.1.[2] In the less-developed regions, the average number of children born to each woman dropped from 6.2 to 2.9. Regional differences are substantial. In China at the turn of the millennium the fertility rate stood at 1.8; in India, 3.0; and in Eastern, Western, and Middle Africa, at more than 5.5 children per woman (United Nations 2002: 5–6).

During the same period mortality declined among the young but also among the elderly and the already old. The average life expectancy of a person born in the 1950s was 46.5 years; for someone born at the turn of the millennium, the figure had increased by almost twenty years. Improved and more accessible healthcare, maternal welfare and childcare programs, better basic education, higher standards of living, and successful vaccination programs have all helped people in most countries – not just in the North – live longer. In 2000, the global life expectancy at age 60 was 18.8 years. The corresponding figure for age 80 was 7.2 years, and these figures are expected to continue increasing (United Nations 2002: 6).

There are also contrary trends. AIDS has led to high mortality among the adult population in some countries in sub-Saharan Africa, mainly because it is young adults who die. Old people and young children – who may also be infected – are left to care for each other. As a result, the number of children living in households headed by grandparents has increased; of the 8.2 million AIDS orphans recorded in 1997, 95 percent lived in sub-Saharan Africa, where grandparents, most often grandmothers, served as the main caregivers for many of these children (United Nations 2001: 77).

In prosperous Western countries, the growing numbers of elderly have caused considerable concern. Most notably, the German parliament launched an *Enquête-Kommission* to examine the issue: "*Demographischer Wandel–Herausforderungen unserer älter verdenden Gesellschaft an den Einzelnen*

9

und die Politik." The commission's final report introduces the issue of an aging population in the very first sentence: "The population pyramid in the Federal Republic of Germany stands on its head" (Deutscher Bundestag 2002). This statement reflects a strong normative view of what the age composition of national populations should be, as does the notion of a "population pyramid" itself. For several decades, the population diagrams of Germany and most other European states have resembled boxes more than pyramids. Another increasingly common German concept, "over-aging" (*Überalterung*[3]), reflects the same concern – that population norms have gone awry. The population norm implicit in the commission's report reflects the age composition of some Western countries fifty years ago, which coincides with the period when important social security systems such as pensions and child allowances were constructed in those same countries.

Such systems were mainly designed when these countries had smaller percentages of elderly citizens and expected life spans were shorter. Post-war economic growth created the possibility of distributing new wealth, and a number of Western European countries focused on ensuring reasonable economic standards for families with young children and for the elderly. Pension systems that included all workers, rather than just the higher-income earners covered in earlier plans, became a feature of the new welfare systems. The new pension systems were constructed differently in different countries; some covered all citizens regardless of labor-market status, while others were restricted to people with paid work. Minimum qualification periods differed, as did maximum benefits. Since the early 1990s, however, when both the numbers and proportions of old-age pensioners grew, policy-makers have been concerned about the systems' sustainability.

In some Organisation for Economic Co-operation and Development (OECD) countries where low birth rates have been seen as problematic, policy-makers have proposed increased access to affordable childcare as a suitable solution. Other suggestions have included tax incentives for having children or improved conditions for parents in the labor market, etc. But in certain respects, the problems associated with obtaining childcare are easier than, and certainly different from, those related to caring for the elderly. A healthy child's care needs can be roughly predicted. Minors often live with at least one of their parents. When everything is as it should be, a child grows up and acquires new abilities and increasing independence. In addition, not everyone becomes a parent and some people do not want to be one. Bringing children into the world today is to some extent a choice. Influencing this choice has been a high priority for some policy-makers in countries with both low and high birth rates.

Parents, on the other hand, are not a matter of choice: everyone has or had them. The care needs of an individual elderly person, parent or not, cannot be predicted, neither in terms of time nor amount. The number of elderly people in a population is, unlike many other social phenomena, easy to forecast. All the people who will be 65 or older in the first half of the twenty-first century have already been born. Their present health status is roughly known, as are their different patterns of living. On a general level, we can make many prognoses for the future of the elderly, with great accuracy.

The conditions of providing care for the elderly are changing rapidly, both for care workers and recipients of care. In a well-developed Western country, for instance, there is a large gray area between the care work a family is able to provide for an aging relative and medical treatment that is obviously too extensive to be furnished within the family circle. An elderly stroke patient in an affluent country may receive extensive specialist care to help her regain lost abilities. In a less-developed country, however, she may stay with her family, receiving only basic care and no rehabilitation at all. Migration, both between countries and within a single country, reduces the abilities of people to provide daily care of elderly relatives; the distances between families may simply be too great. Also, the family disruption that follows migration will diminish family networks. Finally, the disadvantaged positions of migrants in most social hierarchies will make it more difficult for these families, in particular, to care for their older members (Gail Wilson 2002).

Old people make their own choices and claims within the limitations they experience, just as younger people do. The act of growing older does not change these essential aspects of being human. But aging may lead to deteriorating abilities and decreasing independence. The physical, financial, medical, and emotional conditions of aging are, possibly even more so than the conditions of early childhood, the results of class, gender, ethnicity, sexual orientation, etc., and in addition they reflect the life the old person has led and the resources to which she has had access.

AGING IS A GENDERED ISSUE

In most countries, older women greatly outnumber older men. In many cases, the difference is so large that the concerns of the older population should in fact be viewed primarily as the concerns of older women. This is especially true in the case of the oldest-old populations, as the female share increases markedly with age. (United Nations 2002)

A significantly larger proportion of men than of women are married or cohabiting with a partner when they die. This situation results not only from the longer expected life spans of women but also from social convention. In heterosexual partnerships all over the world, the man is often older than the woman. Remarriage after divorce or death of a partner is more common among men, and their new marriage partners are again women younger than they are. In Sweden in 1940, the mean age of first marriage for women was 26.3 years; in 1960, the figure dropped to 24.3 (the lowest in the entire twentieth century), and by 2000 the mean age at which women first married had risen to 30.6 years.[4] The corresponding ages for men's first marriages were three years older than for women in 1940, decreasing to 2.5 years older in 2000. For second or later marriages, the mean age for women in 1940 was 37.7 years; in 1960, 37.8; and, in 2000, 43.2 years. For men in 1940, the age of second or later marriage was six years older than for women; by 2000, this age gap decreased to a little more than four years (Statistics Sweden 2003: Table 5.9 "Mean, median and quartile age at marriage 1940–2002"). The UN reports similar age differences for most parts of the world, with even wider gaps in those countries where women marry youngest, including those of southern Asia and sub-Saharan Africa, except southern Africa (United Nations 2000: 24–5).

The effect of the age gap is that many more men than women spend their last years in households with spouses or partners and that much higher proportions of women are widows than men are widowers (United Nations 2000: 29–30; 2001: 70; Richard A. Posner 1995: 139, 277). Seventy-nine percent of older men are married, against only 43 percent of older women (older most often being defined as 60 plus), and these percentages are virtually identical in more and less developed countries. Most older people who do not have spouses have been widowed (United Nations 2001: 75–6). In the West, many old people, especially women, live alone rather than with other family members. The increase of Western single-person households has largely resulted from female longevity.

In countries with pension systems that cover large sectors of the population, men usually age and die in two-income households (or in households that live on one pension income constructed for a typically male wage earner and his home-working wife). In such households, the most common situation is that the wife provides unpaid care for her husband during the last period in his life, sometimes assisted by children or outside services. She helps contact other relatives, arranges for market services, contacts medical services and home help, and provides company and support. In countries that lack widespread pension coverage, the wife cares for the husband in much the same way, but she has smaller economic resources and often has less assistance from actors outside the family.

The world's women much more often spend the last years of their lives as widows (or are divorced or never-married). They age and die on just one income – their own – but only if there is a pension system covering them or if they generate income from work or other sources. As the husband or partner is dead, they must receive unpaid, family-based care from children, children's spouses, or other relatives, or they must pay for assistance from outside the family. But their pension incomes are typically smaller than men's are, so they find it more difficult to pay for care.

Thus, paradoxically, the people who receive the most unpaid care from their spouses are men, who as a group also have higher retirement incomes. The people who receive much less unpaid care from spouses are women, who as a group have lower retirement incomes. Also, men and women tend to receive their family-based care from different family members. Men more often receive such care from their wives, while women are given care by daughters or daughters-in-law. "Family care," then, will have different meanings for women and men. Receiving help with personal hygiene will, for instance, be qualitatively different when provided by a partner in a long marriage than when provided by a daughter-in-law.

The core of the UN statement quoted earlier is that "the concerns of the older population should in fact be viewed primarily as the concerns of older women." Alan Walker, writing on politics and aging in Europe, takes an optimistic view of this fact:

> Because women outnumber men in old age the new politics will be feminized increasingly.... Of course women will also form an increasing proportion of voters as European societies age. This raises the prospect of issues that affect women in particular gaining a higher political profile – issues such as the long-term care of older people and the rights of family carers. (Alan Walker 1999: 23–4)

It is, however, hard to find the perspective of older women in current European policy debates on pensions, care for the elderly, healthcare, and long-term care for the old and frail. Neither are important groups of women of any age well represented in high-level decision-making in these areas. Instead, middle-aged and elderly men dominate. Very few signs of "new politics" and policy-making are discernible during the first years of the millennium. A parallel may be drawn: increasing numbers of poor women and men will not necessarily lead to poverty issues becoming central in politics. The power aspect of "class" has been recognized for a long time. The same aspect of "gender" should not be disregarded. Women must start moving into the political positions now dominated by men and make the decisions that will deeply affect their own futures.

CARE FOR THE ELDERLY – FOUR INSTITUTIONS ORGANIZE CARE WORK

Four institutions play particular, key roles in organizing care work for the elderly. The starting point for each is *a person who needs or desires a good or service that includes care work provided by other people.* To whom or where can she or he turn?

Examples are a person who wants a haircut, a person who needs medical treatment, a disabled person who needs assistance with personal hygiene, or a person suffering from dizziness who is no longer able to go for the walks she once enjoyed. How do these people get what they want, and under what conditions?

The four institutions are: the family, the market, the public sector, and *voluntary organizations.*[5] These four are here seen as social and complex organizations.[6] They are used to analyze how care work for the elderly is organized and to discuss how different needs and desires may be met. What is required by the person with a need and desire to approach the different organizations? Which needs are seen as legitimate, and what are the bases for legitimacy? To some extent I also discuss the conditions for the people carrying out the care work in the four organizations. For in-depth explanations of the four institutions used in a more general model for analyzing work, for background, and for the different parts of the model see Agneta Stark and Åsa Regnér (2002). While these four institutions have many purposes and functions, I focus here on their role in care work. This role includes connecting a person with a care need to someone who can do the work needed under existing conditions and finding resources of time, knowledge, and money. There are vast differences among a private company, a small family, the Red Cross/Red Crescent, and publicly organized home help. Payment – when it occurs – is differently organized, the amount of formal or informal planning differs, and the relationship between the elderly person and the carer is also different.

What someone needs or desires may be dispensable or vital. I make no distinction here between fundamental needs, such as food or rest, and desires or wishes, such as for cinema tickets or fashionable clothes. Consequently, levels of needs or desires are not classified here in order of precedence, nor are certain phenomena classified as needs and others as desires. Care organizations usually do distinguish between needs and luxuries; a family celebration may be a legitimate reason for asking a family member to prepare a rich and expensive meal, while making the same request of a voluntary organization delivering "meals-on-wheels" would be considered inappropriate. Publicly financed or subsidized services are generally limited to what are regarded as basic needs, while market services that are privately paid for do not have such restrictions. For policy-making purposes, the definition of needs and establishing of hierarchies between needs and wishes or desires would be crucial. But policy is not the issue here. Rather, it is the daily care work that older people request and receive.

Care work for the elderly is defined here as *a set of activities useful and often necessary to daily life that an elderly person is not – or most often no longer – able to provide for herself.* Self-care is thus excluded, even if such care forms a large part of most elderly people's daily lives. Those activities that we are able to continue doing for ourselves generally do not cause problems as we age. Instead, the aging process often involves losing earlier capabilities, in turn requiring assistance from others.

The definition is connected to other people's work, and it focuses on activities, rather than motives or settings. It does not assume payment or nonpayment to the person performing the work, and it does not connect care work to specific attitudes in the recipient or the care worker. However, these conditions are not incompatible with Joan Tronto's view: "Caring seems to involve taking the concerns and needs of the other as a basis for action" (1993: 105). The care work provided by a specialized physiotherapist, a paid cleaner, a more-or-less willing teenager who helps a grandparent go shopping, a wife who checks on her sick husband at midnight, or a volunteer who drives an elderly person to the dentist may involve different motives and attitude; yet the older person's need is still the basis for it.

The boundary between what someone can or cannot do is not clear-cut, and overprotective care workers may not distinguish it very well. For instance, an aging man who had never cooked would perhaps be physically able to prepare a meal for himself and mentally able to learn cooking techniques. An Alzheimer patient's ability to perform daily activities may differ from day to day. Thus, while a negligent care worker may ignore an older person's needs, an overprotective one may not fully understand them.

Payment for care work may exist in all of the four institutions.[7] Pay levels and conditions are important factors influencing care work in a multitude of ways, and I argue that the monetary aspects of care work are important. Julie Nelson, in discussing payment for care work, and the uses the worker may have for her earnings, poignantly states: "Squeamishness about money is a luxury only affordable to those who can assume that someone else will take care of them. The rest of the world knows all too well that gaining access to money is a necessity" (1999: 49).

The four institutions organize care work for the elderly all over the world, in widely differing proportions. For an individual elderly person, only one institution may provide care work, for instance, either the family or the public sector. But care work for the elderly as a group is provided by a combination of the four institutions everywhere in the world.

THREE EUROPEAN COUNTRIES AND CARE FOR THE ELDERLY

The following discussion of conditions in three countries within the European Union, all with rapidly aging populations, will briefly highlight some differences and similarities in care for the elderly in three comparatively affluent countries.

Spain

Spain serves as an example of a comparatively affluent country that bases its care regime for the elderly on the family. Very few outside resources are available to help or support family carers. Local authorities assist only economically disadvantaged elderly people, and only about one-tenth of all local authorities have a developed home help service. As a result, approximately 2 percent of the elderly with help needs received such home help in the late 1990s (Lorenzo Cachon 1998). The market organizes little care for the elderly. Some part is probably organized by families hiring labor without paying tax or social insurance, or hiring illegal immigrants, but these figures are not available. Few people can afford to pay for commercial services or for private nursing homes (OECD 1996). Two Eurobarometers from spring 1993 report that 3–5 percent of the Spanish elderly in need of care receive private, paid assistance, and 3 percent receive assistance from voluntary organizations (SOU 1993: 111).

The solution for Spanish families is often that elderly parents move between their children's homes, a phenomenon now so common that it has been given a name by some sociologists, who call it the "modified extended family" ("*familia extensa modificada*") (Inés Alberdi 1999). The parent continues to be registered as having a home of his or her own, but in practice moves around between the children. Generations often live close, and have frequent contacts. A third of those responding to a government survey say that parents and adult children meet every day, and nearly 70 percent report at least weekly meetings (Ministerio de Trabajo y Asuntos Sociales 1997).

Of all people reporting that they needed daily assistance, 35 percent were helped by a daughter, 18 percent by a spouse, 6 percent by a daughter-in-law or other female family member, and 5 percent by a son (Victor Perez-Díaz, Elisa Chulia, and Berta Alvarez-Miranda 1998).

With a rapidly aging population, birth rates among the lowest in the world, and a growing economy, there are conflicting demands on Spanish families today and especially on Spanish women. In order for Spain to live up to the EU employment goals – to which the Spanish government is firmly committed – almost twice as many women as those who now have paid jobs will have to find their way into the labor market in a few years. At the same time, increasing numbers of older people need care, and the government's plans target helping older people to stay at home, cared for by families. Women, especially middle-aged women with brief formal educations, stand in the middle of this conflict of time use. Very few activities focus on increasing Spanish men's unpaid care work, although both elderly people and their daughters think that men should make themselves more useful in this respect (Perez-Díaz, Chulia, and Alvarez-Miranda 1998). The low birth rate means that in the not-too-distant future, many older people will not have children to provide practical care for them.

A care crisis seems to threaten. If it is not averted, the country will be in the position of tolerating the unmet care needs of elderly people at the same time that standards of living for the not-yet-old are increasing rapidly. The country lacks a profession of care work with corresponding professional standards, a situation that will probably be less acceptable in the future than it has been. The willingness of families to provide care may not decrease, but with the increasing proportion of elderly in the population, and with a foreseen general lack of labor, the pressure on Spanish women's time will increase. Including men as carers would expand family care possibilities. But an infrastructure of care for those without family members seems necessary. Such an infrastructure has yet to be constructed. The sustainability of the present Spanish care for the elderly must be questioned.

Germany

The family as the antithesis of the state has a prominent place in social thought and legislation in Germany. The role of the family is laid down in the Constitution, which was created after World War II and built on an analysis of what made the Nazi regime possible. It includes special measures to limit the role of the state. In order to avoid too strong a state, the family is deemed central, but the Constitution also regulates the roles of churches, trade unions, and other voluntary organizations. A person needing help should primarily be assisted by the family, then by other social organizations, and only thirdly by the government/Bundesland/municipality.

In 1995, the country introduced a universal Care Insurance (*Pflegeversicherung*), financed by employers and employees together. Any elderly person who considers herself or himself in need of care may apply for an assessment to the care-insurance administration or to a health and advice center (*Sozialstation*). During this procedure, an independent physician assesses the degree of the applicant's care needs according to the very detailed insurance regulations, which strictly prescribe the needs that entitle the person to assistance. Twenty-one categories are listed; care of the body, for instance, includes the seven categories of washing, showering, dental care, combing, shaving, and voiding the bowels and bladder. Hair washing and nail cutting are not included, as they are not classified as daily needs. Other needs covered are nutrition, mobility, and domestic work such as shopping, cooking, and care of clothes (Andreas Jürgens 1996: 40–6). There are three levels of needs, with the first and lowest level implying a "considerable" ("*erheblich*") need. The third level is reserved for people who require attendance day and night.

Benefits may take the form of monthly payments or material help including home help, specialist treatment, or time in a nursing home. A fundamental precept of the insurance is that help should primarily be given in the home and principally arranged by relatives, neighbors, and volunteers. This is consistent with the basic German principle that the family – rather than the individual – is the basic unit of society, and that only when the family is unable to cope with its responsibilities should outside resources be made available.

The most common option, and least expensive one for the insurance, is providing money that the elderly person may use to pay a helper. The recipient is asked to designate a carer, who may or may not be a relative.[8] The money, a fixed sum for each level of need, is paid to the recipient, and does not qualify the care worker for more than rudimentary social insurance: it covers accidents that occur during the actual performance of care work, includes retraining when the responsibility for care ends, and provides a minimal pension scheme. Care workers do not have any legal claim on the money paid from the insurance, and are not classified as economically active in labor statistics.

If no relative or other person is available, or if the elderly person prefers professional help, the aid is financed by the insurance and takes the form of material help, provided by trained staff from a voluntary organization that has entered into an agreement with the municipality. This is more costly for the insurance (Jürgens 1996: 129–33). However, even the highest level of insurance payment does not fully cover nursing home costs. If such care is necessary, the recipient's children are means tested by the social services to establish their ability to pay for it. If they can pay only a part – or none – of the costs, social services will pay the difference.

Home care performed by a relative is a common situation in Germany. Of the 1.3 million elderly people who live at home and need care, three-quarters receive it from relatives. In more than 80 percent of these cases, wives, daughters, and daughters-in-law perform the care. Among adult children with parents older than 80 needing care, 61 percent of daughters and only 6 percent of sons provide such care (Bundesministerium für Familie Senioren Frauen und Jugend 2001: 84–5).

The German system has been criticized by feminists and others for putting pressure on women to stay at home as housewives, for conserving old gender patterns, and for the low remuneration of the relatives who perform care; the system is set up so that hourly earnings actually decrease when care needs increase (Ute Behning 1997). Others have argued that the insurance enables women, who would perform the care work anyway, to receive some payment for their work, which is better than none at all. Yet payment from the care insurance is never enough to live on, and the legislation clearly states that money paid to the elderly person is an insurance benefit rather than a grant intended to pay another's wages.

Policy-makers generally recognize that the strain on family care workers can be considerable. Therefore, projects and help lines have been set up to address risks of violence towards the elderly. One project manager in Hanover estimates that about 6 percent of all the elderly people in that city with care needs have been assaulted in their home environment. The majority of victims are women, as are the majority of the batterers. Men are, however, over-represented among the abusers in relation to their proportion of care workers.

One class-based consequence of the insurance is that some low-income families tend to keep elderly relatives at home, since they need the insurance money, even if the elderly person might fare better in a nursing home.

The case of Germany, where as previously mentioned voluntary organizations have a strong legal position, shows how voluntary work can be integrated into ideology and have strong gendered norms. Gertrud Backes (1987) traces the historical background of the concept of *ehrenamtliche Arbeit*, a specifically German concept that signifies work that is done without payment,[9] in connection with different voluntary and public organizations. The concept is unique to Germany and difficult to translate, but it is connected to *Ehre*, honor, and *Beamter*, an employee with a privileged and protected position. In Germany, *ehrenamtliche Arbeit* has a fairly strict gender division: men dominate the administration of both the public and voluntary sectors, a continuation of a long tradition of male citizenship. Women dominate in the area of social work, especially in providing concrete assistance of people in need. For women, Backes describes such work as an intermediary form between (family-based) household work and gainful employment in a market (1987: 103–23). Similarly, she characterizes *ehrenamtliche Arbeit* in the social sector as another intermediary form, an area, which has often been a compromise between the privatization of certain tasks in the family and their being performed by professional care organizations.[10]

In Germany, a large part of publicly financed care for the elderly is organized by voluntary organizations, again as a consequence of the Constitution's limiting the role of the state. Some such organizations have no unpaid volunteers, while others do. A formal system of carefully specified rules governs their activities.

The quality of services that elderly people receive, especially from for-profit organizations, has been a subject of debate in the German media. Private contractors that own nursing homes can do little to increase their incomes. Reimbursement levels are fixed in contracts with the care insurance, and patients and their relatives are generally not able to contribute much more for extra services. The road to profit is cost-cutting, but this tactic can be difficult, since the numbers, qualifications, and training of personnel are also regulated by the insurance contracts. Yet inspections of nursing homes are rare. Thus, the media have reported instances of personnel that exist on paper only, or have no formal training at all. The development of care aids to save on labor costs is also profitable. In the spring of 2002, for instance, a diaper with an absorption capacity of 3.4 liters was demonstrated in a ZDF program (a national German television channel) on care for the elderly. A weak person wearing a wet diaper of that weight cannot rise from a chair.

The sustainability of the German care insurance is under debate, as mentioned. Financing the foreseen increase in needs is one problem. The lack of personnel in the professional part of the care system, especially with the necessary training, is often discussed. Hopes are often expressed that trained people from Eastern Europe will solve the problem. Yet although some trained care personnel have been recruited from abroad, their numbers have not been enough. Another problem is a foreseen shortage of labor in general, as exists in Spain.[11] The low pay for family carers that the insurance provides is not attractive for women with other labor-market options, and it attracts very few men at all. As labor-force participation increases among women, and divorce continues to be not unusual, there are reasons to expect that in the future, fewer elderly than today will be cared for by middle-aged daughters and daughters-in-law.

However, a German infrastructure is in place for care for the elderly, with professional training and corresponding standards. The work provided by family members is recognized. Attention is paid to important problems in care for the elderly, like violence. For women and a few men who provide care for elderly family members, the system means that they may receive some payment, which is better than none at all. The system does conserve gender roles, and for women and men who are dissatisfied with these roles, this is a considerable disadvantage.

Sweden

In the Nordic welfare systems, the individual is the smallest unit – rather than, as in Germany and Spain, the family. This concept is reflected in the legal framework of the Swedish system for care of the elderly. Every individual with a need for assistance has a formal right to it, provided by the local authority and paid for according to means testing of the old person or couple. Married people have a duty to assist each other, but adult children in Sweden, after 1979, no longer have a legal responsibility to pay for or perform care of aged parents. This formal picture does not, however, reflect everyday reality.

Sweden and the other Nordic countries have the largest publicly financed and organized care sector for the elderly among the EU members. Services play a comparatively large part in the welfare systems compared to the role they play in other industrialized countries, and such services are essentially tax financed. A small but increasing part of care work is contracted to private agencies while publicly employed workers still perform the majority of services to the elderly. Both the home services and the special accommodations for the elderly are considered to be of internationally high standard.

In contrast to the procedure in Germany, the assessment of needs is not performed by an independent specialist, but by social-service assessors of care needs. These individuals are supposed to evaluate needs regardless of current budget restrictions, but in practice budgets influence their decisions considerably. Thus, although no changes have occurred in the legal framework, rationing of care services has in the last decade tightened, so that it is now very rare for a married person, with a healthier partner, to receive any assistance. The National Board of Health and Welfare (*Socialstyrelsen*) has observed that social-service personnel increasingly concentrate on what services can and must be provided for an elderly person, rather than on assessing the old person's needs (Socialstyrelsen 1997: 62). The key issue is the definition of a "need." Examples of activities that used to be "needs" but are now generally cut are cooking in the older person's home (replaced by delivered ready meals, not always of high standard) and cleaning (replaced by lists of firms from which the person may hire at her own cost). A large proportion of places in nursing homes have been closed, and hospitals send elderly people home as soon as they no longer require hospital-based medical care – even if they still need care day and night. Thus, local authorities now devote many more hours than formerly to very sick and frail people, and a large proportion of elderly with considerable care needs receive little or nothing from the public services (Marta Szebehely 2000).

Contrary to what non-Swedes sometimes assume, the networks of family and friends surrounding elderly people in Sweden are comparatively large and close. Sixty-four percent of people older than 75 who lived at home met one or several of their children at least once a week. Ninety-three percent speak with their children on the phone at least once a week (Socialstyrelsen 2000: 16–17). These figures compare with those reported in Spain, as discussed above. The geographical distance between elderly parents and adult children has not increased appreciably since the 1950s, and the majority of people over 75 have children living within twenty to thirty kilometers (Regeringens proposition 1997/98: 113: 2).

As public services have suffered cutbacks, social service workers have assisted, and sometimes pressed, relatives to take up more care work. A system similar to the German one described above allows relatives to be employed to care for an aging person. It is still in use but covers fewer people than before, even though the number of people needing care has grown and public services have been reduced. Ann-Britt Mossberg Sand (2000: 145) reports on two cases within the same local authority. A woman, 52 years old, whose husband suffered a stroke, was subjected to hard pressure to reduce her paid working hours and accept part-time employment as a hired carer for her husband. When she hesitated, she was branded "reluctant to care." She says, "The home help assistants would come to my home and ask if I had taken a lover, since I did not want to – or did not have the energy to – take my husband home." A man of similar age chose to work as the hired carer for his wife. As a first alternative, the couple had been offered professional care in the home, during both weekdays and weekends, for the wife. No one in social services counted on the husband's assuming the care work, and officials exerted no pressure on him to leave his job, which had required less education and training than that of the woman above.

Although no laws support the practice, social workers routinely reject elderly persons' requests for assistance, referring instead to the existence of daughters or daughters-in-law. Social services' expectations of relatives are gendered.

With the cutbacks in public services, husbands are now expected to provide care for wives to the same extent that wives do for husbands, which was not the case twenty years ago. As a result of demographics, however, there are many more wives than husbands available; in 2003, in the age group 85 – 89, 14 percent of women were married (86 percent were widows, divorced, or never married), as opposed to 52 percent of men. The group contained twice as many women as men. Of the 90 + group, 5 percent of women and 36 percent of men were married – and there were three times as many women as men in the group (Statistics Sweden 2004: 15).

In paid as in unpaid care work for the elderly, women dominate. In Sweden, unlike both Spain and Germany, more of this work is performed on the labor market and is professionalized. According to a recent government report, the two largest occupations in Sweden are "assistant nurses and hospital ward assistants" and "home-based personal care and related workers," both of which employ more than 90 percent women (Statistics Sweden 2004: 56). Such figures contribute to making the Swedish labor market more gender segregated than markets in other countries.

Among Swedish residents, publicly organized care for the elderly enjoys strong public support. In opinion polls, the public year after year expresses willingness to pay high taxes, and even increase taxes, if the money is used for care for the young, the old, the sick, and for education. The problem of sustainability concerns financing this public-sector care and to some extent also finding qualified personnel. High employment levels are needed to generate tax income for the state, and unemployment is a severe strain on such income. The sensitivity of the care system to state financial problems was demonstrated during the 1990s.

In conclusion, an infrastructure for care of the elderly exists in all of Sweden. There are education and training programs, and satisfaction with the services is reasonably high among the elderly and their families. One problem is that many who need help do not receive it. The gender segregation of care workers is high, both for paid and unpaid work, with the exception of married men, who now provide care work as often as married women – if they are alive when their wives need care. As in Germany, payment for professional care work is low. However, Sweden's public system does not have the formal rule structure of the former nation, which in practice has proved a disadvantage, since unmet needs remain invisible in Sweden.

In addition, there is a tendency to disregard the care work performed by family members in Sweden. In public discourse it is often mentioned that family members provide the vast majority of all such care, but policy-makers may then make assumptions about unused capacity in families, or about family members' habit of ignoring the elderly, without any factual basis, or even in contrast to what statistics or well-researched facts demonstrate.

A RESPONSE TO AGING – TRANSFERRING WORK BETWEEN INSTITUTIONS

In Germany, Sweden, and other countries, stretching resources and cutting public spending has been tried through reorganizing care work. Many transferals of care work between institutions are taking place, often with significant impact on the daily lives of elderly needing care and their relatives, as well as on professional care workers. These transferals merit attention in a comparison between countries, since in a national context "other countries" are often described as having organized care more efficiently, more cheaply for the taxpayer, or with more choice for the elderly person. Underlying assumptions behind such transferals are also of interest.

In Sweden, some policy-makers and researchers argue that elderly people in southern Europe, for instance in Spain, are more respected, enjoy more contact with their families, and lead better lives since they receive care from their loved ones, rather than from impersonal, publicly organized care. Implicit in the argument is that cutting back the public-sector services would improve the lives of the elderly, since their relationships with their families would improve. The German system, with its separate care insurance, has been praised for lightening the burden on the taxpayer. And the US market-based care for the elderly has been presented as providing more free market-based choice for the elderly than do the restricted choices in Sweden. In Germany and elsewhere, politicians of the left and the right have presented Sweden as providing affordable, good quality services to those who need them or as a country in which no one cares about the old, care is cold and impersonal, and interference from the public sector is dissolving families.

One transferal has attracted a lot of attention, not only in wealthy countries, but globally: the movement of public services to other sectors.[12] Often this has been labeled "privatization." But the term is deceptive since it covers very different changes, with very different contents and meanings of "private."

A few examples, all of them labeled "privatization": a voluntary organization takes over a service that had been run by publicly employed carers, a public service is discontinued in the hope that volunteers will continue to run it without payment, or hospitals provide shorter care after an operation and send patients home earlier. Backes (1987) uses "privatization" to signify the transferal of paid work into unpaid work carried out within the family. As a consequence, she regards voluntary work as an intermediary form between paid wage work and unpaid domestic work.

The aim of such transferals is often to reduce the size, or rather the cost, of the public sector, and to make sure that some types of services are not run with public personnel or public funding. The hope of greater effectiveness may be a main ingredient, but ideological reasons have often been important driving forces.

Decision-makers sometimes move work out of the public sector without evaluating the results. When a hospital's resources are insufficient, family members might be expected to provide patients' food or take up nursing tasks. When care for the elderly is cut back, through more restrictive assessments of who should receive help, there is at times no follow-up of the consequences. The older person's needs might remain unmet, or she might be able to buy what she needs on the private market, or family members or voluntary organizations might assist.

Another kind of transferal of care work takes place when the market begins to offer certain services or goods that satisfy needs another institution previously met. One example of this kind of transfer is the new abundance of convenience foods in the grocery store; cooking has moved from being unpaid work in the family to paid work on the market. Yet another example is a voluntary organization that relieves relatives by opening a day center for elderly people who need care.

All in all, many kinds of transfers are taking place all the time. For those who need or desire a commodity or service, changes such as those mentioned above might be easy and cause them no difficulties in finding what they want. But some transfers cause problems. Finding a private provider of cleaning services may seem too hard when the former, publicly organized cleaning help for the elderly has been closed. A main deterrent is lack of money to pay for the service. For an aging person who has never purchased cleaning services before and finds the necessary negotiations difficult, a list of recommended cleaning companies might be of little use.

And class, color, or other structural issues may restrict choice. For instance, a person who used to work as a cleaner may find it harder to hire someone to clean her or his home than someone who formerly worked as a personnel manager, even if the payment is guaranteed by public or insurance funding. Finally, some language skills are necessary to find information or negotiate terms, which may be an obstacle for migrants.

In short, when transferals occur, people who need information must learn to find it in new ways. As this discussion has shown, the methods and rules of the family, the voluntary sector, the market, and the public sector are very different. As a result of transferals from one sector to another, there is a risk that people who cannot find the new information or understand the changing rules will have their important needs go unmet.

A problem not often discussed is how aging migrant workers find help for their care needs. Navigating public and private organizations that are completely different from those in one's home country, identifying rules perhaps in a new language, and approaching the right institution are not easy tasks. Doing so when communication has become difficult, mobility is reduced, and previous knowledge becomes less useful can be extremely hard. When, in addition, the rules of one's adopted country suddenly change – and responsibilities for care of the elderly move between institutions – the extra effort required may prevent the person who needs help from finding her way at all.

FAMILY-ORGANIZED CARE – A SUSTAINABLE SOLUTION?

The family, in different forms, plays a major role in providing care for the old everywhere, and its importance is most vital in less-developed countries. When other sources of care work are unavailable or malfunctioning, the last resort is often the family, whose members have difficulty saying, "This is not our responsibility." But family-organized care may also be a preferred option, offering closeness and high-quality care to those who need it, by family members who know they are doing what they can for a loved person.

Is family-based care sustainable as care needs of the elderly increase?

Family support is particularly crucial in the case of the oldest-old, whose physical and economic needs are usually greater. The parent support ratio gives an indication of the overall demand for family support for the oldest-old. The continuing increase of this ratio implies that more and more frequently the young old will find themselves responsible for the care of one or more oldest-old family members. (UN 2002: 2)

The parent support ratio, as defined by the UN, is the number of persons 85 years old and older per 100 persons aged 50 to 64 years. Thus, it is a general measure that disregards specific family ties and is only usable as a very rough indicator. In 2000, the parent support ratio was 4.3 for the world, 1.6 for Africa, 2.6 for Asia, 8.6 for Europe, 3.5 for Latin America and the Caribbean, 9.9 for Northern America, and 7.2 for Oceania. In principle, this measure implies that many people aged 50 to 64 years are available, willing, and equipped to care for the old. In practice, both specific family ties and the gender of the 50-to-64-year-olds – as well as those of younger and older family members – determine who provides actual family-organized care for the elderly.

Families are changing rapidly, and countries that depend almost exclusively on family care for the elderly may face considerable difficulties in sustaining the quality of such care. But countries in which family care is taken for granted, even if combined with other care sources, also need to consider supporting family carers better.

Some conclusions we can draw from the above discussion of elderly care follow.

From the elderly person's perspective:

- Men receive more care from partners than women do, and such care is largely unpaid.
- Men seem to pay less often for care work than women, in spite of larger economic resources.
- Women, more than men, receive care from female relatives other than partners.
- Women and men who lack access to family members may experience difficulties in receiving necessary care, but where other institutions organizing elderly care exist, these may play an important part.

From the care worker's perspective:

- The majority of care work for the elderly is not paid. However, paid work exists in all four institutions. For family members, payment is not common or is nonexistent in most of the world. But in some countries, like Germany, a person who needs care may receive money with which to pay a family carer. In others countries, family members may be employed by the public sector to provide care. For care work organized by the market or the public sector, payment is the norm. In voluntary organizations, both paid and unpaid work is common. Thus, labor-market conditions cut across all four institutions. Assuming that "family-organized work" and "voluntary work" by definition always mean "unpaid work" may be misleading as regards care for the elderly.
- If the work is paid, the payment and other benefits are generally low compared to levels for other kinds of work in the same country or

region. Absolute levels differ widely, as does the size of the pay gap
between other types of work.

- Conditions for family carers differ vastly among well-developed
  countries and between these countries and those in the developing
  world. Those who provide care for the elderly in their families often
  do so in addition to carrying out other responsibilities, which may not
  diminish as care needs increase.

UNPAID CARE WORK AND LABOR-MARKET WORK – MUTUALLY EXCLUSIVE?

The discussion of sustainability above outlines a time conflict: If women are
to increase their paid labor-market work, can they at the same time
continue providing – or even increase amounts of – unpaid family-based
care for the elderly? An important part of care work lies outside of this
conflict, namely that provided by partners who are past the formal
retirement age and who live in developed countries with adequate pension
systems. But the time conflict does concern adult children, especially
middle-aged women, as well as the many elderly who are still in paid work in
developing countries or in countries with small or no pensions, such as
those in economic transition. Since it is central to the issue of sustainability
of family care, it merits further attention. Is this conflict real and
important?

The United Nations reports that in developed countries, women
performing labor-market work are as likely to be caregivers as women
who do not participate in the labor market; employment outside the home
does not prevent women from care giving (UN 2001: 77).

However, the level of labor-market activity may be influenced by care
responsibilities. A comparative study of twelve European Union countries in
the mid-1990s shows that mid-life women already in the labor market
adapted to starting or increasing informal care work for an elderly person
by decreasing their labor-market hours. When the informal care work
ended or decreased, the women did not increase their labor-market hours;
the response to care responsibilities was thus asymmetrical. The authors
express concern about the longer-term effects of mid-life women
permanently withdrawing partly or wholly from labor-market work after
performing family-organized care work for the elderly (C. Katharina Spiess
and A. Ulrike Schneider 2003).

A Japanese study asks, "Can women do both – hold down a job and
look after the elderly?" The background to the question is the worry of
Japanese policy-makers that women who work may not be willing – or
able – to care for elderly family members at home. According to the
authors, the result that policy-makers fear is fewer women remaining in
the workforce, greater government outlays on care for the elderly, or

both. The authors feel able to reassure policy-makers, and they abstract their work thus:

> Findings from Nihon University's 1999–2000 Japan Longitudinal Study of Aging show that more than half of Japanese women who live with an elderly parent or parent-in-law are employed outside the home. Even in households where the elderly family member is very old or seriously disabled, large proportions of women continue to hold down full- or part-time jobs. These finding [*sic*] should be reassuring to Japanese policymakers who are concerned that middle-aged women remain in the labor force while continuing to care for elderly family members at home. (Naohiro Ogawa, Robert D. Retherford, and Yasuhiko Saito 2003)

One reason given for this outcome is that, although care for the elderly is mainly family-based, long hospital stays are common for elderly with severely restricting disabilities. These care-working women are almost exclusively daughters and daughters-in-law.

A striking result of these studies is that the traditional division of labor expressed as "men earn money working on the market, women provide care by unpaid family organized work" is empirically dissolved. Women are here shown to work both in the labor market and at the same time to provide unpaid care for the elderly in the family. The Japanese study explicitly includes full-time work, and it is also present in the two other studies. The number of labor-market hours obviously has an important impact on the possibilities of performing family-based care work, but it should be noted that full-time and part-time are not absolutes. The OECD defines 30 hours per week as the lower limit for full-time work. Yet there is still a wide gap between the 35-hour work week that constitutes a full-time job in large parts of the German and French labor markets, and the typically much longer hours worked in, for instance, the UK, the US, Australia, the Czech Republic, and Japan[13] (OECD 2001: 224–5). By logic, then, the traditional explanation for men not taking part in such care work can easily be dissolved: If women are already today combining the two responsibilities, why are not men doing the same?

No absolute obstacles to combining labor-market work and unpaid family care for the elderly seem to exist. As conditions on the labor market may be changed, and as care commitments require different levels of time, improving labor-market and care conditions for carers would be a way to improve sustainability. However, plans to increase weekly working hours as debated in, for instance, France and Germany and to push back the formal retirement age in many Western countries may hinder such developments.

PREFERENCES OF THE ELDERLY

What solutions do women and men prefer to the problem of organizing care work for the elderly? Do women and men have a choice regarding who should organize such work, and if not, should they be able to choose? A comparative study examines norms and ideals for the support and care for older people among urban populations in Norway, England, Germany, Spain, and Israel (Svein Olav Daatland and Katarina Herlofson 2003). The study focuses on the relative responsibility for care of adult children and the welfare state.[14] Respondents from all five countries advocate for greater welfare-state responsibility. In Norway and Israel, the relative strengths of formal service and family provision, as indicated by the respondents, approximately reproduce the actual balance in care provision, but among respondents from the other three countries, the expressed preference for formal services is far higher than the actual provision of them.

The authors conclude: "When alternatives are available, today's older people seem more reluctant to receive help from the family than are adult children willing to provide such help, and the young are *more* inclined towards family care provision than the old" (2003: 556, italics in original). The exception is Spain, where the older generation favors family solutions. In each country, the authors find a substantial minority who do not accept filial obligations to parents. The largest such minority is in Germany, where one-third of respondents reject such obligations. As the German system for long-term care for the elderly relies heavily on filial obligation, while in England and Sweden this is not formally the case, the result indicates that there may be considerable discrepancies between formal systems and norms on the one hand, and the preferences of the people concerned on the other. The authors find no consistent gender differences. Gender is, however, treated technically as a variable among others in the study.

It must be kept in mind that the preferences of the elderly will vary considerably and that generalizations should be made with caution. However, there is little doubt that many elderly people are satisfied with partners providing care work for them and that they express more concerns about accepting or requiring assistance from adult children.

General requests for more informal care, more family responsibility, and more care in the community are increasingly common from both politicians and policy-makers in countries where alternatives to family-organized care exist or where such alternatives are contemplated. Such requests rarely mention gender aspects. An exception is William A. Jackson, who discusses gender and informal care, explicitly addressing male nonparticipation:

> There is no pre-existing excess supply of informal carers waiting for someone to look after. The low supply of care from male relatives

could perhaps be interpreted as an untapped source of informal activity. Most males, however, have chosen not to become involved in informal care, and they will be reluctant to participate in caring unless it is made compulsory or induced by financial or other incentives. (1998: 191–2)

He thus does not see increasing family-organized care for the elderly as a viable solution to the new population composition. Instead, he connects care needs to unemployment and underemployment in the labor market. Complicating this argument, at least in Europe, is the forecasted lack of labor, which is expected to result from the present low birth rates and increasing number of elderly. However, Jackson highlights the lack of easy solutions as well as the close interaction between different sectors of the economy that takes place in the family.

One can easily develop Jackson's view that most men have *chosen* not to perform informal, family-based unpaid care. The male choice not to perform such work influences and is influenced by female carers performing it instead – as it is rarely work that both women and men in the family can refuse simultaneously. Whether this situation is best described as a choice for females, and in what meaning of that term, can be debated.

Male care work must not be underestimated. Male partners in heterosexual marriage care for their wives, partners in male homosexual partnership provide care work for each other, and sons to a smaller extent perform care work, too. Exploring the conditions under which sons, especially, and other male nonspouses (choose to) perform care work is important.

CARE FOR THE ELDERLY – FUTURE PROSPECTS

The contributions of feminist research to developing policy for and thinking about the future care of the elderly could have important consequences for that care. Clearly, such contributions would not only enrich policy work, but could also deepen understanding of issues important to the development of feminist economic research itself. A few possibilities will be outlined here.

Interesting opportunities for further research into both male and female care giving are outlined by Michael Bittman, Janet E. Fast, Kimberly Fischer, and Cathy Thomson (2004). They use the concept of "time signature" to explore time-diary surveys, and they present gendered analyses of carers' workdays and the interaction between care responsibilities and other aspects of carers' lives. Corresponding research in other parts of the world could point to ways of assisting family carers and to adapting present systems to different needs.

The relationship between payment and care could be explored further by comparative research on the experiences of family members who receive payment for their care work and the experiences of those belonging to the large majority who do not. There are even care workers in some countries that have moved both in and out of the paid care work sector while caring for the same elderly person. Have payment and pay levels had any influence on the relationship between the person needing care and her carer? If so, what sort of influence have they had?

Payment may play a part in creating either distance or closeness between the person needing care and the carer. Sometimes distance seems desirable; at other times closeness is preferable, depending on what needs are to be met. There are no grounds to expect symmetry between the preferences of the cared for and the carer; both perspectives need to be explored further.

The increasing numbers and proportions of elderly women and men in the world will by necessity mean that more care work will be needed at a societal level. To some extent, the needs for childcare will diminish.

When care work is organized in the market or in the public sector, moving resources from care for the young to care for the elderly is feasible, even if the training and the skills needed are not identical. The same transfer of resources may be valid for some voluntary organizations. But when the work is family organized, the situation is different. Elderly women themselves perform a large proportion of family care work for the elderly, while younger women provide the majority of family childcare, even when older family members assist them. Living conditions and the physical distances between members are important factors that influence who is able to carry out certain tasks. The increasing participation of women in the formal labor markets of many countries is another consideration. As I emphasize above, many countries expect women to increase their labor-market participation – to increase economic growth, to meet future shortages of labor, or to be eligible for a pension of their own – while at the same time insisting that care for the elderly should take place unpaid in the home.

This expectation creates an interesting opportunity for research into the social demands made on women and men. Are there areas in which society asks men to pursue contradictory activities to the same extent it asks women who have elderly family members needing care? What are the class, race, caste, and religious intersectional aspects of such requirements on women and men?

Moving care work from one institution to another may change the conditions of the work, but there is little empirically grounded evidence to support the view that these transfers will change the gendered structure of the work, unless other action is taken at the same time. No organizational changes will by themselves draw men into performing care work.

How might care work for the elderly be distributed in a fairer and a more sustainable way? The question leads into the area of policy, and the brief discussion here will be restricted to developed and fairly affluent countries, not because they are more important than other areas of the world – the opposite is rather the case – but because of my own restricted knowledge and experience.

There is little reason to expect that any one of the four institutions will be the single key to future care for the elderly. Women and men of different ages need to perform different parts of such work. Organizing paid labor-market work so that people also have time for family-based work or voluntary work is in my mind a core requirement. This will be more difficult in those countries with cultures of long paid work hours (the US, the UK, Australia, and the Czech Republic) than in Germany, Norway, or the Netherlands.

Encouraging women and men to share care work more equally, not only "in principle" but also in practice, is even more important. Developing the knowledge and affordable everyday technology to make heavy and difficult care tasks easier would enable elderly people to keep their independence longer and would also help carers. Volunteer organizations and others are developing support structures for the elderly and for their carers, but these structures need more attention.

All of us, women and men, will probably need care in our old age. At present, women are the ones caring for the elderly, and they are doing it unpaid, underpaid, half-paid, or just reasonably paid. Women are even combining full-time labor-market work with considerable care responsibilities for the elderly. Men are under-represented in all types of such care. Now that the world is aging, a new world order of care is needed. The absurd fact is that I have been unable to find any but very marginal suggestions of policies to include men as carers. In childcare, the connection of giving birth physically and providing practical care for the baby and the young child is often emphasized. In care for the old, such a visceral connection is not evident. The starting point for exploring the possibilities of men performing care work for family members should be the sharing of new and increasing burdens. And yet emphasizing the burdening aspect of providing care would be a mistake. The fact that more people lead long lives and thus grow old represents tremendous progress. Providing practical help and assistance to people close to you can give satisfaction to both the carer and the cared for. As men share care-giving responsibilities, traditional, stereotypical male traits such as physical strength may be extremely useful. Innovative technology might also be introduced, not because care-working women are not using and developing technology already, but because new actors may bring new perspectives. In addition, since men generally have more economic resources than women, they might target these resources to increasing the quality of care. New caring skills might be developed, adding new and deeper dimensions to life for the elderly. Finally, perhaps younger men, who have more experience caring for their children than their predecessors did, will be better prepared to care for elderly people than men in earlier generations.

The possible inclusion of men in family-organized care for the old would mostly concern sons and sons-in-law. Given current demographics, husbands are simply not available when their elderly wives and partners need care, or are there much less frequently than wives are there for their aging husbands.

The present world is deeply gendered, and so is its care.

If economic conditions, including pay, insurance, and pension rights, were improved for care workers, living conditions would be better both for them and for the elderly in their care. It is important that care workers receive such benefits, whether they perform their work in the family, in market-based organizations, in the public sector, or in voluntary organizations. Improved wages and conditions would acknowledge the value of good care work, and they would make the care workers' own old age easier. They might also attract more men to such work. Bettering economic conditions would be a small step, and even as such, not easily accomplished. But it would be a good first step towards a new world order of care for the elderly.

And then? Finding a marriage partner is of course a deeply personal issue. It may be seen as a sign of the gendering of such deeply personal and intimate issues that the age differences between women and men in marriage are so uniform all over the world, and seem quite stable over time. Not until men stop sub-viving women, and not until heterosexual partnerships are formed as often with the female partner older than the man as with the male partner older than the woman, will married men as a group be able to provide their wives as much care work as married women as a group provide their husbands today. Other possibilities exist: heterosexual women could live with men during part of their life cycles only, moving in with other older women and providing mutual care in their old age, in another kind of partnership.[15] Would that be breaking the rules of nature? Or trespassing into the individual choice of modern women and men? I would prefer to see it as a bold vision of a future, when liberation from stereotyped gender roles frees women and men to fully express their caring abilities.

Agneta Stark, Dalarna University,
SE-791 88 Falun, Sweden
e-mail: Agneta.Stark@du.se

ACKNOWLEDGMENTS

I thank Nancy Folbre and Lois Shaw for their many thoughtful comments and suggestions and a number of participants in IAFFE conferences and other readers for comments on earlier parts and versions of this work.

NOTES

1 David R. Phillips (2002: 43) mentions China, Japan, and Singapore – countries in which filial piety has an important role – where a single child potentially may have responsibility for up to six direct adult relatives (parents and grandparents).

2 In nineteen countries, the rate is below 1.3. Population change patterns are sometimes described in terms of crises and in violent metaphors: "population explosion," "the aging bomb." Such metaphors seem misleading, since aging on an individual as well as to some extent on a societal level is a comparatively slow and steady process. It should also be noted that a population unchanged in size should not be seen as a goal in itself, just as growing or diminishing populations are not necessarily good or bad.

3 See for instance, Angelika Hensolt (2002: 6).

4 It should be noted that the mean age for a woman giving birth for the first time at the turn of the millennium was almost two years younger; in Sweden marriage often comes after a period of cohabitation, and after the birth of at least a first child.

5 These organizations are in alphabetical order here, and the order does not reflect any normative view.

6 This view of the market is shared by Julie A. Nelson and Paula England (2002).

7 The issue of commodification or decommodification of care work will not be discussed here, as the definition of care work used does not necessitate any specific distinction between market-organized work on the one hand and work organized by the other institutions on the other.

8 Cases are reported in which the elderly person designates a carer, especially a spouse, without asking that person first (Stark and Regnér 2002: 155).

9 However, it is not unusual that compensation for expenses is paid, for example, for transportation in connection to the work.

10 "Consequently there is an attempt at getting the social '*Ehrenamt*' accepted as a *compromise between privatization in the family and professionalization* (as the most far-reaching process of *socialization*)" (Backes 1987: 101, italics in the original); ("Folglich wird soziales Ehrenamt als *Kompromiss zwischen familialer Privatisierung und Verberuflichung* (als weitgehendste *Vergesellschaftung*) durchzusetzen versucht").

11 In the political debate 2000 on recruiting labor abroad, the Christian Democrats used the slogan "Kinder statt Inder" (Children instead of Indian people) to promote support for families with children instead to solve the labor shortage. The slogan was quickly withdrawn after criticism that it fueled hostility towards immigrants.

12 This is certainly not a phenomenon only, or even mainly, connected to policy responses to aging populations.

13 It should be noted that Japanese labor market hours per person have shortened considerably since 1990.

14 A representative age-stratified sample of 6,016 people aged 25 and older, living in the community (not institutions) in urban areas, and in each country 400 people aged 75 or older and 800 from ages 25 to 74 years were interviewed.

15 This connects to existing patterns: older women have long lived with other older women, as relatives, sisters, and friends.

REFERENCES

Alberdi, Inés. 1999. *La Nueva Família Española*. Madrid: Taurus.

Backes, Gertrud. 1987. *Frauen und soziales Ehrenamt: Zur Vergesellschaftung weiblicher Selbsthilfe*. Augsburg: MaroVerlag.

Behning, Ute, ed. 1997. *Das Private ist ökonomisch: Widerspruche der Ökonomisierung privater Familien- und haushaltsleistungen* Berlin: Edition Sigma.

Bittman, Michael, Janet E. Fast, Kimberly Fischer, and Cathy Thomson. 2004. "Making the Invisible Visible: The Life and Time(s) of Informal Caregivers," in Michael Bittman and Nancy Folbre, eds. *Family Time: The Social Organization of Care*. New York: Routledge.

Bundesministerium für Familie Senioren Frauen und Jugend. 2001. *Bericht zur Gesundheitlichen Situation von Frauen in Deutschland: Eine Bestandsaufnahme unter Berücksichtigung der unterschiedlichen Entwicklung in West- und Ostdeutschland*. Stuttgart: Kohlhammer.

Cachon, Lorenzo. 1998. *Nuevos yacimentos de empleo en España. Potencial de crecimiento y desarollo futuro. Informes y Estudios. Ministerio de Trabajo y Asuntos Sociales*. Madrid: Ministerio de Trabajo y Asuntos Sociales.

Daatland, Svein Olav and Katarina Herlofson. 2003. "'Lost Solidarity' or 'Changed Solidarity': A Comparative European View of Normative Family Solidarity." *Ageing and Society* 23: 537–60.

Deutscher Bundestag. 2002. *Schlussbericht der Enquête-Kommission "Demographischer Wandel – Herausforderungen unserer älter verdenden Gesellschaft and den Einzelnen und die Politik,"* Drucksache 14/8800, 28.03.2002.

Hensolt, Angelika. 2002. "Überalterung zwingt Politik zum handeln." *Tageszeitung* 18.04.2002.

Jackson, William A. 1998. *The Political Economy of Population Ageing*. Cheltenham, UK: Edward Elgar.

Jürgens, Andreas. 1996. *Mein Recht bei Pflegebedürftigkeit: Das neue Pflegeversicherungsrecht für Betroffene, Angehörige und Helfer*. München: C. H. Beck.

Ministerio de Trabajo y Asuntos Sociales. 1997. *Envejecimento en el sector rural. Problemas y soluciónes*. Madrid: Ministerio de Trabajo y Asuntos Sociales.

Mossberg Sand, Ann-Britt. 2000. *Ansvar, kärlek och försörjning: om anställda anhörigvårdare i Sverige*. Göteborg: Göteborg University.

Nelson, Julie A. 1999. "Of Markets and Martyrs: Is It OK to Pay Well for Care?" *Feminist Economics* 5(3): 43–59.

—— and Paula England. 2002. "Feminist Philosophies of Love and Work." *Hypatia* 17(2): 1–18.

OECD. 1996. *Caring for Frail Elderly People: Policies in Evolution. Social Policy Studies No 19*. Paris: Organisation for Economic Co-operation and Development.

—— 2001. *Employment Outlook*. Paris: OECD.

Ogawa, Naohiro, Robert D. Retherford, and Yasuhiko Saito. 2003. *Caring for the Elderly and Holding Down a Job: How Are Women Coping in Japan?* Honolulu: East–West Center.

Perez-Díaz, Victor, Elisa Chulia, and Berta Alvarez-Miranda. 1998. *Família y sistema de bienestar. La experiencia española con el paro, las pensiónes, la sanidad y la educación*. Madrid: Fundación Argentaria.

Phillips, David R. 2002. "Family Support for Older Persons in East Asia: Demise or Durability?" in United Nations, ed. *Sustainable Social Structures in a Society for All Ages. Prepared in Cooperation with HelpAge International* pp. 42–7. New York: United Nations.

Posner, Richard A. 1995. *Aging and Old Age*. Chicago: University of Chicago Press.

Regeringens proposition. 1997/98. *Nationell handlingsplan för äldrepolitiken.* Stockholm: Socialdepartementet, 1997/98: 113:2.

Socialstyrelsen. 1997. *Behov, bedömning, beslut i äldreomsorgen. SOS-rapport 1997: 8.* Stockholm: Socialstyrelsen.

——. 2000. *Bo hemma på äldre da'r. Äldreuppdraget 2000: 11.* Stockholm: Socialstyrelsen.

SOU. 1993. *Borta bra men hemma bäst? Fakta om äldre i Europa.* Stockholm: Fritzes, 1993: 111.

Spiess, C. Katharina and A. Ulrike Schneider. 2003. "Interaction between Care-Giving and Paid Work Hours among European Midlife Women, 1994 to 1996." *Ageing and Society* 23: 41–68.

Stark, Agneta and Åsa Regnér. 2002. *In Whose Hands? Work, Gender, Ageing and Care in Three EU-Countries.* Linkoping: Department of Gender Studies.

Statistics Sweden. 2003. *Befolkningsstatistik 2002, del 4. kap 5. Födda och döda, civilståndsändringar m.m.* [*Population Statistics 2002, Part 4. Ch. 5. Births and Deaths, Changes in Marital Status etc.*] Stockholm: Statistics Sweden.

——. 2004. *På tal om kvinnor och män. Lathund om jämställdhet 2004.* Stockholm: Statistics Sweden.

Szebehely, Marta. 2000. "Äldreomsorg i förändring – knappare resurser och nya organisationsformer," *SOU 2000: 38*, pp. 171–223. *Välfärd, vård och omsorg.* Stockholm: Fritzes.

Tronto, Joan. 1993. *Moral Boundaries. A Political Argument for an Ethic of Care.* New York: Routledge.

United Nations. 2000. *The World's Women: Trends and Statistics.* New York: United Nations.

——. 2001. *World Population Monitoring 2000: Population, Gender and Development.* New York: United Nations.

——. 2002. *World Population Ageing 1950–2050.* New York: United Nations.

Walker, Alan. 1999. "Political Participation and Representation of Older People in Europe," in Alan Walker and Gerhard Naegele, eds. *The Politics of Old Age in Europe,* pp. 7–24. Buckingham, UK: Open University Press.

Wilson, Gail. 2002. "Globalisation and Older People: Effects of Markets and Migration." *Ageing and Society* 22: 647–63.

ELDERCARE IN THE UNITED STATES: INADEQUATE, INEQUITABLE, BUT NOT A LOST CAUSE

Susan C. Eaton

INTRODUCTION

Eldercare is one of many kinds of care work that feminist economists have explored (Marianne Ferber and Julie Nelson 1993; Nancy Folbre 2001; Jane Jenson and Mariette Sineau 2001). It takes place both inside and outside the formal market, and many aspects are difficult to measure and quantify. Eldercare is embedded in the values of every culture and imbued with meanings that range from respect to denial, from reciprocity to anger, from family-based obligation to humanitarian privilege (Geoff Schneider and Jean Shackleford 2001: 80–1; Heying Jenny Zhan and Rhonda J. V. Montgomery 2003).

Problems with the provision of eldercare in the United States are growing. The supply of family care for the elderly is likely to decline. The overall quality of paid eldercare is low, and access to it is uneven (Susan Eaton 2000). Low-income elderly, who are predominantly women, cannot rely on family care and often end up in nursing homes where the quality of care is woefully poor. The structure of the nursing home industry, in which firms are forced to engage in competitive cost cutting in order to cope with inadequate federal subsidies, deserves much of the blame for low-quality service.

This paper explores and responds to these mounting problems with the current system of eldercare. It looks for lessons from the countries of northwestern Europe, which provide better eldercare than the US. Even given the current institutional environment within the US, there is potential for improvement through state regulation and participation. Additionally, a number of well-organized volunteer efforts provide inspiration for more radical change in the US.

THE SUPPLY OF ELDERCARE

Much of the responsibility for long-term care continues to fall on families, and it is largely women – many of them over the age of 55 – who provide such care. Several factors are likely to reduce the future pool of women available as caregivers: women's increasing participation in the workforce, the restructuring of families that follows divorce, and increasing geographic mobility. Furthermore, growing awareness of the personal costs of assuming care responsibilities is likely to have an increasing deterrent effect.

Men's shorter average longevity often spares them from the worst consequences of aging, such as being institutionalized, poor, sick, and dependent upon others. A large majority of elderly US nursing home residents are widows who cared for their late husbands at home, often with help from home care services or children (Brenda Spillman, William Spector, John Fleishman, and Liliana Pezzin, 2000). When their husbands die, relatively few surviving wives have the resources to pay for their own home-based care, which seldom provides for 24-hour needs for those without a full-time caregiver at home.

Currently, 85 percent of eldercare in the US is provided free of charge by family members and friends, primarily women (US Administration on Aging 2002). The National Alliance for Caregiving estimates that 73 percent of family caregivers are women, most of them employed (1997). Women are also a majority of informal caregivers in Europe. Female unpaid family workers represented nearly 70 percent of the total between 1990 and 1997 in Austria and the United Kingdom, more than 80 percent in Germany and the Netherlands, and 90 percent or more in Denmark and Luxembourg. Only in Ireland (40 percent), Portugal (58 percent), and Finland (32 percent) was the percentage below 60 percent (United Nations Human Development Report 1999). Women also provide the bulk of eldercare in traditional cultures like China, where unpaid daughters and daughters-in-law often provide hands-on assistance, while sons may assume some responsibility for financial support (Zhan and Montgomery 2003).

In the US, informal eldercare may involve inviting an aged parent or relative to live in one's home or building a "mother-in-law" apartment where she can live without sharing fully in family space on a daily basis. It may involve moving an elder to a nearby apartment or turning down opportunities for career advancement that might require relocation away from an aging relative. Or it may mean just being a "good Samaritan" and bringing meals, doing shopping, taking an elderly neighbor to the doctor's office, or helping with other necessary errands. Sometimes an older person, with or without the help of family, hires an informal caregiver who visits regularly to help when she is unable to care for herself. These informal caregivers are often hired "off the books" so families can avoid paying taxes, worker's compensation, unemployment insurance, and Social Security payments or benefits for the worker.

According to the US Department of Labor, 60 percent of adult women were part of the paid labor force in 1997. In the same year, nearly one in four households provided some care to elders, typically by middle-aged employed women providing an average of 18 hours of care a week to a nearby parent for an average duration of 4.5 years. A study by Metropolitan Life Insurance Company (MetLife) estimated the net cost in lost productivity to business at a minimum of $11.8 billion a year (Metropolitan Life Insurance Company 1997: 4). The $11.8 billion calculation makes clear what is most valued (business productivity), while it simultaneously provides an estimate of the value of part of the unpaid work of the women involved. Yearly replacement costs for employees who quit their jobs to care for elders are estimated at $4.9 billion, absenteeism at $398 million, partial absenteeism at $488 million, workday interruptions at 3.76 billion, eldercare crises at $1.1 billion, and supervising caregivers at $880 million.

Costs to caregivers are substantial. They sometimes forgo promotions, overtime, and other work opportunities to take care of relatives. The term "the sandwich generation" was coined to describe mostly middle-aged women taking care of parents on one side of the generation gap and children on the other. Studies have documented the stress that such responsibilities can impose (Elaine Brody 1990). The numbers from MetLife omit several difficult-to-estimate costs, including increased mental health and healthcare costs for caregivers and the impact of leaves of absence and reduced work hours on career advancement.

The MetLife estimate of $11.8 billion should be viewed as a lower bound, since it only includes employed people helping with multiple significant daily tasks and excludes 8.7 million employed people who help with more basic tasks; if they were included, the total estimated costs would reach as much as $29 billion a year.

The US-based National Alliance for Caregiving offers much higher estimates. By their calculations, American family caregivers provide $257 billion in free care annually. Compare this figure with $32 billion per year spent for home-based paid care and $92 billion per year for nursing home care in the US. In the United Kingdom, family caregivers (also known as "carers") provide free care worth US$86 billion, about the same amount the UK spends on its national health service (National Alliance for Caregiving 2002).

Women are also the primary paid caregivers for the elderly in the US, often going into the field because of previous experience caring for an older relative at home (Susan Eaton 2002). Fully 90 percent of direct care workers employed in US nursing homes are women, disproportionately women of color with a high school education or less (Robin Stone and Joshua Wiener 2001). Certified nursing assistants (CNAs) provide most hands-on care to residents in institutional settings. Home health aides and personal care aides working in the community are also mostly women. The experiences of these workers have been the subject of intense scrutiny lately because of a predicted massive workforce shortage that could entail an 11 percent vacancy rate and a 76 percent turnover rate (Barbara Frank and Steven Dawson 2000; American Health Care Association 2005). At least 42 of the 50 states have created task forces to address actual and potential workforce shortages (Paraprofessional Healthcare Institute and the North Carolina Department of Health and Human Services 2002).

Inadequacy and inequality in eldercare

In the US, unlike many other advanced industrial countries, the social safety net is thin and offers no guarantee of long-term care for the elderly or disabled. While everyone over 65 years of age is eligible for Medicare, this social insurance only covers acute illness and hospitalization, sometimes with a short rehabilitation stay in a nursing home. But despite the existence of some pilot projects, no home or community-based care is provided as a universal benefit. Only extremely poor people (with assets less than $2,000) are eligible for Medicaid, a state-based program that pays for a bare minimum of institutional long-term care. Most Americans appear to be badly informed about this basic problem; few have purchased private long-term care insurance or saved enough to pay for institutional care on their own. Yet projections indicate that as many as two-thirds of all adults reaching 65 will require such care at some time in their lives (Walter Cadette 2003).

Paid home and community-based care

A patchwork system of paid home and community-based care supplements informal care. Home health and home care agencies can provide either personal care, which involves light housekeeping, bathing, and perhaps cooking, or health-related care, which includes assisting with medication, rehabilitation, changes in dressing, or other necessities. Medicare pays a portion of the costs of health-related care under strict conditions, such as when the person covered is only able to leave her home for visits to a doctor. Since 1999, new payment systems have reduced the provision of this form of care (Nelda McCall and Jodi Korb 2003). A limited amount of Medicaid-paid care is provided to poor elders under state waivers when this avoids more expensive institutional care. Most home and personal care is paid "out of pocket" either by the older person needing care or by her or his family.

Most US states are trying to redirect public resources away from long-term institutional care and toward home and community-based care, but they are concerned about the "woodwork" effect: latent demand for such services far exceeds the feasible supply if eligibility requirements are loosened. Although a few innovative experiments are under way, such as a home health cooperative in New York City (Cooperative Home Care Associates 2003), most non-nursing home health jobs are poorly paid and offer little job security, training, or even guaranteed hours. Many home health companies do not even pay for transportation between clients' homes, much less provide their employees health insurance.

Formal eldercare

Formal eldercare is provided in "assisted living" facilities or nursing homes. A few "private pay" facilities admit only wealthy people who can afford $60,000 in minimum annual costs, but 95 percent of US nursing facilities participate in the two public programs Medicare and Medicaid. Relatively few elderly can afford private care, and most live in publicly subsidized nursing homes that are run for profit.

"Assisted living" facilities are apartment-like dwellings where elders can get limited help with some activities of daily living (ADLs), reminders to take medication, and usually at least one hot meal a day. Demographic projections led many businesses to consider these a future profit center, but a number of corporate chains, including Marriott and Hyatt, have encountered sizable unanticipated problems related to "aging in place." These problems occur when elders need more than occasional assistance or require more regular nursing or healthcare than these facilities normally provide. Many elders are so fearful of nursing homes that they resist conceding that they need additional care, and it is hard to force people out of housing they rent or own. The exclusion increases the price of assisted living facilities, which in turn reduces the number of elderly who can afford such facilities.

Continuing care retirement communities (CCRCs) offer the elderly opportunities to move through various levels of care as their needs increase, often requiring that elders be ambulatory and reasonably healthy before they enter. Most of these CCRCs, even religious nonprofits, require deposits that run to the hundreds of thousands of dollars and are forfeited to the organization after some period of time, as well as a monthly living fee covering meals and basic services. While these communities offer the most peace of mind, they are available only to the relatively small numbers of elderly that can afford them.

The elderly living in 17,000 nursing facilities (NFs) in the US are most likely to be poor, whether or not they met that description when they entered. Two-thirds of the 1.7 million mostly female residents in US nursing facilities are eligible for Medicaid, which pays for just over half of nursing facility costs. While requirements vary by state, Medicaid eligibility typically means that elders may not possess more than $2,000 in assets (sometimes excluding a home if a spouse is still alive). Also, any income they may have from US Social Security or other sources is paid directly to the facility, where charges for a single resident now average $158 a day for a semi-private room, or $57,670 a year, and much more in some high-cost states like New York and Alaska (Metropolitan Life Insurance Company 2003: 4).

Facilities prefer to admit residents who can pay their own way for some time to come, but they seldom enjoy this opportunity. If middle-class elders arrive in a nursing facility with typically modest financial resources they quickly spend down their funds (at $51,000 per year, on average) and convert to Medicaid status. The worst nursing facilities tend to be those whose populations are more than 75 percent Medicaid-financed (although there are some exceptions, such as the Hebrew Rehabilitation Center for the Aged in Boston, Massachusetts). So-called "Medicaid mills" rely on minimal staffing, turn over Medicaid clients rapidly without providing personal or individual attention to their needs, and often defy federal regulations. Nursing homes face a cost squeeze: direct public payments to nursing facilities, not including individuals' Social Security payments, cover only about 61 percent of total costs (Cadette 2003).

Elders without family members who are willing and able to care for them at home often have a particularly hard time coping with serious illness. Because of cost-cutting in Medicare and other health programs over recent years, hospitals have incentives to shorten the stays of their patients, and often send elderly people "quicker and sicker" to nursing facilities, where average acuity of needs has increased substantially over the last ten years. According to the Online Certification and Reporting System of the Centers for Medicare and Medicaid Services, more than 45 percent of nursing home residents in 2004 suffered from dementia (American Health Care Association 2005).

In sum, formal eldercare in the US fosters even more social inequality than informal care, splitting old persons between "private payers" and the poor (or soon to be poor).

Nursing home quality

The quality of home and informal care is difficult to assess unless it is delivered in a community setting that can be observed or monitored. The quality of nursing home care is difficult to assess for similar reasons, but some indicators are provided by regular inspections by state surveyors who inspect facilities at least once every fifteen months, looking for regulatory violations. Regulations in the US generally focus on indicators of basic clinical care and health rather than quality-of-life concerns.

Problems that cause actual harm to residents or place them in immediate jeopardy have been documented in at least one-quarter of all facilities (US General Accounting Office 2003). Some care problems, such as severe weight loss and serious avoidable pressure sores, are understated by survey agencies and are not included in this estimate. A study in California, the largest state in the US, showed that many elders are dying of preventable problems including untreated infections, repeated falls, and even malnutrition and dehydration (US General Accounting Office 1998).

A shocking number of complaints a year are logged in the US from consumers, their families, and ombudspersons about the quality of nursing home care (US General Accounting Office 2002). The Department of Health and Human Services (DHHS) recently released a report showing that 95 percent of the nation's nursing homes did not meet the staffing threshold below which harm could be shown to occur for residents (US Center for Medicare and Medicaid Services 2001). Yet the administration of George W. Bush decided not to implement the report's recommendations for mandating increased hiring of nursing assistants and nurses, but rather attempted to create more efficient markets by posting information on nursing home quality on a government website (Department of Health and Human Services Secretary Thompson's letter to Congress concerning US CMS 2001; for a response, see Paraprofessional Healthcare Institute and American Federation of State, County, and Municipal Employees 2001). A coalition representing consumers, labor, providers, and the National Citizens' Coalition on Nursing Home Reform (NCCNHR) has documented serious quality and access problems in the nursing home industry and has proposed potential policy solutions. NCCNHR affiliates have focused on quality issues with consumers in every US state (see http://www.nccnhr.org).

The structure of the nursing home industry

The US primarily uses public funds (Medicare and Medicaid plus Social Security) to fund a mostly private, for-profit industry. About 67 percent of US nursing homes are for-profit, 25 percent are not-for-profit, and 8 percent are publicly owned (Eaton 2000). The federal government has

43

delegated to states the power to set specific benefit levels, beyond a bare minimum, and to monitor basic safety and quality standards.

One major problem with ensuring quality of care is, of course, the limited information and consumer choice that exist in this environment. Nursing facilities average 80 percent or higher occupancy rates; the highest quality ones fill quickly and have long waiting lists. As a result, few consumers are able to exercise much choice. Many elderly people transferring to nursing home facilities after a short hospital stay must go wherever they can find a bed. Most states have limited or banned the construction of new nursing home beds, since they would fill up nearly immediately if built, costing the public sector more. Also, it is difficult and dangerous to move elders after they have settled into a facility, so the initial choice is usually the last, allowing little room for trial and error.

Family members may or may not provide a check on quality; too often they live far away and visit only rarely. Finally, the health status of older residents is poor to begin with and tends to worsen unless they only have a short rehabilitative stay. With more than 50 percent of nursing home inhabitants suffering from dementia, the "consumers" themselves are often not able to make their needs understood or to complain about poor conditions. While direct physical abuse is relatively rare, it does occur, and some observers would say that emotional abuse is more frequent though harder to document. Probably the most severe problem is the poor quality of day-to-day conditions that results from inadequate staffing.

Nursing facilities in the US are not just generally unpleasant places to live and die; they are also unpleasant places to work. Wages for direct care workers average under $10 an hour, not enough to put a single mother with one or two children over the poverty line even if she is working full-time all year. Turnover among certified nursing assistants has been documented as more than 100 percent per year and is seldom lower than 30 percent per year (Eaton 2002). Not surprisingly, turnover among administrators and directors of nursing is increasing. Nursing homes are among the least safe workplaces in the US, even worse than construction sites and coal mines. Major complaints include back injuries from lifting and abuse from residents (Service Employees International Union 1999). Nursing facilities offer few benefits to their staffs, whose members are disproportionately women of color and immigrants, typically with low levels of formal education. Only about 10 percent of nursing facilities are unionized (more in highly organized areas like New York City).

Despite their efforts to cut costs, few nursing homes are profitable. Seven of the largest nine for-profit nursing home chains experienced bankruptcy in the last several years, in part as a result of tighter regulations on the amount of physical therapy and real estate transaction costs that can be reimbursed. Nursing facility operators blame many of their difficulties on inadequate government reimbursement and the precarious conditions experienced by their frontline staff (Barbara Bowers 2001).

POLICY ALTERNATIVES

Many countries do a better job than the US in providing for the elderly, although none provides ideal conditions. Advocates for improved eldercare in the US should demand more generous public provision but should also try to explain the limitations of market-based approaches and search for ways of improving eldercare quality.

Public provision

In many Western European countries, policies toward the elderly are designed to provide public support for living at home and aging in place. These policies are complemented by generous health and housing policies. The best examples of entitlement to independence and autonomy while receiving necessary care can be found in the Nordic countries, where governments provide support for elder home care, sometimes with 24-hour-a-day coverage. Sweden provides health and long-term care to all citizens based on need, offering an allowance to elders (or a caregivers' salary to the caregiver) comparable to the salary a state employee would earn, including vacation and pension benefits. Both Israel and Sweden give generous benefits to family members to take leave from paid work to care for an older family member, and long-term care is part of Israel's state-funded social insurance plan (National Alliance for Caregiving 2002: 6–7). Australia has passed a Home and Community Care (HACC) Act that provides respite and support services to caregivers and subsidizes nursing home care so the maximum payment owed by an elder or their family is capped at US$15,000 a year.

In Japan, where life expectancy is the longest, and the proportion of elders the highest in the world (projected to reach 26 percent by 2020), about half of all elders live with family members. Still, in 2000 Japan established the National Long-Term Care Insurance law, which relies on taxes and 10 percent co-payments from beneficiaries to provide residential or in-home care to all persons over 40 years of age who need it (National Alliance for Caregiving 2002: 8). Even in a very traditional culture where most married women do not work at career-type jobs and filial piety is valued, the government has established a right to needed care, whether at home or in an institution.[1]

In the UK, care in nursing homes is free to all. Home caregiver support is far more extensive than in the US, although it is sometimes means-tested to reduce total costs. Even Canada, a country that excludes nursing homes from national health services, provides affordable alternatives for assisted living. Seniors are also entitled to a social insurance payment that allows them more freedom of choice, although the amount of tax subsidy or caregiver support varies by province (National Alliance for Caregiving 2002: 8).

Weaknesses of market-based provision

The case for increased public provision of support for the elderly in the home and community rests on inherent weaknesses of market-based provision. In a wide-ranging essay on optimal contracts for health services, economists Karen Eggleston and Richard Zeckhauser emphasize the problems caused by limited information and the lack of consumer sovereignty (2002: 64–5). These problems suggest that a profit-oriented system can be problematic.

New economic models are needed to conceptualize the work of physical and emotional care for frail elders. As Arlie Hochschild noted many years ago in *The Managed Heart* (1983), corporations can try to make employees "act" friendly and happy, but this is hard on employees if it requires them to act in ways contradictory to their true feelings. In nursing home care, genuine relationships have remarkable healing qualities, but forced or artificial ones seem to burden caregiver and recipient alike.

Both the inputs and the outputs of care work are difficult to measure and monitor. Care work creates new bonds of social obligation and concern that enhance its value but also keep the "carer" feeling obligated to the person rather than to the job. This may mean that caregivers will work for lower wages than they should given the value of their work, and it may also mean that they perform significant unpaid work, resulting in inequities that penalize caregivers. In the long run, potential caregivers may learn to avoid care responsibilities because they create such emotional vulnerabilities (Paula England and Nancy Folbre 2003).

In the US, achieving accountability for private providers of care services who use scarce public dollars has been very difficult. Monitoring daily interactions is impossible, and occasional surveys, while helpful, do not resolve operational problems leading to repeated serious threats to residents' health and well-being. So far, the US government has attempted to regulate eldercare mainly through outcomes-based regulation and the prohibition of certain practices or conditions (cold food, unsafe hallways, insufficient hydration, etc.). But most consumers and even the government oversight agencies see major problems with this approach. Providers accurately complain that they are the most regulated industry in the US, with the possible exception of nuclear power, yet poor and even dangerous conditions continue to plague the industry.

Regulatory alternatives

Given market failures, how can public policy promote positive organizational change at the level of the individual facility or the industry as a whole? One encouraging example is provided by the state of Massachusetts, which inaugurated a Nursing Home Quality Initiative in 2000. The legislation initially had three features: (1) a wage pass-through to give providers more capacity to increase frontline worker wages ($45 million), (2) a scholarship fund for training new certified nursing assistants to come into the field ($1 million), and (3) a career ladder initiative designed to increase skills and retention among caregivers, to provide them with a way to move up occupational ladders in nursing facilities, and to encourage organizational "culture change" promoting more individualized, higher quality care ($5 million). The Commonwealth Corporation, a quasi-public organization that provides a variety of services to Massachusetts businesses, administered the third feature, the Extended Care Career Ladder Initiative (ECCLI). The Massachusetts legislature has refunded ECCLI each fiscal year through 2004, despite serious lapses in funding during state budget delays in 2001 and 2002.

Evaluations of ECCLI have shown that the program was successful in training hundreds of frontline workers in skills related to dementia care, death and dying, basic adult education and literacy, and other areas related to improving patient care (Susan Eaton, Claudia Green, Randall Wilson, and Theresa Osypuk 2001; Randall Wilson, Susan Eaton, and Amara Kamanu 2003). The program also encouraged organizations to create slightly higher-paying jobs (sometimes called Certified Nursing Assistant or CNA 2 and 3) that involved mentoring, supporting registered and licensed nurses, and sometimes doing more skilled work. However, these jobs paid only about 30 to 50 cents an hour in higher wages, which was insufficient to improve the lives of the CNAs involved. Although adoption of the program was associated with increased retention and reduced turnover, it was hard to identify its specific effects independent of macroeconomic trends (Eaton *et al.* 2001; Wilson *et al.* 2003). Changes in organizational culture were more difficult to perceive and measure, although efforts to attribute specific quality-of-care outcomes to particular workforce improvements continue.

Does ECCLI offer potential for improving the quality of care in the US? Although the program includes clearly mandated requirements for participation and expected outcomes, it also allows for a certain amount of flexibility in regard to program development and implementation at the facility level. Such management-based regulation "directs regulated organizations to engage in a planning process that aims toward achievement of public goals, offering firms flexibility in how they achieve public goals" (Cary Coglianese and David Lazer 2002). This decentralized form of regulation differs from technology-based (in which organizations are directed how to implement a program) or performance-based (in which organizations must achieve desired outcomes) regulation.

Management-based regulation seems appropriate for ECCLI because each nursing facility or home healthcare agency possesses a unique CNA population – differing in nationality, primary language spoken, and years of experience, among other variables – that requires flexibility in program and curriculum development. Allowing local, on-site management and leaving decisions up to those affected by the regulations is also in line with an assisted living philosophy that advocates choice. Yet the implementation and evaluation of the program has not yet resolved the problem of achieving accountability for the larger outcomes of promoting personal relationships between staff and clients and enhancing quality of life for elders and employees.

Encouraging and developing best practices

Overall, the 17,000 nursing facilities in the US have shown little eagerness to improve their management or explore new innovations. Most of the care offered is of a type that can be considered custodial, at best. However, some exceptions are emerging, as new, largely volunteer organizations try to encourage "regenerative care" (Eaton 2000, 2002). These include Wellspring (Susan Reinhard and Robin Stone 2001), the Eden Alternative (2005), and the Pioneer Network (2005).

One management reform advocated by the Pioneer Network involves "consistent assignment" of aides to residents, rather than floating or rotating assignments, so that genuine relationships can develop between people, and so local knowledge of daily preferences can be honored and retained" (The Pioneer Network 2005). The Pioneer Network is trying to redefine the very way "old age" and "eldercare" are understood. Their eleven principles include statements that aging is another life stage; that growth is not only possible, but also necessary in this life stage, as in all others; that elders are people to learn from; and that people need to give and receive care. Becoming a "pioneer" caregiver is a journey, not a destination, promoting the kinds of caring interactions between people that are seldom to be found in grim and reeking nursing homes.

So far, the Pioneer Network is only a small, underfunded, voluntary social movement relying on the extraordinary commitment of talented individuals. However, two private foundations, Atlantic Philanthropies and Robert Wood Johnson, have recently teamed up to fund demonstration projects and applied research studies, inspired in part by Pioneer Network culture change initiatives, to put the concept of "Better Jobs and Better Care" into practice (2005). Grantees representing coalitions of consumer advocates, long-term care workers, provider organizations, and various state agencies in Iowa, North Carolina, Pennsylvania, Oregon, and Vermont will implement innovative changes in policy and practice designed to build a stable, high-quality workforce and address problems of high turnover and worker shortages.

These efforts are directed only at the tip of the iceberg. It is unrealistic to expect highly institutionalized organizations to "change their cultures" based on a few thousand dollars in training funds, or to mandate that managers do a better job of building positive relationships between staff and elders. Moving the entire industry toward "regenerative communities" and high-quality care will require even more public policy resources than Massachusetts' ECCLI program. Still, these efforts could help build the sense of possibility needed to mobilize widespread support for change.

Susan C. Eaton, John F. Kennedy School of Government, Harvard University,
Cambridge, MA 02138, USA

Questions about this article may be sent to

Nancy Folbre, Department of Economics, University of Massachusetts,
Amherst, MA 01003, USA
e-mail: folbre@econs.umass.edu

NOTE

1 In China, as Zhan and Montgomery (2003) note, the increased number of women workers since the Cultural Revolution has meant that not only sons but daughters are considered financially responsible for aging.

REFERENCES

American Health Care Association (AHCA). 2005. Member Survey. http://www.ahca.org (accessed February 2005). Also cited in Paraprofessional Healthcare Institute (PHI) and the Catholic Health Association (CHA). 2003. *Finding and Keeping Direct Care Staff*, p. 51. St Louis, MO: CHA. http://www.ahca.org (accessed May 18, 2005).

Better Jobs and Better Care. http://www.bjbc.org (accessed February 2005).

Bowers, Barbara. 2001. *Organizational Culture Change in Long Term Care.* Washington, DC: Urban Institute, US Department of Health and Social Services.

Brody, Elaine. 1990. *Women in the Middle: The Parent Care Years.* New York: Springer.

Cadette, Walter M. 2003. *Caring for a Large Geriatric Generation: The Coming Crisis in US Health Care.* Policy Note 2003–3. The Levy Economics Institute of Bard College. http://www.levy.org/docs/pn/03-3.html (accessed July 2003).

Coglianese, Cary and David Lazer. 2003. "Management-Based Regulation: Prescribing Private Management to Achieve Public Goals." *Law and Society Review*, 37(4): 691–731.

Cooperative Home Care Associates. 2003. http://www.chcany.org (accessed February 2005).

Eaton, Susan C. 2000. "Beyond 'Unloving Care': Linking Human Resource Management and Patient Care Quality in Nursing Homes." *International Journal of Human Resource Management* 11(3): 591–616.

——. 2002. "What a Difference Management Makes! Nursing Staff Turnover Variation within a Single Labor Market," in Abt Associates, *Appropriateness of Minimum Nurse Staffing Ratios in Nursing Homes: Report to Congress, Phase II*. Released June 12, 2002, by the Center for Medicare and Medicaid Services. http://www.cms.gov (accessed February 2005).

——. Claudia Green, Randall Wilson, and Theresa Osypuk. 2001. "Extended Care Career Ladder Initiative (ECCLI): Baseline Evaluation Report of a Massachusetts Nursing Home Initiative," Kennedy School of Government Working Paper No RWP01-035, July 2001. http://www.ksg.harvard.edu (accessed February 2005).

The Eden Alternative. http://www.edenalternative.com (accessed May 17, 2005).

Eggleston, Karen and Richard Zeckhauser. 2002. "Government Contracting for Health Care," in John D. Donahue and Joseph S. Nye, Jr., eds. *Market-Based Governance: Supply Side, Demand Side, Upside, and Downside*, pp. 29–65. Washington, DC: Brookings Institution Press.

England, Paula and Nancy Folbre. 2003. "Contracting for Care," in Marianne Ferber and Julie Nelson, eds. *Feminist Economics Today: Beyond Economic Man* pp. 61–80. Chicago: University of Chicago Press.

Ferber, Marianne and Julie Nelson, eds. 1993. *Beyond Economic Man*. Chicago: University of Chicago Press.

Folbre, Nancy. 2001. *The Invisible Heart: Economics and Family Values*. New York: The New Press.

Frank, Barbara and Steven Dawson. 2000. *Health Care Workforce Issues in Massachusetts*, Massachusetts Health Policy Forum Issue Brief on June 22, 2000. Waltham, MA: Brandeis University.

Hochschild, Arlie Russell. 1983. *The Managed Heart*. Berkeley, CA: University of California Press.

Jensen, J. and M. Sineau. 2001. *Women's Work, Childcare, and Welfare State Redesign*. Toronto: University of Toronto Press.

McCall, Nelda and Jodi Korb. 2003. "Medicare Home Health Use after the 1997 BBA," in *Fact Sheet for the Home Care Research Institute*. New York: Center for Home Care Policy and Research, Visiting Nurse Service of New York.

Metropolitan Life Insurance Company (MetLife) Mature Market Institute. 2003. *The MetLife Market Survey of Nursing Home and Home Health Costs*.

—— and the National Alliance for Caregiving. 1997. *The MetLife Study of Employer Costs for Working Caregivers*.

National Alliance for Caregiving (NAC). 2002. *Conference Report*. Third International Conference on Caregiving, October 12–14,2002. Washington, DC. http://www.caregiving.org (accessed August 2003).

—— and the American Association of Retired Persons (AARP). 1997. *Family Caregiving in the US: Findings from a National Survey* Washington, DC: NAC.

Paraprofessional Healthcare Institute (PHI) and the Catholic Health Association (CHA) of the United States. 2003. *Finding and Keeping Direct Care Staff*. St. Louis, MO: CHA.

—— and the North Carolina Department of Health and Human Services Office of Long-Term Care. 2002. *Results of the 2002 National Survey of State Initiatives on the Long-Term Care Direct Work Force*. http://www.directcareclearinghouse.org (accessed June 2003).

—— and the American Federation of State, County, and Municipal Employees (AFSCME). 2001. *Cheating Dignity: The Direct Care Wage Crisis in America*. Washington, DC: AFSCME.

The Pioneer Network. http://www.pioneernetwork.org (accessed February 2005).

Reinhard, Susan and Robin Stone. 2001. *Promoting Quality in Nursing Homes: The Well Spring Model*. New York: Institute for the Future of Aging Services, American Association of Homes and Services for the Aging.

Schneider, Geoff and Jean Shackleford. 2001. "Economics Standards and Lists: Proposed Antidotes for Feminist Economists." *Feminist Economics* 7(2): 77–89.

Service Employees International Union (SEIU). 1999. *Caring Till It Hurts.* Washington, DC: SEIU. http://www.seiu.org (accessed September 2001).

Spillman, Brenda, William Spector, John Fleishman, and Liliana Pezzin. 2000. *The Characteristics of Long-Term Care Users.* Paper commissioned by the Institute of Medicine Committee on Improving Quality in Long-Term Care, published by the Agency for Healthcare Research and Quality, AHRQ Pub. No 00-0049, September 2000.

Stone, Robin and Joshua Wiener. 2001. *Who Will Care for Us? Addressing the Long-Term Care Workforce Crisis.* New York: The Urban Institute and the American Association of Homes and Services for the Aging.

United Nations Human Development Program (UNHDP). 1999. *Human Development Report.* New York: United Nations.

United States Administration on Aging. 2002. *America's Families Care: A Report on the Needs of America's Family Caregivers.* http://www.aoa.gov/carenetwork/report.html (accessed August 2003).

United States Center for Medicare and Medicaid Services (CMS). 2001. *Phase 2 of the Minimum Staffing Study.* Cambridge, MA: Abt Associates. http://www.cms.gov (accessed February 2005).

United States General Accounting Office (GAO). 1998. *California Nursing Homes: Federal and State Oversight Inadequate to Protect Residents in Homes with Serious Care Problems,* Report GAO/HEHS-99-46 Washington, DC: GAO.

——. 2002. *Nursing Homes: More Can Be Done to Protect Residents from Abuse.* http://www.gao.gov/new.items/d02312.pdf (accessed February 2005).

——. 2003. *Nursing Home Quality: Prevalence of Serious Problems, While Declining, Reinforces Importance of Enhanced Oversight,* Report GAO-03-561 Washington, DC: GAO.

Wilson, Randall, Susan C. Eaton, and Amara Kamanu. 2003. "Extended Care Career Ladder Initiative (ECCLI): Round 2 Evaluation Report," Kennedy School of Government Working Paper No RWP03-006.

Zhan, Heying Jenny and Rhonda J. V. Montgomery. 2003. "Gender and Elder Care in China: The Influence of Filial Piety and Structural Constraints." *Gender and Society* 17(2): 209–29.

GENDER, AGING, AND THE EVOLVING ARAB PATRIARCHAL CONTRACT

Jennifer C. Olmsted

INTRODUCTION

Demographic transitions, whether they involve a growing cohort of youths or elderly persons,[1] concern policy-makers (James Midgley 1996). While in the West concerns have been raised about the growing cohort of elderly, in the Arab world, the policy focus has been on the slow fertility decline (Sulayman Al-Qudsi 1996; Jennifer Olmsted 2003), which in turn is linked to extremely high rates of youth unemployment (World Bank 2004d). The enormity of the problem of rising unemployment, occurring when structural adjustment programs are also being imposed, has tended to limit research examining how the elderly in Arab communities are faring. And yet, as I will argue, the well-being of the elderly is directly linked to the question of youth unemployment, since, in most Arab countries, the primary social safety net remains the family.

Although some recent discussions of aging (for example, United Nations International Research and Training Institute for the Advancement of

Women [UN INSTRAW 1999]) suggest that the elderly are often not respected or valued, evidence from Arab communities challenges this conclusion. While the nature of the patriarchal society constructs a hierarchy where men dominate women, this same hierarchy is age based, suggesting that women may gain power as they age. The patriarchal contract that exists in Arab societies protects most elderly women from economic hardship and facilitates their access to power in certain spheres. At the same time, most women's choices have been limited to participation in the patriarchal contract. In addition, not all women are equally protected by the patriarchal contract. Finally, as Arab society changes, the strength of the patriarchal contract is beginning to erode. Yet the ability of the public sector to provide a social safety net for the elderly is severely limited, particularly in countries where unemployment rates are alarmingly high and poverty remains a serious problem. In the Palestinian case, which I discuss in some depth here, recent, rather draconian, Israeli policies[2] have led to massive unemployment and rapidly rising poverty in the West Bank and Gaza, creating economic hardship not only for the elderly but for many Palestinian households.

THE ARAB PATRIARCHAL CONTRACT

As Nancy Folbre (1994) and others have illustrated, it is necessary to contextualize discussions of patriarchy both culturally and historically to understand the differing ways patriarchal control has developed and been maintained – or challenged – in different communities during various time periods. Carole Pateman (1988), for instance, examines how the structure of the sexual contract in the UK, US, and Australia is shaped by culturally specific notions of the "individual," thereby illustrating the need to examine notions of self in order to comprehend how patriarchy operates. Suad Joseph (1999b, 2000) and Halim Barakat (1985) have pointed out that an examination of identity is also central to understanding the continued strength of patriarchy in the Arab context. Barakat emphasizes the link between family and identity, observing that the "success or failure of an individual member becomes that of the family as a whole" (p. 28). Joseph similarly discusses what she describes as the enmeshed or connective relationships among Arab family members. In doing so, she challenges the notion that patriarchy is necessarily based on the idea of a male separative self,[3] pointing out that in Arab society the construction of a more connective or fluid self is central to patriarchal control. Children are socialized to think of themselves not only as continuations of their parents, but also of their siblings and other family members. Particularly strong may be the bonds between mothers and sons, and brothers and sisters.

The dominant Arab family structure also facilitates the strength of patriarchy, as it is both patrilinear and patrilocal; that is, descent is based on the male line, and adult sons often continue to live with their parents, while daughters marry out (Barakat 1985). As a result, aging parents generally live in extended family households, with one or more of their adult sons. Most women are economically supported first by their fathers, then by their husbands, and eventually by their sons. While women are generally defined as economic dependents during most, if not all of their lives, Deniz Kandiyoti (1991) argues that the power of Arab women increases as they age. This may be particularly true of older widows living in extended households. They may have more powerful voices than younger men and women, not only within the household, where they control the labor of their daughters-in-law and make economic demands on their sons, but also in the public sphere.

Islam has also played a role in shaping the nature of the patriarchal contract in the region. Because Islam is a highly contractual religion, the terms of men's and women's rights and responsibilities are fairly clearly laid out in religious doctrine. In addition, the responsibility of the community to care for members in economic need, especially widows and orphans, is explicitly addressed within Islam through the notion of *zakat*. *Zakat*, one of the five pillars of Islam, defines alms giving as an explicit duty of Muslims, and involves the giving of a percentage of one's income to mosques, which then redistribute the contributions to the poor.

In addition, most Arab countries adjudicate marriage, divorce, and inheritance laws through religious rather than secular courts (Jennifer Olmsted 1999; Joseph 2000). On one hand, this means that marriage laws are explicit about husbands' economic responsibilities toward their wives and children, and that individual marriage contracts often contain provisions stipulating when and what a woman's right to economic support and inheritance is. On the other hand, as Barakat (1985) has pointed out, these security provisions have also meant that women continue to be defined as dependents. And, although women's economic rights are guaranteed under family law, the level of enforcement of this patriarchal contract varies and depends on interpretations made by (male) judges.

Women's access to economic resources

In most Arab societies women's primary, albeit indirect, access to economic assets remains their claim on family resources, although they also have the right to control their own wealth. According to Annelies Moors (1995), *mahr* (dower) is one important way for women to obtain property. In Muslim marriage contracts the amount of *mahr* a woman will receive is explicitly specified. Moors identified two forms of *mahr* – prompt and deferred. Prompt *mahr* involves the transfer of cash, gold, and other forms of wealth from the husband to the wife (and/or the wife's family) upon marriage. The deferred *mahr* generally refers to a woman's inheritance when she becomes a widow (or if her husband divorces her). While, in theory, *mahr* gives women the right to their own wealth, in reality family dynamics often lead to fathers claiming some *mahr* and/or women contributing some of their property to the running of their own household, although according to Muslim law, this is strictly the responsibility of the husband (Moors 1995).

Muslim law also stipulates more generally that women have the right to inherit property, although as both Suad Joseph (1999a) and Moors (1995) point out, women may relinquish their claims to inheritance for a variety of complex reasons. For instance, within the patriarchal contract, siblings are raised with the expectation that if a sister is in economic need, the brother will provide for her. Because women are aware of this implicit contract, they may choose not to claim their inheritances, preferring instead to maintain good relations with their brothers.

Historically, some women have had the choice to opt out of the patriarchal contract, because of access to the labor market or because their families have had enough wealth to enable them to live independently. But for most women this contract remains the norm. In keeping with the strength of the patriarchal contract, marriage has been nearly compulsory. Having children is also virtually compulsory for women in Arab societies, and fertility rates in the region have historically been quite high, although in recent years they have begun declining. Although having children is the norm, the continuing strength of the patriarchal contract, which instills in men the idea that they are economically responsible for all close female kin, ensures that even unmarried women or married women who do not have children, are provided for, generally by close male kin such as uncles and nephews. Still, even within this rather inclusive patriarchal contract, women with few kin members or with kin members who are either unable or unwilling to accept economic responsibility for female family members are at increased economic risk.

Is the contract evolving?

As Barakat (1985) and Hisham Sharabi (1988), among others, have pointed out, modernity,[4] which is often associated with industrialization, the decreased importance of a land-based economy, and the increased importance of education, has reduced the power of the older generation. Data presented in Table 1 (ranked by per capita GDP), illustrate the decreasing economic importance of agriculture and rapidly rising education levels, as well as the fact that countries in the region are in various phases of modernization. The Palestinians, I have argued elsewhere (Jennifer Olmsted 1996), experienced a particularly rapid, forced modernization when many became landless (and stateless) in 1948, with the creation of Israel. As a result, Palestinians also experienced a relatively

Table 1 Socio-economic indicators of modernization by country and region

Country or region	Per capita GDP (US$) 2002[a]	Adult literacy rate 1970[b]	Adult literacy rate 2000[b]	Employment in agriculture 1980[c]	Employment in agriculture 1990[c]	Total fertility rate 1980[d]	Total fertility rate 2000[d]	Females as percent of labor force[d]	Unemployment[e]
Qatar	28,959	58		3		5.6	2.6	15	12*
United Arab Emirates	19,816	52	76	5	8	5.4	3.2	15	3*
Kuwait	13,935	58	82	2	1	5.3	2.7	31	3*
Bahrain	12,012	51	88			5.2	2.8	21	12*
Saudi Arabia	8,169	33	76	44	19	7.3	5.5	16	8*
Oman	7,421	19	72			9.9	4.3	17	10*
Libya	5,453	35	80	25	11	7.3	3.5	23	
Lebanon	5,087			14	17	4.0	2.3	30	7*
Tunisia	2,080	27	71	39	22**	5.2	2.1	32	16
Algeria	1,784	22	67	36	12**	6.7	3.1	28	27
Jordan	1,726	55	90	11	6**	6.8	3.7	25	13*
West Bank and Gaza	1,650[f]			22	14	6.3[g]	5.1		31
Syria	1,543	41	74		28**	7.1	3.6	27	12
Egypt	1,390	32		42	30**	5.1	3.3	30	9
Morocco	1,145	20	49		44**	5.4	2.9	35	12 or 22*
Iraq	881			29	16	6.4	4.3	20	
Yemen	431	14	46	72	54**	7.9	6.2	28	12
Sudan	376			72	70	6.1	4.6	30	
Middle East and Northern Africa	2,160[e]	22	74		27		3.2	28	
Low income	410		63		72			38	
Lower middle	1,220[e]		90					43	
Upper middle	4,640[e]		96	61	40			36	
High	26,900[e]			9	4				

Sources: [a]United Nations (2003); [b]World Bank (2005a); [c]World Bank (2005c), except **World Bank (2004d) (latest available data reported – years vary from 1990 to 2000); [d]World Bank (2005b), except *World Bank (2004b), except *World Bank (2004d); [e]United Nations (2005); [f]World Bank (2004b); [g]Palestinian Central Bureau of Statistics (1998).

rapid rise in literacy. A Palestinian Central Bureau of Statistics (PCBS) study (1996) reported that 65 percent of Palestinians over 65 years of age were illiterate, while among men and women aged 15 to 24, literacy was almost universal.

While some trends suggest rapid modernization, declines in fertility rates and increases in women's labor-force participation rates in the region have been slow relative to other parts of the world, again, particularly among Palestinians. What these trends suggest about the age and gender aspects of the patriarchal contract remains unclear. I hypothesize that traditional family structures and gendered economic relationships have been maintained more in the Arab world than in other modernizing contexts. However, despite the particular resilience of the Arab patriarchal contract, cultural norms are changing, although far more research is needed to determine the extent of these changes. It is not clear how quickly changes are occurring or how various cohorts of women and men are likely to be affected. And, as changes have occurred, the pace at which communities within the region have experienced the shift towards modernity has differed, with members of various communities reacting to and experiencing modernity in differing ways.

Why has the patriarchal contract remained particularly resilient in Arab communities? Doubtless, both economic and cultural factors have played a role. As Joseph (2000) argues, the construction of a fluid self has facilitated the notion of economic responsibility for other family members, particularly among men. Given that the economic well-being of women depends heavily on their sons, mothers have had an incentive to encourage the idea of a fluid or connective self. On the economic side, the strong macroeconomy that prevailed during the oil boom of the 1970s and 1980s helped facilitate the gender division of labor. At that time, male Arab workers could earn relatively high (family) wages, and as a result women's entry into paid employment was slow. Women's major economic contributions thus continued to be in the reproductive and domestic spheres.

While for the most part reinforcing traditional gender roles, the strong oil economy and modernization in general did in some ways contribute to breaking down the extended family and traditional gender roles. Modernization meant increased rural to urban migration, while the oil boom led to increased international migration, with large numbers of men from poorer Arab countries such as Yemen and Egypt migrating to the richer oil states in search of paid employment.[5] Both types of migration contributed to the weakening of the extended family household structure and changing gender roles. Women, for example, often assumed new roles, when their husbands migrated and they stayed behind (Elizabeth Taylor 1984; Annelies Moors 1989; Louhichi Khaled 1995).

More recently, macro developments and political events have reversed a number of these earlier trends. Declining oil prices (which peaked in

1979), followed by the decision of many Gulf countries to replace Arab migrants with non-Arabs, reduced the number of migration opportunities in the region (World Bank 2004d). A number of countries that had come to expect migration opportunities as a means of reducing unemployment[6] now find that they are facing high unemployment rates, especially among the youth cohort. It is unclear what impact these changes will have on family formation and the patriarchal contract. The dissolution of the extended family has already begun and thus is likely to continue to occur. However, the very difficult economic situation in the region may be leading to a reversal, or at least a slowing, of this trend, since younger cohorts have not been able to become economically independent.

(ELDERLY) WOMEN'S ECONOMIC PARTICIPATION/ VULNERABILITY

Data reported in Table 2 (ranked in order of female life expectancy) provide some insights into the gendering of socio-economic conditions in the region. They also illustrate that generalizing across Arab communities is somewhat problematic, given the wide disparity in incomes and political histories in the region. Among Palestinians, for instance, Israeli military occupation has long precluded the development of a state apparatus[7] and also caused high levels of political and economic uncertainty. Communities in Iraq, Algeria, Lebanon, Yemen, and Sudan have also been impacted by extensive military conflicts, which have negatively affected per capita income and exacerbated poverty. The Gulf states, on the other hand, have very high per capita income, as they receive considerable income from oil and natural gas sales. Average life expectancy in the region ranges from 56 to 80 years and fairly closely maps per capita income. Women, who have a somewhat higher average life expectancy (69 versus 66 years) than men,[8] are slightly over-represented among the elderly.[9]

As was noted earlier, participation in the labor market remains low among Arab women. As the structure of Arab economies evolves and women's education levels rise, these employment patterns are shifting, but increases in paid employment have primarily occurred among younger cohorts (Sulayman Al-Qudsi, Ragui Assaad, and Radwan Shaban 1993).[10] Older women more often participate in the economy by contributing their labor to domestic labor and to agricultural production and other family businesses. For the older generation of Arab women, then, lack of access to paid employment is not necessarily the best indicator of relative economic vulnerability.[11]

Data suggest that while marriage rates remain very high, women are less likely to marry than men, and in recent years the number of never-married women has been rising. Among Palestinians, for instance, 2.7 percent of women older than 65, compared with 0.7 percent of similarly aged men, are

Table 2 Socio-economic indicators for the Middle East and Northern Africa

Country	Population[a] (millions)	GDP[b] (per capita)	Life expectancy[a] (female)	Life expectancy[a] (male)	Difference	Population < 15[c]	Population > 60[c] (female)	Population > 60[c] (male)
Kuwait	2.0	13,935	79	75	4	26	3	3
United Arab Emirates	2.9	19,816	77	74	3	25	3	2
Bahrain	0.6	12,012	76	71	5	29	5	4
Qatar	0.6	28,959	75	74	1	26	3	3
Oman	2.4	7,421	75	72	3	37	4	3
Saudi Arabia	20.7	8,169	74	71	3	39	4	4
Libya	5.3	5,453	74	69	5	31	6	6
Tunisia	9.6	2,080	74	70	4	28	9	8
West Bank and Gaza		1,650[d]	74	70	4		3.6[e]	3.3[e]
Algeria	30.4	1,784	73	69	4	33	7	5
Jordan	4.9	1,726	73	70	3	38	5	5
Lebanon	4.3	5,087	72	69	3	29	9	8
Turkey	67.4	2,136	72	67	5	30	9	8
Syria	16.2	1,543	72	67	5	37	5	4
Iran	63.7	1,606	70	68	2	32	6	6
Morocco	28.7	1,145	70	66	4	31	7	6
Egypt	64.0	1,390	69	66	3	35	7	6
Iraq	22.3	881	62	60	2	41	5	4
Sudan	31.1	376	59	56	3	39	6	5
Yemen	17.5	431	57	56	1	49	4	3
Middle East and Northern Africa	294.9	2,160[d]	69	66	3	36.2		
Low income		410	60	58	2	36.4		
Lower middle		1,220[d]	71	67	4	26.7		
Upper middle		4,640[d]	75	68	7	29.0		
High		26,900[d]	81	75	6	18.4		

Sources: [a]World Bank (2005b); [b]United Nations (2003); [c]United Nations (2004); [d]World Bank (2004b); [e]Palestinian Central Bureau of Statistics (1998).

categorized as never-married. Among the group aged 50–54, though, 8.5 percent of women never married, versus 1.0 percent of men (Palestinian Central Bureau of Statistics [PCBS] 1996). In addition, women are more likely to outlive their husbands (who are often older), and they are less likely than men to remarry when their spouses die. Thus, while 87.4 percent of men over the age of 65 report being married, only 34.7 percent of women of this age are. The other 66.3 percent of women are widowed (60.6 percent), never married (2.7 percent), separated (1.1 percent), or divorced (0.8 percent) (PCBS 1996). Older women are thus far less likely to be married than men, for a variety of reasons, and as a result are more likely to be living alone and economically vulnerable. This trend has been noted in many areas of the world, despite the fact that, as pointed out in a recent UN INSTRAW publication (1999), "in most societies there is the expectation that widowed women will remarry or be reabsorbed into extended families" (p. x).

A number of scholars have remarked on the fact that poverty rates in the region are quite low, given GDP figures.[12] Researchers have offered various explanations for why poverty rates in the region are relatively low. The World Bank (1995: 34) argues that "rapid growth in the 1970s and early 1980s and the introduction of generous transfers to large portions of the population" are in part responsible for lower poverty rates. Others have argued that built-in redistribution mechanisms (*zakat* and inheritance laws), enforced by cultural and religious norms, play a role (Riad El-Ghonemy 1998).

Evidence of the impact of sex and age on poverty is mixed,[13] and information on these factors remains extremely limited. El-Ghonemy (1998) cites data limitations as one problem. Gaurav Datt, Dean Jolliffe, and Manohar Sharma (2001) find that in Egypt, female-headed households have a slightly higher rate of poverty, but that this difference is not statistically significant. A 2001 World Bank study noted that among Palestinians, 26 percent of female- headed households were categorized as poor, compared to 20 percent of dual- or male-headed households. Among elderly Palestinians the poverty rate was even higher, at 32 percent, but poverty rates are also high among Palestinian and Egyptian families that have many dependent children. Of course, given that the elderly are usually part of extended families, it is likely that large, poor households, with high dependency ratios, contain both children and elderly household members.

It is also important to note that recent Israeli policies, such as closures, travel restrictions, and curfews, have caused a dramatic increase in the number of Palestinian households experiencing economic hardship. While in 1998, one in four Palestinians was poor (World Bank 2001), by 2002 the estimated poverty rate had risen to an unprecedented 60 percent (UNSCO 2002: 2). This development raises serious concerns about the well-being not only of elderly women, but also of the Palestinian population more generally.

The few studies that have examined the incidence of poverty among the elderly and women acknowledge that only limited conclusions can be drawn, particularly from studies that focus on headship as the category for examining the links among age, sex, and poverty. Such studies do not address how females and the elderly are treated and what their access to resources within households is. The possibility of a gender bias against girls has received more attention than the question of whether elderly women face neglect. Some child health indicators suggest a gender bias, although the evidence is mixed (World Bank 2004a, 2004c). The question of whether elderly women have less access than other household members to available resources also needs to be discussed, but has received only limited attention in the literature.

SAFETY NETS

Given that elderly women often do not have direct control over economic resources, it is important to examine the structure of the safety net in the Arab world. The term safety net is generally used when referring to state-sponsored programs to protect vulnerable populations, but can also refer to more informal mechanisms, particularly the family, by which individuals can make claims to economic support.

The role of the government

Government-sponsored safety nets, while stronger in Arab countries than in other parts of the developing world, remain limited, and do not particularly target the elderly (World Bank 2002). This is of course particularly the case for Palestinians, given their stateless status, although the UN, as well as a range of international nongovernmental organizations (NGOs), have provided a state-like apparatus to some Palestinian communities. In recent years the main institutional providers of social support in the West Bank and Gaza[14] have been the Palestinian Ministry of Social Affairs (MSA), the UN, and various religious institutions (most notably the Islamic *zakat* program).

Other Arab communities have developed state-sponsored social safety nets of varying effectiveness. The oil-rich Gulf states, which have extensive financial resources, have some of the more comprehensive programs. In many of the non-oil-exporting countries historically, the two major components of safety nets in the region were universal food subsidies and employment guarantees (primarily for the educated), both of which are under attack because of structural adjustments. While most government programs are not specifically tailored for the elderly, both Arab culture and Islam recognize the economic vulnerability of widows and orphans; hence, most countries have assistance programs that specifically target these two groups, although payments are often small and coverage incomplete.

In the past, pensions were not a major component of government programs, but in recent years government expenditures on pensions have increased considerably and have often surpassed spending on other kinds of transfers (World Bank 2002). Existing pension programs, though, are generally "pay-as-you-go" systems, based on employment history, and limited to formal-sector employees. Given that both men's and women's participation in formal sector employment remain low, coverage remains limited. This is particularly the case for women, who are far less likely to participate in paid employment. Women who do benefit from such programs tend to do so primarily through the receipt of survivor benefits. Dependent children as well as wives are generally eligible for survivor benefits, which vary from 25 to 100 percent of the benefit provided to the worker, with the percent often depending on the number of other survivors (United States Social Security Association [SSA] 1999).

Pensions are quite scarce among Palestinians. While a study by Marianne Heiberg and Geir Ovensen (1993) indicated that 3 percent of Palestinians surveyed were collecting a pension in 1992, 14 percent of Jordanians surveyed around the same time said that they received a government-provided pension or social security (Jon Hanssen-Bauer, Jon Pedersen, and Age Tiltnes 1998), although the age profiles of both populations are similar. More generally, while the formal safety net provides some assistance to groups identified as particularly needy, there are large gaps in its fabric, and the family remains the primary source of assistance, particularly for elderly women.

The family-based safety net – the Palestinian case

An examination of the household structures within which elderly Palestinians live can provide some insights into the ways elder care is gendered. The data in Table 3[15] group the elderly (aged 60 and higher) by marital status and living arrangement. The average size of households containing elderly members was seven, with a range from one to twenty-three members. The living patterns observed are emblematic of the patriarchal structure of society, with elderly parents generally living with their sons. It is noteworthy that although my sample included both refugees (who had lost their land and thus had been thrust more rapidly into the modern economy) and nonrefugees, there did not appear to be many differences in living arrangements (with the exception that extremely large households were more prevalent among nonrefugees living in villages).

The most common arrangement (seen in 38 percent of households) consisted of a parent or parents living in an extended (mixed) family setting with one or more sons and any unmarried daughters. The next most

Table 3 Elderly Palestinians' living arrangements

	With son(s)		Sons and daughters		With daughter(s)		Alone		Unknown		Total	
	No.	%	No.	%	No.	%	No.	%	No.	%	No.	%
Single male (widowed)	2	40	1	20	1	20	0	0	1	20	5	6
Single female (divorced, single, widowed)	11	30	13 (15)	35 (40)	5 (3)	14 (9)	2	5	6	16	37	47
Married couples	13	36	16	44	5	14	3	6	0	0	37	47
Total number of households	26	34	30 (32)	38 (42)	11 (9)	14 (10)	4	5	7	9	78	100

Note: Numbers in parentheses represent estimates based on an alternative definition of household – cases where the parents were residing with a daughter, but one or more sons were also living in the same building (in separate residences).

common arrangement, which occurred if the daughters had already married and left the household, was for the parent(s) to live with one or more sons, married or unmarried. Only eleven sets of parents (14 percent of the sample) lived with daughters only. In two of these cases, a son was living in the same building; thus, presenting an alternative definition of "household" this arrangement would be added to the "mixed" category. Of the remaining nine, only two cases were documented in which parents were living with a married daughter, and both were quite unusual. The first case was that of a highly educated woman, whose siblings had all emigrated and who was married to a European man. The second was the household of a polygynous man. The remaining seven cases were all instances in which parents were living with an unmarried daughter. In two of these cases the daughter was the only child who had remained in the West Bank, while in one case the couple had had only daughters and were living with the one who had remained unmarried.

While the norm was for elderly parents to live with their sons, as the above cases and others suggest, alternative household arrangements also existed. Two of the four never-married women in my sample, for instance, lived with nephews, while another two lived with brothers. Another unusual household, given that men are not expected to support their wives' parents, was the household of the polygynous man, who was supporting two wives and the elderly mother of one of them.

Most of the elderly in this sample lived in households containing at least some members of another generation, but 5 percent lived either alone or with a spouse only. Three couples and two single women lived in one- or two-person households. More recent surveys covering the entire West Bank and Gaza Strip have also found that the majority of elderly persons lived with at least some kin, although the percentage of elderly living alone was higher than in my sample. Jamil Hilal and Majdi El-Malki (1997: 64) reported that 7.3 percent of the elderly residents of the West Bank and 4.9 percent of those in Gaza lived alone. They found that elderly women – 12 percent of them in the West Bank and 8 percent in Gaza – were far more likely to live alone than elderly men. Jon Pederson, Sara Randall, and Marwan Khawaja (2001: 51) reported that 11 percent of elderly women and 2 percent of elderly men were living alone.[16]

The primary income source for most elderly Palestinians is the income of the children with whom they live. As a result, those who do not live with their children are likely to be at increased economic risk. Four of the five households in my survey containing only elderly members appeared particularly economically vulnerable, despite receiving some form of assistance (remittances or money from the UN or a charity). The dwellings of these individuals were particularly small and spartan. One old woman living alone was widowed and had no children. She was fortunate to have a much younger brother who had emigrated to the US and who provided her with some economic assistance. Still, she appeared to be among the most impoverished individuals we visited. Another elderly woman who was living alone had children – four sons and a daughter – but none of her sons lived in the West Bank. She claimed that she received no assistance from any of her children. Again, these findings suggest that while the patriarchal contract is providing for most elderly women, not all of them are protected by it.

A number of very large households containing elderly people also seemed to be economically vulnerable, because of the large number of dependents in the household. Thirty-nine households with elderly members (50 percent) reported a household size of ten members or more. Almost 40 percent of these households contained a single-income earner, with another 20 percent containing only two earners. The percentage of dependents in the vast majority of these houses (over 80 percent) was 80 percent or higher. As was noted earlier, the depth and rate of poverty have unfortunately increased significantly since 2001, but statistics indicating which households have been affected are not available.

Income-support patterns are also gendered. Daughters on occasion contributed income to the support of their parents but rarely did so once they moved out of their parents' house, which generally occurred when they married. In my sample no daughters who had moved out of the family home were contributing to their parents' income, although ten households received remittances from sons who were living in a separate household.

The only married daughter recorded as being in paid employment and contributing to a parent's income was the woman who had married a European and whose mother lived with her and her husband. In comparison, 25 percent of married sons were supporting their parents financially, again with the majority still living with their parents. Since most daughters continue to live at home until marriage, there were also cases of single daughters bringing in income, but only half as many single daughters as single sons (10 versus 20 percent) were doing so.

Elderly persons also provided income to the family. Thirty-two percent of elderly men and 14 percent of elderly women reported being economically active.[17] Sources of income for elderly women, other than from wage labor, which was rare, included pensions and income from the ownership of physical property. Two women were earning pension income, based on their own labor histories. Some women possessed wealth (particularly in the form of land or gold). Over 50 percent of women reported having received prompt *mahr*, although it is not clear how many of them still had some or all of that wealth. A number of sons reported that their mothers had carefully accumulated savings in order to contribute to their sons' marriage costs or to build a house to accommodate their children. One son reported that his mother, who lived with him, received income from rental properties she owned.

Another woman reported that she had saved some money, with which she bought land that she distributed among her daughter and sons. This woman had become a widow more than fifty years earlier and had raised four children while working as a trader and traditional healer. She lived with her daughter, who was also a widow and who reported she had resisted marriage for a long time, because she "didn't want to take any villager as a husband ..." She went on to explain that she wanted to marry someone educated. The daughter finally married in her mid-30s, but subsequently became a widow. The community then pressured her to remarry, but she refused to do so, because all the men put forth as possible husbands already had wives. Her ability to resist the social pressure to remarry was probably at least in part due to the fact that her mother had given her some land and she was receiving a pension. Her case, however, was unique, because her husband's job had offered a pension with survivor benefits, which was quite rare.

While my data shed some light on whether the elderly have access to income, as in the rest of the Arab world, few studies of Palestinians have examined whether the elderly actually control economic resources within the household. A few researchers have, however, examined the physical and psychological well-being of the elderly. Michel Sansur (1999) finds that elderly Palestinians are particularly prone to depression, with 60 percent of women and 40 percent of men surveyed being classified as "depressed" according to the Geriatric Depression Scale. Unfortunately, his study does not provide any insights into whether depression is linked to household structure or access to economic resources, although he notes that the most economically vulnerable elderly are those living alone, who often lack not only economic resources but also access to physical care.

Another study (Nachman Sharon and Sameer Zoabi 1997) of Palestinians living in Israel finds that the rate of elder abuse is 2.5 percent. The authors state that "[t]his figure is somewhat lower than that reported in the literature for either developed or developing societies" (p. 43) and thus that their study "lends support to modernization theories of aging which link rapid social change, including greater urbanization, with a decline in the standing of the elderly" (p. 55).

EVOLVING INTERGENERATIONAL RELATIONS

Interviews and participant observation can augment statistical surveys, providing information about trends as well as variations in trends.[18] Um Maher[19] and Um Omar were two older women with whom I spent a considerable amount of time. A discussion of their relationship to their children and in-laws can provide more details on intra-family dynamics.

Um Maher[20]

Um Maher was a widow with seven children. When I met her in 1989, two of her sons were in prison,[21] two sons and her only daughter had emigrated, and Um Maher, who was probably about 60, was living with her other two sons in a town in the West Bank. The house that Um Maher shared with the sons, their wives, and three children consisted of three bedrooms, a small living room (little more than a corridor), a medium-size kitchen, and one bathroom. Although I never inquired about finances, I assumed that income was pooled to some degree, since Um Maher did not work and family members shared meals as well as various other household expenses.

Um Maher struck me as a strong, opinionated woman. She spoke forcefully and took a keen interest in politics. Whenever a *bayaan* (an illegal, underground newsletter that provided updates on developments during the first Intifada) was distributed in her neighborhood, she would immediately ask one of her sons to read it to her (since she was illiterate). She also took part in a number of demonstrations against the Israeli occupation when I knew her, and on at least one occasion showed me bruises, explaining that she had been beaten by Israeli soldiers during a demonstration.

She also played an active role in the lives of her sons and daughters-in-law. Um Maher had chosen her sons' wives, going to a nearby refugee camp to locate girls she felt were appropriate brides. The sons were both working when I knew the family during the early 1990s,[22] while the daughters-in-law stayed home. The daughters-in-law cared for the children and did most, if not all, of the housework, meal preparation, and laundry (which was quite labor intensive since the household had neither a washing machine nor hot running water). While they spent most of their time at home, Um Maher seemed to spend her time in political activities or visiting relatives.

I interviewed Um Maher's daughter-in-law Nabiha during my return trip in 1994. Nabiha had completed only eight years of education, although the average amount of schooling for women in her age group was ten years. She complained considerably about her mother-in-law, stating that she felt she had been tricked by Um Maher into a speedy engagement and marriage to Ahmed, then aged 27, when she was 15 years old. She had wanted to take vocational training courses, in order to facilitate finding paid work, but her mother-in-law had objected and in the end she did not pursue this option. When I interviewed her in 1994, she had convinced Ahmed to set up a separate residence so they could live apart from his mother.

Um Maher, in a number of ways, fit the profile of the stereotypical older woman in Arab society, as described by Kandiyoti (1991). She was actively involved in arranging her sons' marriages and acted as a supervisor of her daughters-in-law. She may have deliberately chosen young girls with little education for her sons. Her success in stopping Nabiha from taking training courses and working for pay suggests her desire to maintain control over her daughter-in-law's labor. Within the household, she wielded a considerable amount of power, and she also enjoyed considerable mobility in the community. Although the household was not well off, Um Maher appeared quite comfortable and seemed to have all her material needs fulfilled, thus clearly benefiting from living with her sons, who supported her financially, and daughters-in-law, who shouldered most of the household labor.

Um Omar[23]

While Um Omar and Um Maher were of the same generation and had similar backgrounds, having both become refugees in 1948, their attitudes toward their children differed considerably. Like Um Maher, Um Omar had very little education. She married at 16 and had nine children. She seemed less overtly politically active than Um Maher, although her children were extremely active. Her eldest son Omar had spent time in prison for his political activities[24] and one of her younger sons was in hiding in the early 1990s, since he was wanted by the Israeli military.

I observed very different living arrangements and household dynamics when I visited Um Omar than when I visited Um Maher. Although the family was still living in a refugee camp, Omar and his parents, who lived in the same building, maintained two households, with separate kitchens, bathrooms, and entrances. Um Omar had played no role in choosing Omar's wife. Omar and his wife, Jameela, had fallen in love while students at the university.

Both Omar and Jameela were college graduates with careers, and there was little indication that Um Omar disapproved of her daughter-in-law's working or that having a working daughter-in-law increased Um Omar's unpaid work substantially.[25] The couple's children were enrolled in day care, and although Um Omar sometimes took care of the children, preparing food for them or watching them after school, her contributions did not appear to be significant. Instead, Omar and his wife shared childcare duties and, for the most part, the households of Omar and Jameela and of Um and Abu Omar functioned separately, despite their close proximity.

Um Omar was not only less involved than many Arab mothers in controlling her children's lives, but she was also aware that her behavior was atypical. "I have a daughter," she said. "She is still studying and I will not control her life. She may do as she wishes." When I asked Um Omar if she thought her attitude was typical she replied: "You won't find many people like us. We don't interfere in each others' lives." Interestingly, Jameela explained that her parents had cautioned her not to marry Omar, because they feared his mother was domineering and controlling. Jameela had not found this to be the case and instead had "a very good relation[ship] with my [mother-in-law]." Despite this relationship, she and Omar opted to move away from his parents some time after I interviewed them.

Um Maher and Um Omar not only provide examples of elderly Palestinian women as active agents, but they also provide insights into how intergenerational relationships are changing, and how different women are coping with these changes. Um Maher responded by trying to maintain the traditional age hierarchy and control her sons and daughters-in-law. Um Omar instead recognized her children's need to make their own choices. In both cases, the result was the erosion of the extended household structure. The ultimate fate of Um Maher and Um Omar in terms of the support they will receive from their children as they continue to age remains to be determined.

Implications of the evolving patriarchal contract

Changes in the economic and social structure have implications for the region's elderly and in particular for women. One sign that the patriarchal contract is evolving can be found in the emergence of institutions other than the family to care for the elderly. Studies by Faisal Azaiza, Ariella Lowenstein, and Jenny Brodsky (1999); Stephen Margolis and Richard Reed (2001); and a report included in a recent issue of *Al-Raida* (1999) provide statistics on the number of elderly in Israel, the United Arab Emirates (UAE), and Lebanon who end their lives in nursing homes. The study by Margolis and Reed estimates that the institutionalization rate among the elderly in the UAE remains quite low (7 to 14 persons per 1,000, which they compare to a rate of over 40 for the US). Azaiza, Lowenstein, and Brodsky cite a study by Baer and Factor, who estimate that the institutionalization rate is about the same for Palestinians in Israel. Although these rates are low, there does seem to be an increasing trend towards institutionalization of the elderly, which is no doubt linked to evolving economic and cultural factors.

Other changes have also been taking place in recent years, which may have implications for future cohorts of the elderly. Both the erosion of the extended household structure and high rates of unemployment, particularly among young workers, are likely to increase the economic vulnerability of elderly people. This is not only the case among Palestinians, where unemployment rates in recent years have reached as high as 50 percent, but also in other Arab communities, particularly Algeria and Egypt, where youth unemployment rates are quite high.

Rising female employment rates may also be changing expectations about elderly women's contributions to the household. Under the traditional patriarchal contract, sons are expected to contribute income-generating labor while daughters-in-law and possibly daughters, particularly if they are unmarried, provide unpaid labor. Older men and women are primarily recipients of caring labor, although as Sansur (1999) points out, elderly women are also expected to provide caring labor for their husbands. But as women's labor force participation increases, older women may increasingly be viewed as sources, rather than as recipients, of labor. This pattern has certainly been observed in other parts of the world (UN INSTRAW 1999) but has been less prevalent in Arab countries to date, because the labor-force participation rates of younger women have remained relatively low. Although women's participation in the paid labor market has begun to rise, very little is known about the availability of day care facilities for working women or how much childcare other family members, including the elderly, are providing.

Changes in marriage traditions may be both the cause and consequence of changes in attitudes about caring for the elderly. Although arranged marriages are still prevalent, an increasing number of young people are choosing their own marriage partners. This situation raises the question: as mothers lose influence over their sons' choice of brides, will their power to make demands on their daughters-in-laws' labor diminish? Some young men and women are also rejecting the tradition of *mahr*. While this development is linked to women's increased access to paid employment, it also suggests that women's claims to individual wealth may be reduced.

CONCLUSION

Evidence suggests that the patriarchal contract remains quite strong and effective in the Arab world. Men are socialized to care for their female kin, and most elderly women are cared for under this family-based social security system. As Palestinians, and Arabs more generally, have continued to rely on the patriarchal contract, they have also kept their preference for large families and particularly for sons. This has meant that although the contract has worked for most women, it has also limited women's options, with most marrying and having children. In addition, this contract has failed to serve a portion of elderly women and, in some cases, elderly men. Failure of this contract occurs when men are either unwilling or unable to fulfill their economic obligations toward dependent relatives.

Changing economic conditions may be straining the patriarchal contract, as suggested by changes in marriage patterns (fewer arranged marriages, later marriage, and higher rates of nonmarriage) and the emergence of nonfamily care facilities for the elderly. As the agricultural economic base has disappeared and been replaced by a wage-based economy, the economic strategies Arabs have pursued have increasingly included education and migration (both from rural to urban areas and to other countries). While in the short run such strategies have facilitated the

71

continuance of the patriarchal contract, in the long run these changes suggest the evolution and possible erosion of this contract.

This evolution can be seen in the changing roles played by both young and old women within the family and in particular in the relationships among parents, daughters, and daughters-in-law. The fact that, among Palestinians, a number of elderly are living with unmarried daughters, but few with married daughters, also raises questions about the ways that gender norms concerning the primary responsibility for the elderly are evolving. Smaller families, as well as high rates of male migration, can in part explain the trend of elderly parents' remaining with their daughters. But the fact that it is almost exclusively unmarried daughters who are taking on this role raises the possibility that expectations about daughters' roles may be changing in multiple ways. Because they are choosing not to marry, a group of women may by default be staying with their parents and thus providing them with economic support. But, some women might also be feeling societal or family pressure not to marry so they can care for their aging parents. A married daughter's care for her elderly parents would be a far less acceptable solution, since she is expected to provide caring labor for her in-laws. Meanwhile, her husband is expected to financially support his parents, leaving few resources for the care of the wife's parents.

While still in the minority, the number of Palestinian women remaining unmarried – of whom some are caring for their elderly parents – seems to be rising. The fate of these women as they age is uncertain, since they will have neither husbands nor children to provide them with economic support in the future. In addition, because of high migration rates and decreasing family sizes, these women may be less able to rely on other male kin for support, as previous generations of unmarried women have done.

A number of researchers (Jamil Hilal, Majdi El-Malki, Yasser Shalabi, and Hasan Ladadweh 1998; Edward Sayre and Jennifer Olmsted 2004) have argued that as the predominant household structure changes from an extended to a nuclear one, the need to develop more comprehensive pension systems will increase. The creation of strong state-based social safety nets would increase women's choices and reduce their need to marry and have families in order to assure their own economic futures. It would also reduce social and economic pressures on young men, among whom unemployment rates are extremely high, thus precluding their ability to fulfill the patriarchal contract. Yet precisely because Arab economies are facing considerable hardship, it is unlikely that such a comprehensive social net is likely to develop.

Much of the focus in the literature discussing the political economy of the region emphasizes how high unemployment rates have fueled youth discontent and political instability. Yet one group that is indirectly affected by massive unemployment is the elderly, many of whom are women who rely on their children for their economic support. Particularly in the case of the Palestinian economy, but also in a number of other Arab communities experiencing military conflict (Iraq, of course, comes to mind, as does the Sudan) and changing economic conditions (particularly in poor countries such as Algeria and Yemen, but also the Gulf states), increased attention needs to be paid to the impact this is having not only on the working-age population but also on the elderly. In the absence of effective government programs, international assistance, targeted both at families who support the elderly and the elderly themselves, may be needed.

Jennifer C. Olmsted, Department of Economics, Drew University,
36 Madison Avenue, Madison, NJ 07940, USA
e-mail:jolmsted@drew.edu

ACKNOWLEDGMENTS

Funding for this research was provided by the Economic Research forum for the Arab countries, Iran and Turkey (ERS); the Institute on Global Conflict and Cooperation at the University of California, San Diego; the International Christian Committee in Jerusalem; and the University of Michigan Research Development Fund. I wish to thank guest editor Agneta Stark for encouraging me to write this paper. The comments and suggestions of the anonymous reviewers, Raj Mankad, Polly Maurice, and Diana Strassmann were also most appreciated.

NOTES

1 The literature is not consistent in defining when someone becomes "elderly." While I generally use data for those over 60, in some places I report data for those over 65, for comparability with other studies.

2 As documented by the United Nations Office of the Special Coordinator in the Occupied Territories (UNSCO 2002) and the World Bank (2004b), the imposition of a range of closures, curfews, and travel restrictions on the Palestinian population, has led to massive drops in per capita GDP and increases in poverty.

3 A notion put forth by Nancy Chodorow (1978). See Julie Nelson (1996) for a discussion of this idea in the context of Western economic theory.

4 The term modernity has been problematized by various authors. It is used here to define the transition from a land-based to a wage-labor-based economy, rather than to suggest the notion of a superior economic system.

5 Europe also provided considerable migration options for young men, particularly from Algeria and Morocco (World Bank 2004d).

6 The World Bank (2004d) suggests that as much as 10 and 15 percent of the Egyptian and Yemeni labor forces respectively worked abroad during the 1980s.

7 Even now that a limited state apparatus has been put in place, because of continued violence and ongoing occupation by the Israeli military, its effectiveness has been extremely limited.

8 Research suggests women should live on average five years longer than men (United Nations Development Program 1996: 74). The average woman in the region lives three to four years longer than the average man, suggesting a slight, but not an extreme, gender bias. Considerable variation, though, exists across countries, and higher income does not necessarily lead to women's life expectancy improving relative to men's. For example, in relative terms, Syria, a middle-income country, performed better than Bahrain.

9 Surveys of the United Arab Emirates (Stephen Margolis and Richard Reed 2001) and Egypt (World Bank 2004a), though, find that the number of elderly men is greater than the number of women. Explanations for this include high maternal mortality rates for older generations and the possibility that older women may be under-counted in some surveys.

10 As in other parts of the world, Arab women who enter the paid labor market are likely to face discrimination and occupational segregation (Richard Anker 1998; Jennifer Olmsted 2001).

11 One can in fact make the argument that increases in female labor force participation may be a sign of increased economic vulnerability.

12 As illustrated in Tables 1 and 2, it should be noted that GDP per capita varies considerably in the region. Generally poverty rates are higher in countries with lower levels of national income.

13 More generally, whereas there appears to be a consensus that poverty is extremely feminized in the industrial North, evidence from the South is less compelling, in part because female headship rates remain low. Agnes Quisumbing, Lawrence Haddad, and Christine Pena (2001), for instance, do not find significantly different poverty rates among households with a greater percentage of females or those headed by females. See Nilifur Cagatay (1998) for an excellent discussion of the links between gender and poverty.

14 Large Palestinian populations also live in Jordan, Lebanon, as well as a number of other countries.

15 I collected the data in the Bethlehem area in 1991. Following the model of Leslie Kish (1965), a randomized sample of rural and urban households was surveyed. One household member was asked to provide socio-economic information about him/herself and all other household members. See Jennifer Olmsted (1994) for more detail. In order to gauge reliability of the sample, data were compared with a survey encompassing the entire West Bank and Gaza, which was carried out by the Norwegian Fafo Institute for Applied Social Sciences in 1992 (Marianne Heiberg and Geir Ovenson 1993).

16 Their numbers only included loner households and excluded elderly couples living together.

17 Some were wage laborers, but most worked in family businesses, particularly in farming or running small shops.

18 For further discussion of feminist economic methods, see Jennifer Olmsted (1997), as well as other contributions to the special issue of *Feminist Economics* edited by Michelle Pujol (1997).

19 In Arab society, parents are known by the name of their first-born son. Women are called Um (mother of) and men Abu (father of), followed by the given name of their first son. This naming is emblematic not only of the patriarchal structure of society, but also of the way in which naming reinforces the fluid, connective notions of self.

20 Although I never formally interviewed Um Maher, I had many conversations with her while visiting her household first in 1988–89 and then again in 1990–91.

21 During the first Intifada, many forms of political activism, including participation in student politics, were considered suspect by the Israeli authorities and punishable by imprisonment.

22 This was before the Palestinian economy began experiencing unemployment rates has high as 30 percent in the late 1990s. By that time one son had emigrated to the US. As I have since lost touch with the family, I am not sure what employment opportunities the sons who remained in the area currently have.

23 I was fortunate to have observed this household extensively, as well as interviewing both Um Omar and one of her daughters-in-law.

24 He was imprisoned after being elected to the student government at his university.

25 I have argued elsewhere (Tarek Maassarani and Jennifer Olmsted 2004), though, that Israeli occupation does increase women's unpaid work burden.

REFERENCES

Al-Qudsi, Sulayman. 1996. "Labor Markets in the Future of Arab Economies: The Imperatives and Implications of Economic Structuring," in Ismail Sirageldin and Eqbal Al-Rahmani, eds. *Population and Development Transformations in the Arab World*, Vol 9, *Research in Human Capital and Development*. London: JAI Press.

——, Ragui Assaad, and Radwan Shaban. 1993. "Labor Markets in the Arab Countries: A Survey," presented at the First Annual Conference on Development Economics, Cairo, Egypt.

Al-Raida. 1999. "Caring Institutions in Lebanon," Vol. XVI, No 85, Spring, pp. 35–8.

Anker, Richard. 1998. *Gender and Jobs: Sex Segregation of Occupations in the World* Washington, DC: International Labor Office.

Azaiza, Faisal, Ariella Lowenstein, and Jenny Brodsky. 1999. "Institutionalization for the Elderly is a Novel Phenomenon among the Arab Population in Israel." *Journal of Gerontological Social Work* 31(3/4): 65–85.

Barakat, Halim. 1985. "The Arab Family and the Challenge of Social Transformation," in Elizabeth Warnock Fernea, ed. *Women and the Family in the Middle East: New Voices of Change*, pp. 27–48. Austin, TX: University of Texas Press.

Cagatay, Nilufer. 1998. "Gender and Poverty," UNDP Working Paper No 5. http://www.undp.org/poverty/publications/ wkpaper/wp5/wp5-nilufer.PDF (accessed 2004).

Chodorow, Nancy. 1978. *The Reproduction of Mothering: Psychoanalysis and the Sociology of Gender*. Berkeley: University of California Press.

Datt, Gaurav, Dean Jolliffe, and Manohar Sharma. 2001. "A Profile of Poverty in Egypt." *African Development Review* 13(2): 202–37.

El-Ghonemy, Riad. 1998. *Affluence and Poverty in the Middle East*. London: Routledge.

Folbre, Nancy. 1994. *Who Pays for the Kids? Gender and the Structures of Constraint*. London: Routledge.

Hanssen-Bauer, Jon, Jon Pedersen, and Age Tiltnes, eds. 1998. *Jordanian Society: Living Conditions in the Hashemite Kingdom of Jordan*. Institute for Applied Social Sciences (Fafo) Report No. 253 Oslo: Fafo.

Heiberg, Marianne and Geir Ovensen. 1993. *Palestinian Society in Gaza, West Bank and Arab Jerusalem: A Survey of Living Conditions*. Institute for Applied Social Sciences (Fafo) Report No 151. Oslo: Fafo.

Hilal, Jamil and Majdi El-Malki. 1997. *Informal Social Support System (Non-Institutionalized) in the West Bank and Gaza Strip*. Jerusalem: Palestine Economic Policy Research Institute (MAS).

——, Majdi El-Malki, Yasser Shalabi, and Hasan Ladadweh. 1998. *Towards a Social Security System in the West Bank and Gaza Strip*, Palestine Economic Policy Research Institute (MAS) Jerusalem and Ramallah: MAS.

Joseph, Suad. 1999a. "Brother–Sister Relationships: Connectivity, Love, and Power in the Reproduction of Patriarchy in Lebanon," in Suad Joseph, ed. *Intimate Selving in Arab Families: Gender, Self, and Identity*, pp. 113–40. Syracuse: Syracuse University Press.

——. 1999b. "Introduction: Theories and Dynamics of Gender, Self, and Identity in Arab Families," in Suad Joseph, ed. *Intimate Selving in Arab Families: Gender, Self, and Identity*, pp. 1–24. Syracuse: Syracuse University Press.

——. 2000. "Civic Myths, Citizenship, and Gender in Lebanon," in Suad Joseph, ed. *Gender and Citizenship in the Middle East*, pp. 107–36. Syracuse: Syracuse University Press.

Kandiyoti, Deniz. 1991. "Islam and Patriarchy: A Comparative Perspective," in Nikkie Keddie and Beth Baron, eds. *Women in Middle Eastern History: Shifting Boundaries in Sex and Gender* New Haven, CT: Yale University Press.

Khaled, Louhichi. 1995. "Migration and Women's Status: The Jordan Case." *International Migration* 33(2): 235–50.

Kish, Leslie. 1965. *Survey Sampling*. New York: John Wiley.

Maassarani, Tarek and Jennifer Olmsted. 2004. "Gendered Occupation and Resistance in Palestine." *Middle East Women's Studies Review* 19(1/2): 1–4.

Margolis, Stephen and Richard Reed. 2001. "Institutionalized Older Adults in a Health District in the United Arab Emirates: Health Status and Utilization Rate." *Gerontology* 47: 161–7.

Midgley, James. 1996. "Challenges Facing Social Security," in James Midgley and Martin Tracy, eds. *Challenges to Social Security: An International Exploration*, pp. 1–18. Westport, CT: Auburn House.

Moors, Annelies. 1989. "Gender and Hierarchy in a Palestinian Village: The Case of Al-Balad," in *The Rural Middle East: Peasant Lives and Modes of Production*, pp. 195–209. London: Zed Books and Birzeit University.

——. 1995. *Women, Property and Islam: Palestinian Experiences 1920–1990*. Cambridge, UK: Cambridge University Press.

Nelson, Julie. 1996. *Feminism, Objectivity and Economics*. London: Routledge.

Olmsted, Jennifer. 1994. "Family Investment in Human Capital – Education and Migration among Bethlehem Area Palestinians." PhD dissertation, University of California, Davis.

——. 1996. "Women 'Manufacture' Economic Spaces in Bethlehem." *World Development* 24(12): 1829–40.

——. 1997. "Telling Palestinian Women's Economic Stories." *Feminist Economics* 3(2): 141–51.

——. 1999. "Economic History, Middle East and North Africa," in Janice Peterson and Margaret Lewis, eds. *The Elgar Companion to Feminist Economics*, pp. 219–26. Cheltenham, UK: Edward Elgar.

——. 2001. "Men's Work/Women's Work: Employment, Wages and Occupational Segregation in Bethlehem," in Mine Cinar ed., *The Economics of Women and Work in the Middle East and North Africa*, Vol. 4, *Research in Middle East Economics*, pp. 151–74. Amsterdam: JAI Press.

——. 2003. "Reexamining the Fertility Puzzle in the Middle East and North Africa," in Eleanor Doumato and Marsha Pripstein-Posusney, eds. *Middle Eastern Women in the Age of Globalization: Gender, Jobs and Activism*. London: Lynne Rienner.

Palestinian Central Bureau of Statistics (PCBS). 1996. *The Demographic Survey in the West Bank and Gaza Strip: Preliminary Report*. Ramallah, Palestine: PCBS.

——. 1998. *Women and Men in Palestine: Trends & Statistics*. Ramallah, Palestine: PCBS.

Pateman, Carole. 1988. *The Sexual Contract* Stanford, CA: Stanford University Press.

Pedersen, Jon, Sara Randall, and Marwan Khawaja, eds. 2001. *Growing Fast: The Palestinian Population in the West Bank and Gaza Strip,* Institute for Applied Social Sciences (Fafo) 353. Oslo: Centraltrykkeriet AS.

Pujol, Michelle, ed. 1997. "Feminist Methodology." Special Issue, *Feminist Economics* 3(2).

Quisumbing, Agnes, Lawrence Haddad, and Christine Pena. 2001. "Are Women Overrepresented among the Poor? An Analysis of Poverty in 10 Developing Countries." *Journal of Development Economics* 66(1): 225–69.

Sansur, Michel. 1999. "Older Adult Men and Women in Palestine: Towards a Better Life?" *Al-Raida* 16(85): 25–34.

Sayre, Edward and Jennifer Olmsted. 2004. "Structuring a Pension Scheme for a Future Palestinian State," in David Cobham and Nu'man Kanafani, eds. *The Economic Policy of Palestine.* London: Routledge.

Sharabi, Hisham. 1988. *Neopatriarchy: A Theory of Distorted Change in Arab Society.* Oxford, UK: Oxford University Press.

Sharon, Nachman and Sameer Zoabi. 1997. "Elder Abuse in a Land of Tradition: The Case of Israel's Arabs." *Journal of Elder Abuse and Neglect* 8(4): 43–58.

Taylor, Elizabeth. 1984. "Egyptian Migration and Peasant Wives." *Middle East Reports (MERIP),* 124: 3–10.

United Nations. 2003. *Statistics Division. Social Indicators.* http://unstats.un.org/unsd/demographic/products/socind/inc-eco.htm (accessed July 21, 2003).

——. 2004. *Statistics Division. Social Indicators. Indicators on Youth and Elderly Populations.* http://unstats.un.org/unsd/demographic/products/socind/youth.htm (accessed December 22, 2004).

——. 2005. *Statistics Division. Social Indicators. Indicators of Unemployment.* http://unstats.un.org/unsd/demographic/products/socind/unempl.htm (accessed March 6, 2005).

United Nations Development Programme (UNDP). 1996. *Human Development Report, 1995.* New York: Oxford University Press. http://hdr.undp.org/reports/global/1995/en/ (accessed March 6, 2005).

United Nations International Research and Training Institute for the Advancement of Women (UN INSTRAW). 1999. *Ageing in a Gendered World: Women's Issues and Identities* Santo Domingo, Dominican Republic: INSTRAW.

United Nations Office of the Special Coordinator in the Occupied Territories (UNSCO). 2002. *The Impact of Closure and Other Mobility Restrictions on Palestinian Productive Activities.* www.un.org/News/dh/mideast/econ-report-final.pdf (accessed March 6, 2005).

United States Social Security Administration (SSA). 1999. *Social Security Programs Throughout the World.* http://www.ssa.gov/policy/docs/progdesc/ssptw/1999/#toc (accessed March 6, 2005).

World Bank. 1995. *Claiming the Future: Choosing Prosperity in the Middle East and North Africa.* Washington, DC: World Bank.

——. 2001. *Poverty in the West Bank and Gaza,* 22312-GZ. Washington, DC: World Bank. http://www.wds.worldbank.org/servlet/WDSContentServer/WDSP/IB/2001/08/04/000094946_01072104010092/Rendered/INDEX/multi0page.txt (accessed May 12, 2005).

——. 2002. *Reducing Vulnerability and Increasing Opportunity: A Strategy for Social Protection in Middle East and North Africa.* Washington, DC: World Bank.

——. 2004a. *Egypt: Gender Assessment Report.* Washington, DC: World Bank.

——. 2004b. *Four Years – Intifada, Closures and Palestinian Economics Crisis: An Assessment.* Washington, DC: World Bank.

——. 2004c. *Gender and Development in the Middle East and North Africa: Women in the Public Sphere.* Washington, DC: World Bank.

——. 2004d. *Unlocking the Employment Potential in the Middle East and North Africa: Toward A New Social Contract.* Washington, DC: World Bank.

——. 2005a. *EdStats, Global Country Data, Data Query System.* http://devdata.worldbank .org/edstats/(accessed March 6, 2005).

——. 2005b. *GenderStats: Database of Gender Statistics.* http://devdata.worldbank.org/ genderstats/home.asp

——. 2005c. *Quick Query.* http://devdata.worldbank.org/query/default.htm (accessed May 12, 2005).

Australia's "Other" Gender Wage Gap: Baby Boomers and Compulsory Superannuation Accounts

Therese Jefferson and Alison Preston

INTRODUCTION

In 1992, Australia introduced a system of "forced saving" for retirement to address the projected income needs of an aging population (Hazel Bateman, Geoffrey Kingston, and John Piggott 2001). This new system took the form of compulsory employer contributions to individual retirement accounts for employees, known in Australia as compulsory superannuation accounts. We understand that the term superannuation as it is used here differs considerably from its meaning in other countries. In Australia the term refers to a specific contributory system of retirement saving covered by legislative provisions. Contributions are made to individual accounts, and withdrawal restrictions apply until specific age and employment criteria are met. In the tradition of Susan Himmelweit's work (2002), this paper offers a gendered perspective of this policy that establishes a strong nexus between retirement savings and participation in the formal labor market.

Compulsory superannuation, as it now operates in Australia, represents one form of private capital accumulation of the type often promoted as the answer to demographic trends (Patrick Bolle 2000: 206) and projected fiscal stresses. However, schemes that privilege the role of private savings also increase the risk that those in less advantaged labor market positions will be unable to achieve an adequate retirement income. Australia's evolving structure privatizes the risks associated with saving for retirement (Natalie Gallery, Kerry Brown, and Gerry Gallery 1996; Rosemary Kelly 1997) and neglects an important social feature inherent in Australia's traditional age pension scheme, that of redistribution. Without redistribution, there is a reduced ability for different generations to share the risks of low lifetime incomes caused by war and depression or to enable those outside the paid workforce to access the benefits of national economic growth (Colin Gillion, John Turner, Clive Bailey, and Denis Latulippe 2000: 11).

This paper projects employment participation and superannuation accumulations of women and men who are entitled to compulsory superannuation contributions during their working lives. It illustrates Australia's "other" gender wage gap, the superannuation accumulation gap. We focus on baby boomers because of their impending retirement needs. Our projections of Australian employment patterns suggest a lifetime gender employment experience gap of 35 percent among baby boomers. Since superannuation accumulation is directly dependent upon time spent in paid employment, a 35 percent gap in the latter will translate to a gender superannuation accumulation gap of at least 35 percent. Other factors known to affect gender earnings differentials (e.g. occupational distribution, gender differences in rates of return to experience, and unobservable factors such as discrimination) will serve to widen the final superannuation accumulation gap.

THE AUSTRALIAN PENSION SYSTEM

The Australian retirement income system is a hybrid system. It consists of three components or "pillars": (1) a means-tested system of publicly financed transfers, known as the age pension; (2) a compulsory system of private savings through occupational superannuation schemes; and (3) voluntary savings, including privately financed pensions and occupational superannuation arrangements in excess of the mandated minimum. Recent regulations have changed the emphasis from the first pillar to the second. In comparison, the third pillar has not been as significant a focus of public policy.

The age pension

Since the introduction of the age pension in 1909, Australia has relied heavily on government transfers as a key element of retirement income provision. Contributions to specific individual accounts do not form part of the Australian age pensions system, which is funded from current government revenue. Entitlement to an age pension and the amount received depend on an individual's or a couple's income and assets. The application of these tests can be complex. In simple terms, the assets tests mean that for every A$1,000 of assets in excess of the threshold the fortnightly age pension is reduced by A$3.00. The asset threshold, which does not include the value of a residence, is currently set at A$153,000 for single homeowners. The income test applies an implicit tax rate of 40 percent to income that exceeds a specified threshold (currently A$122 per fortnight for single people). The smaller amount calculated from these two tests comprises an individual's age pension entitlement.

The importance of age pensions as a source of retirement income for all retirees, and especially for women, is well established (Linda Rosenman and Jeni Warberton 1996; Department of Family and Community Services 1999; Anthony King, Hans Bækgaard, and Ann Harding 1999; Anthony King, Agnes Walker, and Ann Harding 1999; Department of Family and Community Services 2001). In June 2002, 61 percent of age pensioners were women, of whom 69.2 percent received the full age pension rate of 25 percent of male average weekly earnings. The age pension is indexed to the consumer price index and male total average weekly earnings.

The age pension system has been described as a system of intergenerational transfers. This is because it represents "a compact between successive generations; generation B supports generation A in the expectation that it will be supported by generation C, and so on" (Keith Hancock 1981: 11). Since payments are made regardless of patterns of paid work prior to retirement, the age pension has a redistributive effect. Those with limited workforce participation who have paid relatively low tax are entitled to the same level of benefits as those who have paid relatively high tax during their years in paid work (subject to the means test).

Occupational superannuation system

Occupational superannuation in Australia refers to a specific system of private capital accumulation. The Superannuation Guarantee Charge Act of 1992 governs the compulsory component of this system. The Act's legislative provisions require employers to make contributions equal to 9 percent of base salary to an employee's individual superannuation account unless they are: paid less than A$450 per month; aged 70 or over; aged under 18 years of age and do not work more than thirty hours a week; or performing work of a domestic or private nature for not more than thirty hours a week for a nonbusiness employer. As women are concentrated in workforce sectors with lower pay and casual working hours, they are less likely to be eligible for employer contributions to occupational super-annuation. It should also be noted that the law omits the self-employed from this system and implicitly assumes that they will make their own retirement income provisions. Available data indicate that this occurs on a relatively limited scale (Therese Jefferson and Alison Preston 2003).

In addition to accumulation through the compulsory system, employees have the option of making voluntary contributions to a superannuation account. Once contributions have been made to an account, restrictions and penalties apply that limit access to the funds prior to retirement.

Payments made through compulsory occupational superannuation are generally made to defined contribution accounts. This means that the contributions to the fund, rather than the benefits, are specified. Often the funds are not capital guaranteed, do not offer a guaranteed rate of return, and have fees deducted for administrative and other purposes. By 2000, three-quarters of the Australian pre-retired population had some super-annuation coverage. Of those with coverage, 81 percent of women and 79 percent of men were covered by defined contribution accounts. The remainder had either defined benefit or hybrid accounts (Australian Bureau of Statistics 2000). Defined benefit funds are generally associated with schemes predating the introduction of compulsory contributions and/or public service employee schemes.

Upon retirement, former employees may access funds either withdrawn as a lump sum, converted to an annuity, or taken as a combination of both. These options are associated with significant taxation implications, with lump and income stream benefits above certain thresholds being subject to tax. Further, as discussed above, the existence of means tests involving both assets and income indicates these decisions can also affect age pension eligibility.[1] In the case of converting superannuation entitlements to an annuity, entitlement to continued payments upon the death of a spouse depends specifically on the terms of the annuity purchased.

PROBLEMS FOR WOMEN AND MEN WITH BROKEN WORK PATTERNS

Since its introduction in 1992, compulsory occupational superannuation has become a central pillar of Australia's retirement income framework. Yet two decades of research in Australia have consistently highlighted the risks for women inherent in the shift away from intergenerational transfers through publicly financed pensions to private capital accumulation schemes (Mary Owen 1984; Julia Perry 1988; Economic Planning Advisory Council 1994; Senate Select Committee on Superannuation [SSCS] 1995;

Susan Donath 1998; Phil Gallagher 2001; Diana Olsberg 2001; Alison Preston and Siobhan Austen 2001; Sheila Shaver 2001). These studies show that inequities flow from gender differences in patterns and forms of labor market attachment and a significant gender pay gap. That is, persons with broken work patterns and low earnings will find it difficult to save an adequate retirement income through defined contribution superannuation schemes. A large and diverse literature from other countries supports the same conclusion.[2] This literature gives insights into key policy issues that were identified over twenty years ago (Barbara Bergmann 1982) and that are of continuing importance in feminist debate (Virginia Richardson 1999).

However, public debate surrounding pension reform in Australia has done little to address the gender implications of the current system. Instead, current debate is largely concerned with the taxation arrangements of such schemes (SSCS 2002) and on policies to encourage older workers to remain in employment beyond the traditional retirement age of 65 years.

Limited measures have been recommended to assist women and others with broken work patterns in accumulating an adequate private income in retirement. These include the removal of work tests for voluntary contributions, extending government co-contributions, and removing eligibility rules which discriminate against those on low incomes (SSCS 2002: 64). One may speculate as to why such critical gender inequities fail to attract public interest and debate in Australia. It may relate to the concept of retirement, which, as John Larkin (1994: 64) explains, is problematic for those not in paid employment:

> The rationale for providing tax concessions for superannuation is to encourage savings which will replace salary and wages income on retirement and thus enable them, as far as practicable, to maintain a standard of living in retirement which is related to their pre-retirement standard of living. Taking this line to its logical conclusion, it follows that persons who are not in paid employment, or whose income comprises "unearned or passive income" (that is, income from other investments) do not generally experience a drop in income on retirement and therefore do not have the same need for superannuation to generate replacement income. In fact, the very notion of "retirement" for such people is something of a misnomer.

The absence of public concern on the issue of women and pension adequacy may also reflect information limitations. There is, for example, a lack of information on pension projections disaggregated by gender. At present, around 66 percent of women and 61 percent of men receive the full rate of the publicly financed age pension, a means-tested social welfare payment. As access to the age pension is means tested, it is expected that as the system of occupational superannuation matures, the number in receipt of the full age pension will decline dramatically, from about two-thirds of all age pension recipients to around one-third by 2050 (SSCS 2002: 138). Missing from these projections, however, is an insight on the gender composition of recipients. How many will be women?

ISSUES FACING WOMEN BABY BOOMERS IN AUSTRALIA

The changing structure of retirement income provision is particularly relevant for the baby boom generation. Born between 1946 and 1964, most baby boomers entered the workforce when the age pension was the dominant form of retirement income and long before the introduction of compulsory superannuation contributions in 1992. The shift towards a system of private capital accumulation has occurred during the years in which most baby boomers have been in employment and/or carrying out unpaid work associated with childrearing and caring for elders in the community.

Although more than 90 percent of baby boomers in paid employment have superannuation coverage, few are making voluntary contributions. Their accumulations are almost entirely dependent on compulsory employer or business contributions (see Table 1). Affordability is the main reason that baby boomers do not make personal contributions (Australian Bureau of Statistics 2000: 37).

Notwithstanding the relatively high rates of coverage, balances within superannuation accounts are low. In 2000, for example, the median balance for women was A\$4,896 while for men it was A\$9,535 (Australian Bureau of Statistics 2002: 28). Data on the distribution of balances (presented in Figure 1) illustrate the extent of these gender differences: in 2000, 39.1 percent of women aged 35–44 had less than A\$5,000 in their account; the comparable share for men in the same age group was 17.6 percent. These shares were reversed at the other end of the distribution: 30.8 percent of men and 15.1 percent of women aged 35–44 had A\$40,000 or more in superannuation accumulations.

Underpinning these patterns are gender differences in labor market attachment and employment. Figures 2 and 3 clearly illustrate these gender differences in employment patterns.

The data for Figures 2 and 3 are drawn from the 1997 Negotiating the Life Course Survey (NLCS) (Peter McDonald, Janeen Baxter, Frank Jones, and Deborah Mitchell 2000).[3] In this survey, 2,000 randomly selected participants were asked wide-ranging questions about their lives at home and at work. Using all the records for those born in 1950 (34 women and 32 men) we are able to illustrate, graphically, the actual employment histories of this birth group, disaggregated by gender. Figures 2 and 3 illustrate the actual employment histories (up to 1996) of women and men born in 1950.

84

Table 1 Superannuation coverage of persons aged 35–54 with one or more jobs,[a]
June 2000

	Men aged		Women aged	
	35–44 %	*45–54* %	*35–44* %	*45–54* %
Employer or business contributions only	44.3	37.8	55.8	51.1
Personal/spouse and employer/business contributions	31.7	35.0	22.9	29.3
Personal/spouse contributions only	6.0	9.0	3.1	3.7
Has superannuation but no contributions currently being made	9.5	9.5	7.6	5.5
No superannuation	8.6	8.8	10.5	10.4
Total	100.0	100.0	100.0	100.0

Notes: [a]Excludes workers in family business and those paid in-kind in their main job.
Source: Australian Bureau of Statistics (2002) *Labour Force Australia Catalogue 6203.0*, Table 10.

There are two obvious features: (1) the high incidence of continuous full-time work patterns for men and (2) the absence of any clear "typical" work pattern in the lifetimes of women. The same exercise repeated for men and women born in 1960 showed similar results.

By 1996, men born in 1950 had, on average, spent 27 years in full-time employment; this compares with 14 years for women born in 1950. Similarly by 1996, men born in 1960 had spent an average of 19 years in full-time employment compared with 10 years for women of the same age. Women spent more time in part-time employment than men.

OCCUPATIONAL PROFILES

Although not shown in Figures 2 and 3, analysis of the NLCS reveals another important gender dimension to the employment patterns displayed: the occupational profiles of respondents during their working lives. An analysis of "first" occupation since completing education and 1996 occupational data suggests that, over their lifetimes, men are more likely than women to move into higher status occupations. For example, of the sample of men born in 1950, 34.4 percent indicated that their first occupation was in one of the skilled job categories of "managerial, professional, or para-professional." By 1996, this proportion had grown to 50 percent. Of the women born in 1950, 20.5 percent categorized their first job as managerial, professional, or para-professional. By 1996, the share of

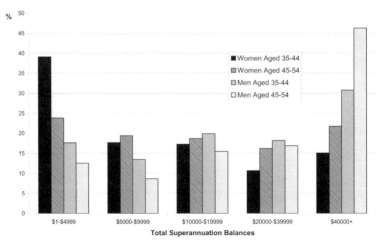

Figure 1 Pre-retired baby boomer population with superannuation accounts and known balances, 2000

Notes: Final balances could not be determined for around 12 percent of the pre-retired baby boom population with superannuation accounts.

Source: Derived from Australian Bureau of Statistics. 2000. *Superannuation Australia: Coverage and financial characteristics: April to June 2000, Catalogue 6360.0,* Table 9.

women born in 1950 employed in these occupational categories remained unchanged at 20.5 percent.

Marriage and family formation

While many women and men have planned their retirement income within the context of a marriage partnership, the growing incidence of divorce adds another risk dimension (John Dewar, Grania Sheehan, and Jody Hughes 1999). Legislation has recently been passed in Australia allowing superannuation to be considered an asset for distribution in divorce proceedings. The first cases are only now coming before the courts, and the basis for the division of this asset is yet to become clear. A 50 percent split in accumulated balances at the time of divorce may not be sufficient to cover the costs of an interrupted work life on future earning (and super-annuation accumulation) potential. Moreover, baby boomers divorced prior to the legislation coming into effect have had no claims on their spouse's superannuation. In common with international literature (see, for example, Stanley DeViney and Jennifer Crew Solomon 1995; Karen C. Holden and Hsiang-Hui Daphne Kuo 1996; John B. Williamson and Tay K. McNamara 2003), Australian studies show that divorce has significant, adverse consequences for women's retirement income (Richardson 1999; Ruth Weston and Bruce Smyth 2000; Peter Whiteford and Kim Bond 2000).

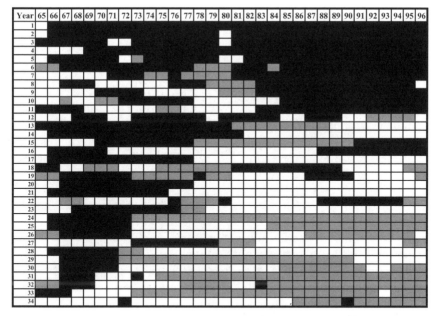

Figure 2 Patterns of workforce participation: women born in 1950
Notes: Sample size is 34 respondents. Each row of this grid represents the working life of an individual respondent. Rows are ordered in terms of the amount of time spent in full–time, paid employment. Black rectangles denote a year of full-time employment, grey denotes part-time employment and white denotes a year of not being in paid work.
Source: McDonald *et al.* (2000).

It has been argued that the above legislative changes will have a limited impact on divorced women's relative position in retirement (Geoff Maloney *et al.* 2000; Danny Sandor 2001).

National statistics indicate that in 2001, 75 percent of women in the 50–54-year age group were married, about 15 percent were divorced, and 10 percent were either never married or widowed (Australian Bureau of Statistics 2002: 57). These statistics have obvious implications for a retirement income system constructed on the assumption of shared resources between couples.

In summary, the life-course experiences of women and men vary significantly. Most men exhibit a strong degree of long-term, full-time attachment to the workforce, but the same cannot be said for many women. Women present a diverse range of employment patterns. While a few may have long-term periods of full-time employment, it is more typical for women to combine periods of full-time employment, part-time employment, and time out of the formal labor market as they meet a range of paid

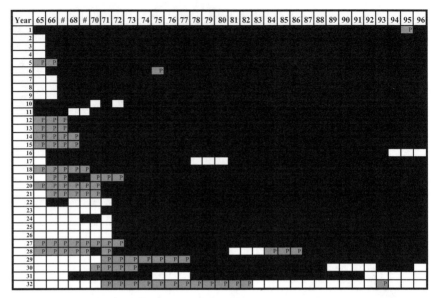

Figure 3 Patterns of workforce participation: men born in 1950
Note: Sample size is 32 respondents. See also notes attached to figure 2.
Source: McDonald *et al.* (2000).

and unpaid responsibilities. They are also more likely to be in lower paying occupations, to have relatively flat career paths, and to have limited access to superannuation contributions made on their behalf. Partnering patterns mean that a significant minority of baby boomers are unlikely to have a partner with whom financial resources will be shared, making access to individual sources of retirement income particularly important.

PROJECTING THE EMPLOYMENT EXPERIENCE AND SUPERANNUATION ACCUMULATIONS OF BABY BOOMERS

In this section, we project comparative employment experience and superannuation accumulation of men and women baby boomers over their life course and highlight the degree to which women are disadvantaged within a retirement income system centered on occupational super-annuation. Australia does not have an official longitudinal database that can be used in studies such as this one. Since the early 1980s, the development of simulations which estimate variables such as labor force attachment, family formation, wage rates, and contributions to retirement schemes has been a significant method of demonstrating policy implications (see, for example, Colin Brown 1994; Steven Ross 1994; Donath 1998;

Anthony King 2001; Preston and Austen 2001; Simon Kelly, Ann Harding, and Richard Percival 2002). The aim of this section is to develop a simple model, using actual work histories, that demonstrates the gendered nature of retirement savings schemes based on an employment nexus.

Data, approach, and assumptions – projecting employment experience

As a starting point, we use actual employment histories for men and women born in the period 1950–60 (inclusive) compiled from the Negotiating the Life Course Survey (McDonald et al. 2000). While this survey will become a longitudinal database in future years, the work histories available in the first wave of data consist of respondents' recollections of their work history up until 1996. These data give the actual work histories of 442 women and 367 men. In estimating average accumulated years of labor market experience, we assumed that each person's stated employment status in a particular year (full-time, part-time, not working, or not in the labor force) was characteristic of their actual status throughout the whole year. We then assumed that, for each year of full-time employment, their accumulated labor market experience would increase by one year. Consistent with Australian data showing that the average number of hours worked by part-time workers approximates "half-time" employment, we have added half a year's labor market experience for each year of part-time employment. We also assumed that time in unemployment or out of the labor force left accumulated labor market experience unchanged.[4]

To project employment patterns beyond 1996, we use Australian Bureau of Statistics actual 1997–2002 employment participation rates disaggregated by gender and age to construct profiles up to 2002 (Australian Bureau of Statistics 1997–2002). For the period 2003 and beyond, we construct two scenarios. In the first scenario, we assume that women in different age groups continue to participate in employment at known 2002 rates until they retire at age 65. To demonstrate the effect of this assumption, we construct a second series where women's total employment participation rates after 2002 are set equal to the corresponding male age–employment participation rates. In both scenarios, we hold each group's full-time and part-time employment distribution shares constant at 2002 levels. This assumption reflects historical data in Australia that show that while women's overall employment participation rates have significantly increased, virtually no change has occurred in the share of women participating in full-time work over the span of two decades (Alison Preston and John Burgess 2003). A sample of the data and calculations used in this process is shown in Table 2. The process illustrated in Table 2 was repeated for each gender, year of birth, and scenario. We averaged projected years of employment experience for each cohort to give average years of experience for baby boomers in the total population group 1950–60.

Table 2 Sample of projections for years of employment experience: women baby boomers born 1950, scenario 1

Age of respondent in year being projected	Year being projected	Year of Australian Bureau of Statistics participation data	Participation rate for women in this age group (%)	Participating women in full-time employment (%)	Participating women in part-time employment (%)	Total estimated average years of employment experience
	(i)	(ii)	(iii)	(iv)	(v)	(vi)
47	1997	1997	68.9	56.6	38.7	17.8
48	1998	1998	69.8	56.7	39.0	18.3
49	1999	1999	71.1	56.1	40.2	18.9
50	2000	2000	70.7	57.4	38.8	19.4
51	2001	2001	67.4	54.9	41.1	19.9
52	2002	2002	71.5	57.3	39.3	20.5
53	2003	2002	71.5	57.3	39.3	21.1
54	2004	2002	71.5	57.3	39.3	21.6
55	2005	2002	50.5	51.1	45.9	22.0
56	2006	2002	50.5	51.1	45.9	22.4
57	2007	2002	50.5	51.1	45.9	22.8
58	2008	2002	50.5	51.1	45.9	23.1
59	2009	2002	50.5	51.1	45.9	23.5
60	2010	2002	26.8	39.6	39.6	23.7
61	2011	2002	26.8	39.6	39.6	23.9
62	2012	2002	26.8	39.6	39.6	24.1
63	2013	2002	26.8	39.6	39.6	24.3
64	2014	2002	26.8	39.6	39.6	24.4

Notes. As described in the main text, we use actual employment histories for men and women born in the period 1950–60 (inclusive) compiled from the Negotiating the Life Course Survey (McDonald *et al.* 2000). Data consist of respondents' recollections of their work history up until 1996 for 442 women and 367 men. In the sample above, these data give an average employment experience for women born in 1950 of 17.3 years.

To project employment patterns beyond 1996, we use Australian Bureau of Statistics actual 1997–2002 employment participation rates disaggregated by gender and age to construct profiles to 2002 (Australian Bureau of Statistics 1997–2002, Catalogue 6203.0). For the period 2003 and beyond, we construct average additions to workforce experience by continuing with employment experience patterns indicated by the 2002 ABS data.

Additional average years of experience are calculated by total workforce experience [full-time participation + part-time participation (0.5)]. Full-time participation plus part-time participation do not add to 100 percent because unemployed persons are included in workforce participation statistics. Periods of unemployment are assumed to not add to years of workforce experience for the purposes of these calculations.

Over their entire work life, with an assumed age of retirement set at 65, men will, on average, accumulate 39.3 years of work experience. If women continue with 2002 patterns of participation in paid employment, they will, on average, accumulate 25.5 years of work experience. In the second scenario, where women participate in paid employment from 2002 at the same rate as men, they accumulate 29.2 years of work experience. The gender gap in average years of accumulated work experience over the life course is therefore around 35 percent or 26 percent if women are assigned men's participation rates. Based on these data we can confidently say that the gender gap in baby boomer lifetime superannuation accumulation will, at a minimum, be around 26 percent. The more likely scenario is a superannuation accumulation gap of around 35 percent and more if we take into account other important determinants such as the gender pay gap.

Projecting superannuation accumulations

To estimate the average superannuation accumulations, we need to construct average earning profiles for each individual. This, in turn, requires lifetime individual employment histories for all individuals in the sample born between 1950 and 1960 until age 65. Whilst we have been able to use information on average work participation rates together with gender/age full-time and part-time employment shares to construct profiles of average baby boomer lifetime experience profiles, we are unable to use this approach at the individual level. Therefore, for illustrative purposes, we take the sample of individuals born in 1950 and 1960 and, in the case of women, apply two different employment patterns from 1997 onwards. Under scenario A, we assume all women are employed full-time in each year until they reach 60 years of age and thereafter work part-time until they reach age 65. Under scenario B, women are assumed to work part-time until they reach age 65. Employment patterns for men are assumed to be full-time until age 60 and part-time thereafter until age 65.

Having constructed experience profiles for each individual, we then use the 2001 average annual salaries of young (aged 20–24) Australians equal to A$26,416 for men and A$24,440 for women (Australian Bureau of Statistics 2001). These data are applied to information on returns to experience to develop a lifetime earnings profile for each individual.[5]

The profiles estimated by adopting this approach are shown in Figures 4 and 5. Figure 4 displays the earnings profiles over the period for which actual employment histories are available. Figure 5 shows the effects of our alternative scenarios of women's employment participation from 1997 until age 65.

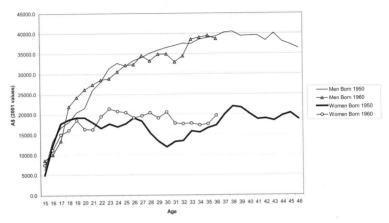

Figure 4 Estimated earning profiles based on actual experience data

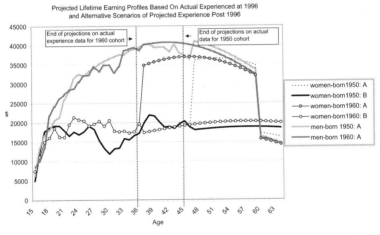

Figure 5 Projected lifetime earning profiles based on actual experience at 1996 and alternative scenarios of projected experience post 1996

In studies of age – earning profiles, it is common to find that earnings increase at a decreasing rate, that profiles are higher and steeper for more educated people, and that profiles are steeper for men (Paul Miller 1982). Our age – earning profiles take on similar characteristics. The flatter female profile, however, reflects the fact that the earnings represent an average of the total female sample for each age/birth group and that at each point in time some of the group will be in full-time employment, some will be in part-time employment, and some not in paid employment.

To estimate the level of superannuation accumulated by each group of baby boomers, we make the following assumptions:

- Contributions to superannuation savings comprise only the minimum amounts mandated by the SGC.[6] The SGC was gradually phased in between 1992 and 2002; the rate of compulsory contributions is now set at 9 percent of base salary.
- Earnings in the superannuation funds increase at a real rate of interest equal to 3.25 percent per annum.[7]
- A 15 percent tax is levied on contributions. No allowance is made for a superannuation surcharge or other taxes (including taxes on retirement income).
- Contributions are made until individuals reach 65 years.
- The respondent makes no additional contributions.[8]

Table 3 shows the gross lifetime income and minimum compulsory superannuation accumulations of baby boomers born in 1950 and 1960. It is apparent that women's gross lifetime income and superannuation balances are directly related to the amount of time they spend in paid employment. Under scenario B (where women are assumed to work on a part-time basis from 1997 until age 65) a paid-employment experience gap of around 15.8 years (or 37.3 percent) separates women and men born in 1950. This translates into an estimated lifetime earnings gap of around 45 percent and an annual private pension gap of around 50 percent.

Scenario A shows the estimated balances based on the unlikely assumption that, post-1996, all women participate in employment on a full-time basis until they reach age 60 and then work part-time until age 65. Even under this assumption, we see a gap in the annual private pension streams of women and men. In the case of baby boomers born in 1960, the gender pension gap is equal to about 24 percent. Of perhaps more concern is the finding that even if women in this birth cohort were to take on men's employment participation patterns until age 65, their private annual pension, estimated at 18.7 percent of male average weekly total earnings (MAWTE) in 2001, would still fall below the minimum adequacy standard of 25 percent of MAWTE.[9,10]

Moreover, it is unlikely that our estimates will be reflective of what people would actually get from insurers. The main limitation with our calculations is the artificial assumption that the period of annuity exactly matches the length of a person's life. In other words, we assume complete exhaustion of capital by the time of death. In reality, the actual age of death is unknown and some individuals may have strong motivations to

Table 3 Gross lifetime income and accumulated superannuation savings

	Estimated years of lifetime labor market experience (i)	Estimated lifetime earnings (A$) (ii)	Lump-sum invested (A$) (iii)	Private pension (per annum) (A$) (iv)	Percent of MAWTE May 2001 (v)
Men born 1950					
Scenario A: projected experience assumed to be full-time*	42.4	160,8642	64,775	5,110	12.4%
Women born 1950					
Scenario A: projected experience assumed to be full-time*	33.1	110,0451	57,940	3,957	9.6%
Scenario B: projected experience assumed to be part-time	26.6	882,452	36,684	2,505	6.1%
Men born 1960					
Scenario A	44.3	1,601,465	128,440	10,133	24.6%
Women born 1960					
Scenario A	38.2	1,283,451	112,516	7,684	18.7%
Scenario B	26.7	934,865	68,803	4,699	11.4%
Gender ratios (%)					
Born 1950					
Women A/Men A	78.1	68.4	89.4	77.4	77.4
Women B/Men A	62.7	54.9	56.6	49.0	49.0
Born 1960					
Women A/Men A	86.2	80.1	87.6	75.8	75.8
Women B/Men A	60.3	58.4	53.6	46.4	46.4

Notes:
*Under scenario A individuals are assumed to work part-time over the age range 60–64.
Amounts shown are in real 2001 Australian dollars. The reported accumulated balances are at age 65 (which is 2015 for those born in 1950 and 2025 for those born in 1960).
The net present value estimates in column 3 are derived using a divisor of 12.675 for men and 14.643 for women. The difference reflects gender differences in average life expectancy at age 65.

94

leave a bequest, so actual annuities are likely to be less than that calculated here.

SUMMARY AND CONCLUSION

In this paper, we have used simulations to project the superannuation accumulations of women, particularly the baby boom cohort who will be retiring in the near future. It is apparent that women's gross lifetime income and superannuation balances are directly related to the amount of time spent in paid employment. Our projections on average employment for baby boomers born between 1950 and 1960 show a gender employment experience gap of around 14 years (or 35 percent) over their working life (aged 15 to 65). In other words, over their lifetime, relative to male baby boomers, women baby boomers will spend around 35 percent fewer years in paid employment. The gender gap in baby boomer superannuation accumulations and annual pension flows will be similarly large. Our predicted 35 percent gap is based only on gender differences in time in paid employment. Once we take into account other factors known to affect lifetime earnings (e.g. gender differences in returns to experience, the occupational structure, discrimination in relation to training and promotion), and make allowance for the longer life expectancies of women, the lifetime gender superannuation accumulation gap and annual gender pension gap is much more than the base 35 percent gap predicted here. Even under the highly unlikely scenario of women baby boomers taking on men's employment participation patterns in later life (in this study from 1997 until age 65), a substantial gender gap in accumulated years of experience (and thus, base gender pension gap) would still prevail, equal to 21.9 percent. In the absence of other private income streams, either from voluntary contributions to superannuation or private savings, our estimates suggest that the average baby boomer (male or female) will struggle to generate a private annual pension that meets even the minimum of adequacy standards of 25 percent of MAWTE.

Our results show that the publicly financed age pensions will remain a significant source of retirement income for most baby boomers and for women in particular. From a policy perspective, it is important to direct attention to this pillar of the Australian retirement income framework and to consider the gender biases inherent within the current system. Minor changes to superannuation policy will not address the gender disparities inherent in a framework based on a nexus with paid employment. The question as to how all older Australians can secure their income needs in later life needs to be addressed. At a minimum, it requires explicit commitment to the maintenance of an adequate age pension safety net. This research may provide a useful example for economists in other countries such as the United States that are considering privatizing their social insurance systems for the elderly.

Therese Jefferson, Women's Economic Policy Analysis Unit,
Graduate School of Business, Curtin University of Technology,
PO Box U1987, Perth, Western Australia, 6845
e-mail: jeffersont@cbs.curtin.edu.au

Alison Preston, Women's Economic Policy Analysis Unit,
Graduate School of Business, Curtin University of Technology,
PO Box U1987, Perth, Western Australia, 6845
e-mail: prestona@cbs.curtin.edu.au

ACKNOWLEDGMENTS

This paper was financed, in part, by an ARC Linkage Grant (LP0347060), the Western Australian Office for Women's Policy, and Office for Senior's Interests and Volunteering. It was completed while Alison Preston was on study leave at Stirling University, Scotland, and she would like to thank the Department of Management and Organization for the hospitality provided while there. The authors gratefully acknowledge the constructive and helpful comments and suggestions provided by the guest editors of *Feminist Economics* and three anonymous referees.

NOTES

1 The taxation of superannuation is an issue of ongoing debate in Australia, particularly as fund managers perceive current taxation arrangements as providing disincentives to invest in superannuation. See for example, Association of Superannuation Funds of Australia (2004).
2 See, for example: Madonna Harrington Meyer (1990); James E. Pesando, Morley Gunderson, and John McLaren (1991); Kathleen Perkins (1993); Eileen J. Feurbach and Carol J. Erdwins (1994); Stanley DeViney and Jennifer Crew Solomon (1995); Annika E. Sundén and Brian J. Surette (1998); Vickie L. Bajtelsmit, Alexandra Bernasek, and Nancy A. Jianakoplos (1999); Ellen A. Bruce (1999); Jay Ginn and Sarah Arber (1999); Virginia Richardson (1999); Barbara Butrica and Howard M. Iams (2000); Leslie A. Morgan (2000); Alexandra Bernasek and Stephanie Schwiff (2001); Mary Condon (2001); Sun-Kang Koh *et al.* (2001); Susan Gee *et al.* (2002); Thomas K. Gregoire, Dieth Kilty, and Virginia Richardson (2002).
3 While the data are drawn from the Peter McDonald *et al.* NLC survey, the authors of this article bear full responsibility for the analysis and interpretation of the data as presented in this paper.
4 We did a check on the suitability of this 0.5 weighting given to part-time employment and found that of those employed part-time in Australia (defined as less than 35 hours per week) average part-time hours per week were around 21.4 for men and 19.1 for women in 2000/01. In other words, if a person works part-time then, on average, they are employed roughly half the time as their full-time counterpart.

96

5 Rates of return to labor market experience

	Men	Women
Experience (β_1)	0.0385	0.0384
Experience^2 (β_2)	-0.000774	-0.000835

Notes: These coefficient estimates on the rates of return to additional years of labor market experience are taken from a standard wage equation for persons with average educational attributes. Full details of the model are reported in Alison Preston and Siobhan Austen (2001: 295). In this equation, labor market experience was estimated using the standard measure of potential experience (i.e., age minus years of formal schooling minus age when school first commenced). We appreciate that this potential measure may overstate the returns to actual experience, especially in the case of women. In the simulations presented here, this overstatement will simply narrow (rather than widen) the estimated gender gap in superannuation accumulations. In other words, it will produce a more conservative estimate than might otherwise have been the case.

6 This assumption is reasonable. According to ABS data collected in 2000, only 18.7 percent of women in employment have superannuation funds that consist of personal/spouse contributions *and* employer/business contributions. Among men, the corresponding share is 25.2 percent (ABS 6361.0, Table 15).

7 This equates to the standard investment real rate of interest recommended by the Australian Securities and Investment Commission (ASIC) for use when calculating investment returns on a balanced style investment portfolio.

8 Table 1 shows that, for women, this is a fair assumption. Around 70 percent of female baby boomers make no voluntary contributions (either in the form of own, spouse, or voluntary employer contributions) into their superannuation funds.

9 A target level frequently referred to in the Australian literature is that of 70–80 percent of pre-retirement expenditure or approximately 60–65 percent of gross pre-retirement income (Senate Select Committee on Superannuation 2002: 53). The social welfare measure of the age pension in Australia is set at 25 percent of MAWTE, which, in May 2001, equated to A$10,286 per annum (seasonally adjusted, Australian Bureau of Statistics 2001).

10 The formula used to compute the annual annuity (R), with the principal (A) completely exhausted, may be written as follows:

$$R = \frac{A}{\left(\dfrac{1 - (1 + r)^{-n}}{r}\right)}$$

where r measures the real rate of interest (as before, assumed to be equal to 3.25 percent) and n measures the number of payments. Based on 1997–99 life tables, Australian men and women who reach 65 may expect, on average, to live for another 16.6 and 20.2 years, respectively; in other words n is equal to 16.6 years for men and 20.2 years for women. We assume that the lump sum used to purchase the annuity is not subject to tax. There is no adjustment for inflation; estimates provided are in real 2001 Australian dollars.

REFERENCES

Association of Superannuation Funds of Australia. 2004. "Australian Superannuation Tax Arrangements Compared with Other Countries." Sydney: Association of Superannuation Funds. On-line. Available http://www.superannuation.asn.au/super/Factsheet2004_2.pdf (accessed June 30, 2004).

Australian Bureau of Statistics. 1997–2002. *Labour Force Australia Catalogue 6203. 0.* Canberra: Australian Bureau of Statistics.

——. 2000. *Superannuation Australia: Coverage and Financial Characteristics: April to June 2000, Catalogue 6360. 0.* Canberra: Australian Bureau of Statistics.

——. 2001. *Average Weekly Earning Australia Catalogue 6302. 0.* Canberra: Australian Bureau of Statistics.

——. 2002. *Marriages and Divorces Australia Catalogue 3310. 0.* Canberra: Australian Bureau of Statistics.

Bajtelsmit, Vickie L., Alexandra Bernasek, and Nancy A. Jianakoplos. 1999. "Gender Differences in Defined Contribution Pension Decisions." *Financial Services Review* 8(1999): 1–10.

Bateman, Hazel, Geoffrey Kingston, and John Piggott. 2001. *Forced Saving: Mandating Private Retirement Incomes.* Cambridge, UK: Cambridge University Press.

Bergmann, Barbara R. 1982. "The Housewife and Social Security Reform: A Feminist Perspective," in Richard V Burkhauser and Karen C. Holden, eds. *A Challenge to Social Security: The Changing Roles of Women and Men in American Society*, pp. 229–33. Toronto: Academic Press.

Bernasek, Alexander and Stephanie Schwiff. 2001. "Gender, Risk, and Retirement." *Journal of Economic Issues* 35(2): 345–56.

Bolle, Patrick. 2000. "Pension Reform: What the Debate Is About." *International Labour Review* 139(2): 197–213.

Brown, Colin. 1994. "The Distribution of Private Sector Superannuation by Gender, Age, and Salary of Members." Retirement Income Modelling Task Force Conference Paper 94/2, Canberra.

Bruce, Ellen A. 1999. "The Application of Unisex Annuity Tables to Retirement Plans." *Journal of Aging and Social Policy* 11(1): 27–38.

Butrica, Barbara and Howard M. Iams. 2000. "Divorced Women at Retirement: Projections of Economic Well-Being in the Near Future." *Social Security Bulletin* 63(6): 3–12.

Condon, Mary. 2001. "Gendering the Pension Promise in Canada: Risk, Financial Markets, and Neoliberalism." *Social and Legal Studies* 10(1): 83–103.

Department of Family and Community Services. 1999. *Income Support Customers: A Statistical Overview 1999.* Canberra: Commonwealth of Australia.

——. 2001. *Income and Support Related Statistics: A Ten Year Compendium, 1989–1999.* Department of Family and Community Services Occasional Paper No 1, Canberra: Commonwealth of Australia.

DeViney, Stanley and Jennifer Crew Solomon. 1995. "Gender Differences in Retirement Income: A Comparison of Theoretical Explanations." *Journal of Women and Aging* 7(4): 83–100.

Dewar, John, Grania Sheehan, and Jody Hughes. 1999. "Superannuation and Divorce in Australia." Australian Institute of Family Studies Working Paper 18, Melbourne.

Donath, Susan. 1998. "The Continuing Problem of Women's Retirement Income," presented at the 7th Australian Women's Studies Association Conference, April 16–18, University of South Australia.

Economic Planning and Advisory Council (EPAC). 1994. *Women and Superannuation: Selected Seminar Papers: EPAC Background Paper No. 41.* Canberra: Economic Planning and Advisory Council and Office for the Status of Women.

Feurbach, Eileen J. and Carol J. Erdwins. 1994. "Women Retirement: The Influence of Work History." *Journal of Women and Aging* 6(3): 69–85.

Gallagher, Phil. 2001. "Challenges of the Past, Present, and Future: Women and Retirement Income." Paper presented to the Economic Policy Summit, September 7, University of New South Wales.

Gallery, Natalie, Kerry Brown, and Gerry Gallery. 1996. "Privatising the Pension." *Journal of Australian Political Economy* 38: 98–124.

Gee, Susan, Sik Hung Ng, Ann Weatherall, Jim Liu, Cynthia Leong, and Te Ripowai Higgins. 2002. "Savings Ourselves: Gender Issues in Making Provision for One's Own Retirement." *Australasian Journal on Ageing* 21(1): 30–5.

Gillion, Colin, John Turner, Clive Bailey, and Denis Latulippe, eds. 2000. *Social Security Pensions: Development and Reform.* Geneva: International Labour Organization.

Ginn, Jay and Sarah Arber. 1999. "Changing Patterns of Pension Inequality: The Shift from State to Private Resources." *Ageing and Society* 19: 319–42.

Gregoire, Thomas K., Dieth Kilty, and Virginia Richardson. 2002. "Gender and Racial Inequities in Retirement Resources." *Journal of Women and Aging* 14(3/4): 25–39.

Hancock, Keith. 1981. "The Economics of Retirement Provision in Australia." *Economic Papers* 20(36): 1–23.

Harrington Meyer, Madonna. 1990."Family Status and Poverty Among Older Women: The Gender Distribution of Retirement Income in the United States." *Social Problems* 37: 551–63.

Himmelweit, Susan. 2002. "Making Visible the Hidden Economy: The Case for Gender Impact Analysis of Economic Policy." *Feminist Economics* 8(1): 40–70.

Holden, Karen C. and Hsiang-Hui Daphne Kuo. 1996. "Complex Marital Histories and Economic Well Being: The Continuing Legacy of Divorce and Widowhood as the HRS Cohort Approaches Retirement." *The Gerontologist* 36(3): 383–90.

Jefferson, Therese and Alison Preston. 2003. "Bargaining for Welfare: Gender Consequences of Australia's Dual Welfare Model." *Australian Bulletin of Labour* 29(1): 76–96.

Kelly, Rosemary. 1997. "Superannuation and the Marketisation of Retirement Incomes." *Labour and Industry* 8(1): 57–80.

Kelly, Simon, Ann Harding, and Richard Percival. 2002. "Projecting the Impact of Changes in Superannuation Policy: A Microsimulation Approach." Presented at the 10th Annual Colloquium of Superannuation Researchers, July 8–9, 2002.

King, Anthony. 2001. "Superannuation – The Right Balance." CPA Australia. http://www.cpaaustralia.com.au (accessed July 2003).

——, Hans Bækgaard, and Ann Harding. 1999. "Australian Retirement Incomes." National Centre for Economic Modelling Discussion Paper No. 29, NATSEM, University of Canberra.

——, Agnes Walker, and Ann Harding. 1999. "Social Security, Ageing, and Income Distribution in Australia." National Centre for Applied Economic Modelling Discussion Paper No. 58, NATSEM, University of Canberra.

Koh, Sun-Kang, Mary Winter, Earl W. Morrise, Krystyna Gutkowska, and Marzena Jeżewska-Zcyhowcz. 2001. "Gender and Productive and Retirement Incomes in Poland in the Initial Stages of Transformation." *East European Quarterly* 35(1): 59–86.

Larkin, John. 1994. "Occupational Link: Eligibility and the Two Year Rule," in Economic Planning and Advisory Council and Office for the Status of Women. *Women and Superannuation: Selected Seminar Papers.* EPAC Background Paper No. 41, Economic Planning and Advisory Council and Office for the Status of Women, Canberra.

Maloney, Geoff, Justin Marshall, Anne McConnell, Julie Elliot, Alastair Banks, and Peggy Hausknecht. 2000. "Retirement Incomes of Women Who Divorce." *Australian Social Policy* 2000(1): 3–24.

McDonald, Peter, Janeen Baxter, Frank Jones, and Deborah Mitchell. 2000. *Negotiating the Life Course 1997* [computer file]. Canberra. Social Science Data Archives, The Australian National University.

Miller, Paul. 1982. "The Rate of Return to Education." *Australian Economic Review* 59(3): 23–32.

Morgan, Leslie A. 2000. "The Continuing Gender Gap in Later Life Economic Security." *Journal of Aging and Social Policy* 11(2/3): 157–65.

Olsberg, Diana. 2001. "Women and Retirement Savings – Ways Forward? Lessons from Overseas Initiatives and Proposed Australian Strategies." Presented to the Economic Policy Summit, University of New South Wales, September 7.

Owen, Mary. 1984. "Superannuation was Not Meant for Women." *The Australian Quarterly* 56(4): 363–73.

Perkins, Kathleen. 1993. "Working Class Women and Retirement." *Journal of Gerontological Social Work* 20(3/4): 129–46.

Perry, Julia. 1988. "Income Support for Older Women." Social Security Review Research Paper No. 43, Commonwealth Department of Social Security, Canberra.

Pesando, James E., Morley Gunderson, and John McLaren. 1991. "Pension Benefits and Male–Female Wage Differentials." *Canadian Journal of Economics* 24(3): 536–50.

Preston, Alison and Siobhan Austen. 2001. "Women, Superannuation, and the SGC." *Australian Bulletin of Labour* 27(4): 272–95.

—— and John Burgess. 2003. "Women's Work in Australia: Trends, Issues, and Prospects." *Australian Journal of Labour Economics* 6(4): 497–518.

Richardson, Virginia. 1999. "Women and Retirement." *Journal of Woman and Aging* 11(2/3): 49–66.

Rosenman, Linda and Jeni Warberton. 1996. "Restructuring Australian Retirement Incomes: Implications of Changing Work and Retirement Patterns." *International Social Security Review* 49(4): 5–25.

Ross, Steven. 1994. "Taxation, Superannuation, and Women," in Economic Planning and Advisory Council and Office for the Status of Women. *Women and Superannuation: Selected Seminar Papers*. EPAC Background Paper No. 41, pp. 105–14 Canberra: Economic Planning and Advisory Council and Office for the Status of Women.

Sandor, Danny. 2001. "To Have and to Hold Till the Super Do We Part – Women and Marital Separation: Superannuation Implications." Presented to the Economic Policy Summit on Women and Retirement Savings, University of New South Wales, September 7, 2001.

Senate Select Committee on Superannuation. 1995. *Super and Broken Work Patterns, 17th Report of the Senate Select Committee on Superannuation*. Canberra: Parliament of the Commonwealth of Australia.

——. 2002. *Superannuation and Standards of Living in Retirement: Report on the Adequacy of the Tax Arrangements for Superannuation and Related Policy*. Canberra: Parliament of the Commonwealth of Australia. http://www.aph.gov.au/senate/committee/superannuation_ctte/living_standards/report/report.pdf (accessed March 2003).

Shaver, Sheila. 2001. "Pension Reform in Australia: Problematic Gender Equality," in Jay Ginn, Debra Street, and Sarah Arber, eds. *Women, Work, and Pensions: International Issues and Prospects*, pp. 179–98. Buckingham, UK: Open University Press.

Sundén, Annika E. and Brian J. Surette. 1998. "Gender Differences in the Allocation of Assets in Retirement Savings Plans." *AEA Papers and Proceedings* 88(2): 207–11.

Weston, Ruth and Bruce Smyth. 2000. "Financial Living Standards after Divorce." *Family Matters* 55: 11–15.

Whiteford, Peter and Kim Bond. 2000. "Trends in the Incomes and Living Standards of Older People in Australia." Policy Research Paper No. 6, Department of Family and Community Services, Commonwealth of Australia, Canberra.

Williamson, John B. and Tay K. McNamara. 2003. "Interrupted Trajectories and Labor Force Participation." *Research on Aging* 25(2): 87–121.

SOCIAL ASSISTANCE, GENDER, AND THE AGED IN SOUTH AFRICA

Justine Burns, Malcolm Keswell, and Murray Leibbrandt

INTRODUCTION

The social pension system in South Africa is among the most far-reaching and generous in the developing world (Armando Barrientos and Peter Lloyd-Sherlock 2002). Representing the core component of the South African social safety net, the pension is a noncontributory, means-tested pension that is payable to women aged 60 and above and men aged 65 and above. The pension has a strong gender dimension: different age eligibility rules and different male and female mortality rates ensure that the pension reaches significantly more elderly women than men. Moreover, key demographic trends, such as the large population share of school-going youth, very high unemployment rates, and the devastating impact of the HIV/AIDS epidemic on younger age cohorts have placed the social old-age pension and the elderly[1] at the center of the livelihood strategies of many South African households. In this context, the social pension plays a vital role as a poverty-alleviation mechanism, with the effect of pension income on the welfare of other household members being strongly conditioned upon whether or not the pensioner is female (Marianne Bertrand, Sendhil Mullainathan, and Douglas Miller 2003; Esther Duflo 2003; Malcolm

Keswell 2004b; Dori Posel, James Fairburn, and Frances Lund 2004). Thus, while elderly women benefit significantly from the pension system, important externalities such as changes in household composition and allocation of labor time, as well as changes in child health and educational status, are also associated with pension receipt, especially if the pensioner is female.

A HISTORY OF THE SOUTH AFRICAN SOCIAL PENSION

The South African social pension and its evolution from a grant that only went to white South Africans to one that went to all South Africans regardless of racial categorization[2] has an interesting history. The grant was first introduced in 1928 as a form of income support for poor elderly whites (Andreas Sagner 2000). Only in 1944 did the pre-apartheid state extend the social pension to include members of other race groups, and even then, pension payment size was determined by race at a ratio of 4:2:1 respectively for Whites relative to Indians and Coloreds relative to Black South Africans.[3] In practice, actual payment ratios were on the order of 12:6:1 using rural Black pensioners as the baseline group for comparison (Stephen Devereux 2001: 4).

From the late 1970s onward, these racially-based pension gaps were significantly reduced. To reduce these gaps, the apartheid state allocated large additional funds to social assistance schemes, particularly the pension. The state made these allocations in an attempt to legitimize the fiction of sustainable, self-governing states, also called homelands, for Black South Africans. These homelands were deliberately created to keep Black South Africans outside of the increasingly integrated legal and political structures for those categorized as Whites, Indians, and Coloreds (Servaas Van der Berg 1998). During the 1980s, the size of pensions more than doubled for Black South Africans while it declined by 40 percent (in real terms) for Whites (Monica Ferreira 1999: 55). By 1985, White pensions were only 2.5 times higher than those for Blacks and 1.5 times higher than those for those categorized as Coloreds and Indians (Lawrence Schlemmer and Valerie Moller 1997). Take-up rates,[4] particularly among elderly Black South Africans, increased markedly during this time.

By the end of the 1980s, the divide-and-rule tactics of the apartheid state had failed, but the social pension had come to dominate the South African social assistance landscape for all race groups. There would have been major social resistance to any attempt by the apartheid state to cut back on the scope of the pension policy during the negotiations that preceded the transition to a post-apartheid era. Indeed, stakeholders in the negotiations never placed the issue of pension payout reduction on the agenda over the 1990–94 period. On the contrary, the *Social Assistance Act of 1992* provided steps to deracialize pensions and achieve pension parity, which was finally achieved in 1993, just one year prior to the first democratic elections. By 1993, the take-up rate among eligible Black South African men and women stood at 80 percent.[5] At this time, the maximum benefit was R370 (about US$3 per day at the prevailing exchange rate), an amount equal to twice the median per capita income in rural areas (Duflo 2003) and three times the level of the least generous World Bank poverty line.

In 2002, the pension was raised to R700 per month,[6] a level that represents more than twice the median monthly individual earnings of Black South Africans (Malcolm Keswell 2004a). The pension, funded out of general government revenues that are derived from progressive income taxes, costs approximately 1.4 percent of GDP each year. With 1.9 million beneficiaries, it constitutes the largest social assistance program in South Africa (Department of Social Development 2002a), with important redistributive and poverty-alleviation impacts.

THE EFFECT OF PENSIONS ON POVERTY

Social pensions for the elderly in South Africa are widely viewed as a key aspect of the South African government's poverty-alleviation program. While there are few good estimates of poverty rates among the elderly, the South African Department of Social Development (2002a, 2002b) has estimated that over 80 percent of the elderly have no access to income apart from the social pension and that the pension reduces the poverty gap (defined as the difference between the poverty line and observed income for an individual living below the poverty line) of the elderly by 94 percent. In addition to the social pension, the elderly are also eligible to receive free primary and secondary healthcare,[7] a generous housing subsidy,[8] and under certain conditions, additional grants such as a care dependency grant, disability grant, or child support grant.

Developed countries face a situation where the increasing elderly population imposes a rising financial burden on less populous younger generations. South Africa faces a different situation. South Africa's elderly account for only 7 percent of the total population, a relatively small percentage (Department of Social Development 2002a).[9] The largest share of the South African population is composed of school-age youth. These trends, taken together with very high unemployment rates and the devastating impact of the HIV/AIDS epidemic on the younger cohorts of the working-age population, have placed the social pension at the center of household livelihood strategies for many South African households. As shown in Table 1, the social pension represents a vital source of household income, particularly for households in the lower income quintiles. For households in these quintiles, remittances and social pensions constitute a significantly larger share of household income than for richer households (Murray Leibbrandt, Christopher Woolard, and Ingrid Woolard 2000).

Table 1 Income by sources by quintiles of per capita household income, 2000 IES
($N = 26,263$)

| Variable | Quintile | | | | | Total |
	1	2	3	4	5	
Aggregate estimates						
Income per capita*	691	2,041	4,092	8,922	40,150	11,156
Percent Black South African	91.6	92.9	86.7	76.9	48.2	78.0
Number in household	5.54	5.01	3.81	2.97	2.50	3.97
Number under age 15	2.37	1.87	1.11	0.73	0.51	1.32
Number aged 60 +	0.29	0.42	0.33	0.27	0.19	0.30
Source of income disaggregated by income class (percent)						
Wage and salaries	35.3	42.2	61.7	72.7	85.3	60.2
Profits	6.0	5.3	5.0	4.4	4.2	4.9
Rent	0.8	0.4	0.6	0.6	0.4	0.5
Interests and dividends	0.1	0.1	0.2	0.3	0.9	0.3
Private pension	0.8	1.2	1.2	2.1	4.7	2.0
Alimony	3.4	2.4	1.8	1.1	0.4	1.8
Remittances	25.3	16.4	9.9	5.2	1.5	11.2
Disability grant	2.9	4.6	2.7	1.9	0.2	2.4
Social pension	17.6	22.1	13.6	10.1	1.4	12.8
Distribution of social pension by income class (percent)						
Percent receiving social pension	19.8	28.5	21.2	17.5	6.4	18.8
Percent of income from pensions for recipient households	88.5	74.0	60.8	63.1	33.6	68.8

Source: David Lam and Murray Leibbrandt (2003).
Note: *Income per capita in South African rands.

Most notably, pension income constitutes almost 90 percent of household income for households in the poorest quintile and almost three-quarters of total household income for households in the second quintile. In the absence of these social grants, the incidence and severity of household poverty would be substantially worse.

Using 1993 household survey data for South Africa, Anne Case and Angus Deaton (1998) estimate that the poverty headcount ratio among Black South Africans is reduced by 5 percentage points through the introduction of the pension, assuming no offsetting changes in pre-pension incomes. In order to check for the robustness of this key finding over the post-apartheid period, Figure 1 shows the distribution of total household

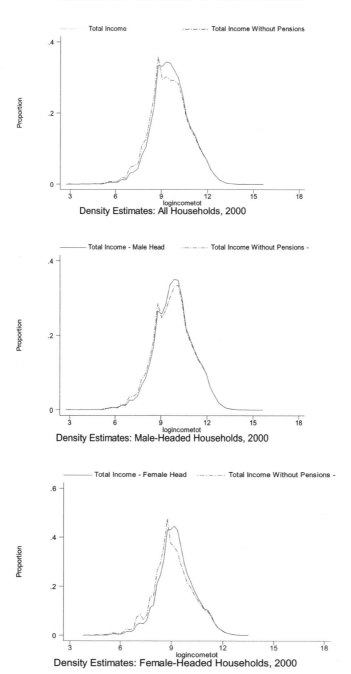

Figure 1 Distribution of Household Income, with and without pension income, by gender of household head

income, both with and without pension income, using data from a national household income and expenditure survey undertaken in 2000. These distributions confirm that in the absence of pension receipt, household income is significantly reduced, causing a leftward shift of the distribution, particularly for households in the middle and lower end of the income distribution.[10] A similar comparison for male- and female-headed[11] households respectively further suggests that female-headed households are particularly vulnerable in this regard. Not only do female-headed households experience lower mean household income, but the absence of pension income also causes a larger leftward shift in their distribution than in the distribution for male-headed households.

The old-age pension reaches a clear majority of female recipients. This is due to a combination of demographic trends and the eligibility rules of the social pension: not only do South African women enjoy greater longevity than men, constituting just over three-fifths of those aged 60 and above, but the age-eligibility requirement for women to receive a pension is 60, whereas men are age-eligible at age 65.[12] These two factors give the social pension a significant gender dimension, with pensions reaching almost three times as many women as men (Case and Deaton 1998; Department of Social Development 2002b).

Of those aged 60 and above, two-thirds are Black South Africans, who, owing to the legacy of residential segregation imposed under apartheid, still largely reside in rural areas. Whites comprise 22 percent of the elderly population. Whites are over-represented in this cohort relative to their weighting in the total population, while Blacks are relatively under-represented. These differences reflect the different life expectancies in these racial groups. The over-representation of Whites in the elderly cohort, however, does not map onto the pensions take-up rates by race. Because eligibility for the social pension is means tested,[13] nearly all Whites are screened out. Black South Africans are on average one of the poorer racial cohorts and tend to meet the means test, enabling them to receive pensions. While only 1 percent of age-eligible White elderly receive the social pension, over 80 percent of age-eligible Black South Africans receive the pension. The existing literature provides a compelling case that most eligible Black South Africans receive the maximum social pension payment and that the social pension is particularly well targeted at elderly, rural Black women. Furthermore, as an outcome of these two forces, the social assistance program does have a substantial positive impact on household poverty. In light of these facts, an emerging literature has developed that tries to tease out more detail on the adjustments *within* households in response to the social pension. Two themes have featured prominently. The first key theme is the literature investigating adjustments to household composition, while the second is program-evaluation literature attempting to investigate whether there are differential impacts on labor supply, intrahousehold allocation of resources, child nutrition, and unemployment within households if the social pension comes to an eligible female rather than an eligible male.

BEHAVIORAL RESPONSES

Changes in living arrangements and caregiving

As Table 1 shows, the households that rely most heavily on the social pension are not only mostly Black and poorer, but are also larger in size. Multi-generational households are common amongst Black South African families, accounting for the larger household size at the bottom of the income distribution. Thus, unlike the experience of developed countries, pension receipt in South Africa does not increase the propensity of the elderly to live alone (Valerie Moller and Ayanda Sotshongaye 1996; Eric Edmonds, Kristin Mammen, and Douglas Miller 2003). Rather, it is associated with increases in household size and changes in household composition, with a larger number of children, especially those aged 0 – 6, migrating into pensioner households (Eric Edmonds 2004). Case and Deaton (1998) estimate that 60 percent of all Black pensioner households are three-generation households with children, compared to only 9 percent of White pensioner households. A further 14 percent of Black pensioner households are skip-generation households containing only grandparents and young children, while there are no such White pensioner households in their sample. This finding resonates with other research showing that the elderly, particularly elderly Black women, are increasingly assuming the role of primary caregiver, as the middle generation is either forced to migrate out of the household in search of scarce employment opportunities or have been lost to the HIV/AIDS epidemic (Helena Legido-Quigley 2003; Edmonds 2004).[14] Pension incomes are thus an important income source, in conjunction with child support grants, through which the elderly caregivers are able to meet these additional childcare and educational costs. (Table 2 provides a summary of other such grants available to the elderly.)

Available evidence also suggests that South Africa's social pensions are vitally important for the welfare of these unintended beneficiaries, in that pension receipt is positively and significantly associated[15] with improvements in child health status (Esther Duflo 2000; Anne Case 2001), particularly for female children living with pension-eligible maternal grandmothers (Duflo 2000). Pension receipt is also positively and significantly associated[16] with increased school attendance and decreased child labor (Edmonds 2004). Moreover, it would appear that there are differential impacts within households if the social pension comes to an eligible female rather than an eligible male.

Table 2 Menu of social assistance grants

Grant type	Value in rands
Grant for the Aged[a]	700
War Veterans Grant[b]	718
Grant for Disability[c]	700
Care Dependency Grant[d]	700
Child Support Grant[e]	160
Foster Child Grant[f]	500
Grant-in-Aid[g]	150

Notes:

[a]Paid to women 60 years and older and men aged 65 and older.

[b]Given to those who are 60 and older who served in the South African army during the world wars.

[c]Paid to those 18 years and older who have been disabled for six months or more. Individual must have been declared medically unfit by a district surgeon, and be unable to support themselves or find employment. If individuals are 60 or older, they are not eligible to receive both the pension and disability grant.

[d]For children who are severely disabled and may need special care.

[e]Paid to primary caregiver (defined as anyone who takes care of the daily needs of children and is not receiving any income for caring for the children) who takes care of children, up to a maximum of six children. To qualify, household income for urban households must not exceed R800, and for households in rural areas or informal settlements, household income must not exceed R1,100.

[f]Paid to foster parents in respect of children placed in their care through a court order.

[g]Payable to an individual taking care of another person in need of full-time attention, and who is a recipient of a grant.

Source: Department of Social Development (2002a).

Changes in labor supply and the gender of the pension recipient

Evidence of the impact of pension receipt on labor supply in South Africa is mixed. Unemployment in South Africa is higher than any other country with a similar level of GDP per capita, with estimates ranging anywhere from 30–40 percent, depending on whether the so-called "non-searching unemployed" are included (Keswell 2004b). But unlike other developing countries with large reservoirs of surplus labor, South Africa does not have a large informal sector that can absorb these individuals (Geeta Kingdon and John Knight 2003). In the face of such scarce job opportunities, pensions represent a stable source of household income. Moreover, as argued previously, evidence exists that this additional pension income supports a change in household living arrangements to maximize the comparative advantage of prime-age women in labor markets, allowing out-migration in search of work and leaving the elderly (elderly women in particular) to care for children (Edmonds, Mammen, and Miller 2003). Household income in the form of pensions has been shown to be positively associated with changes in child health and educational status (Duflo 2000; Edmonds 2004), particularly for female children living with maternal grandmothers.

Some evidence shows that unemployed individuals tend to attach themselves to their grandparents in order to access the pension income, and this attachment often results in the unemployed moving from urban to rural areas, thereby further reducing their employment chances (Stephen

Klasen and Ingrid Woolard 2000). Bertrand, Mullainathan, and Miller (2003) argue that pension receipt is associated with a substantial and statistically significant[17] reduction in employment and labor supply responses by prime-age individuals living in a three-generation household containing pension-eligible individuals. Moreover, these effects have two important gender dimensions: not only is the negative labor supply effect larger for those living with pension-eligible females than for those living with pension-eligible males, but the negative labor supply effect is strongest for prime-age males, eldest sons in particular, in households containing female pensioners. Bertrand, Mullainathan, and Miller (2003) interpret this as evidence in favor of a bargaining model of the household in which dominant men with greater power inside the household are able to capture a larger share of the surplus when the pensioner is female.

More recent work, however, suggests that the negative labor supply response associated with pension receipt is strongly conditioned on the occurrence of negative shocks in rural areas and on the way in which households are defined. South Africa has a long history of individuals who *temporarily migrate* to places of employment, but who retain original household membership. Posel, Fairburn, and Lund (2004) show that when the definition of household is extended to include these nonresident household members, the negative relationship between the social pension and labor force participation disappears. In particular, rural Black women are significantly more likely to be migrant workers when they are members of a household in receipt of a pension, especially when a female receives the pension. Similarly, using data collected in the KwaZulu-Natal province, home to some of the poorest areas in South Africa where households are subjected to frequent weather and health shocks, Keswell (2004b) finds that, after controlling for negative shocks experienced by the household, the employment elasticity for prime-age individuals in pension households is positive and significant[18] when the pensioner is female and zero when the pensioner is male. Both sets of results reinforce the notion that pension income received by women specifically may be important not only because it helps prime-age individuals, women in particular, overcome income constraints to migration, but also because it enables grandmothers to support grandchildren. As in the case of improvements in child health status described above, however, the gender of the pension recipient is key, with the evidence suggesting that female pensioners are more prone to sharing their pension income with other household members for such purposes than male pensioners.

CONCLUSION

One of the strongest recurring themes in the body of literature concerning the South African pension scheme is the importance of gender. Not only does the pension reach significantly more women than men, but the effect of pension income on the welfare of other household members and changes in the intra-household allocation of labor depends vitally on whether or not the pensioner is female (Bertrand, Mullainathan, and Miller 2003; Duflo 2003; Keswell 2004b; Posel, Fairburn, and Lund 2004).

However, while positive externalities such as improved child health are arguably desirable, it does mean that the intended effect of the transfer on the target group, namely, the elderly, is reduced. Moreover, there is evidence of negative externalities associated with the pension, namely increased household sizes and an associated increase in the care-giving burden for elderly women in particular, and potential negative labor supply effects (although this appears to be strongly conditioned on how the household is defined, household location, and the occurrence of negative shocks). While the labor supply results have been interpreted by some as evidence of negative incentive effects induced by large cash transfers to the elderly, in this paper, we also cite work arguing that the unemployed attach themselves to pensioner households as part of a survival strategy. This ambiguity will not be resolved until the quality of data improves.

Collectively, the weight of evidence around the social pension makes a clear argument that social security assistance targeted at the unemployed would complement the welfare impact of the pension. The fact that the pension program is having a large number of desirable outcomes does not obviate the need for additional social security assistance for other vulnerable groups in society. Two obvious cases are the current "unintended beneficiaries" of the social pension, namely, children up to the age of 18, and the unemployed, who face bleak employment prospects in the context of massive structural unemployment. The Committee of Inquiry into a Comprehensive System of Social Security for South Africa (Department of Social Development 2002b) has recently recommended that a basic income grant (BIG) of R100 per month (just less than US$20) for all South Africans be phased in, targeting children under the age of 18 in the initial stages and then expanding to cover the broader population in time, once the relevant administrative systems are in place. The South African government has thus far resisted implementing this recommendation, and the social pensions remain as the largest welfare program in South Africa. The introduction of such additional social security programs seems not only inevitable, but also critical if South Africa's elderly are truly to receive the poverty-alleviation assistance they require.

Justine Burns, School of Economics, University of Cape Town, Rondebosch,
Cape Town, 7700, South Africa
e-mail: jburns@commerce.uct.ac.za

Malcolm Keswell, School of Economics, University of Cape Town, Rondebosch,
Cape Town, 7700, South Africa
e-mail: mkeswell@commerce.uct.ac.za

Murray Leibbrandt, School of Economics, University of Cape Town, Rondebosch,
Cape Town, 7700, South Africa
e-mail: mleibbra@commerce.uct.ac.za

NOTES

1 The elderly are defined as people who are 60 years or older. For simplicity, this convention is followed throughout this paper despite the differences in pension-age eligibility rules by gender.

2 Racial categorization was institutionalized by the apartheid state. The Population Registration Act of 1950 required that all South Africans be racially classified, and this resulted in the legal construction of four main race groups: White (European descent), Black (African), Indian (predominantly descendants of South Indian indentured laborers brought to work on British-owned sugar plantations on the southeast coast of South Africa) or Colored (of mixed-race descent). Classification into these categories was based on appearance, social acceptance, and descent, and was vigorously enforced by the apartheid state.

3 See note 2 for discussion of race categorizations.

4 Take-up rates are the rates of enrollment for a program.

5 The remaining age-eligible Black South Africans were either in richer households with a private pension or were the very poor who had difficulty accessing pensions (Anne Case and Angus Deaton 1998).

6 This is approximately US$132 in PPP adjusted terms.

7 Primary healthcare is free for all South Africans. With respect to secondary healthcare, the elderly in receipt of a pension are eligible to receive free secondary healthcare services at public hospitals.

8 The housing subsidy scheme makes special provision for the elderly, and the value of the subsidy for the elderly exceeds the maximum value of subsidies for other beneficiaries.

9 The elderly account for 8 percent of the total population in developing countries, 5 percent in other African countries, and 19 percent in developed nations (Department of Social Development 2002a).

10 These estimates, however, assume the absence of any crowding out of informal assistance or remittances as the result of pension receipt. Robert Jensen (2003) presents evidence to suggest a 20 – 30 percent reduction in remittances for every rand of pension income received by South Africa's elderly, implying that the poverty-reducing effects of the pension may be lower than previously thought. However, Dori Posel (2001) argues that remittances are more strongly influenced by the characteristics of the remitting household than by the pension status of the recipient.

11 Headship is a self-identified concept reported by the interview respondent.

12 This differential age-eligibility rule has been contested in post-apartheid South Africa. In the latest challenge, the Communicare Residents Association has taken a class action suit before one of South Africa's provincial high courts, arguing that this law embodies discrimination against men (*Cape Argus* June 20, 2002).

13 In the case of a single individual, the means test is calculated by taking the sum of the individual's income and an income value assigned to the assets that the individual owns. For married individuals, the means test is calculated by taking the mean of the

pooled income (actual income and the income value of owned assets) of the pensioner and their spouse. The means test does not take the income of other household members into account, thus removing any incentive for households to rearrange themselves in order to become eligible for pension receipt. If the individual's income exceeds the means test, the size of the pension payment is reduced on a rand-for-rand basis, in line with their income status.

14 According to a National Food Consumption Survey (Department of Social Welfare 2002a), 40 percent of households are now headed by elderly persons as a direct result of the HIV/AIDS epidemic. These households would be characterized as skip-generation households.

15 Significant at 1 percent level.

16 Significant at 1 percent level.

17 Significant at 1 percent level.

18 Significant at 1 percent level.

REFERENCES

Barrientos, Armando and Peter Lloyd-Sherlock. 2002. "Non-Contributory Pensions and Social Protection." Discussion paper at University of Manchester, UK, and University of East Anglia, UK.

Bertrand, Marianne, Sendhil Mullainathan, and Douglas Miller. 2003. "Public Policy and Extended Families: Evidence from Pensions in South Africa." *The World Bank Economic Review* 17(1): 27–50.

Cape Argus. 2002. "Give Us Pensions at 60 Too, Say Men." June 20.

Case, Anne. 2001. "Does Money Protect Health Status? Evidence from South African Pensions." Discussion paper at National Bureau of Economic Research.

—— and Angus Deaton. 1998. "Large Cash Transfers to the Elderly in South Africa." *Economic Journal* 108(450): 1330–61.

Department of Social Development. 2002a. "National Report on the Status of Older Persons: Report to the Second World Assembly on Ageing." Discussion paper Government of the Republic of South Africa Pretoria: Government Printer.

——. 2002b. "Report of the Committee of Inquiry into a Comprehensive System of Social Security for South Africa." Consolidated Report Government of the Republic of South Africa Pretoria: Government Printer.

Devereux, Stephen. 2001. "Social Pensions in Namibia and South Africa?" Discussion Paper No 379, IDS, University of Sussex, UK.

Duflo, Esther. 2000. "Child Health and Household Resources in South Africa: Evidence from the Old Age Pension Program." *American Economic Review* Papers and Proceedings (May): 393–8.

——. 2003. "Grandmothers and Granddaughters: Old Age Pension and Intrahousehold Allocation in South Africa." *The World Bank Economic Review* 17(1): 1–26.

Edmonds, Eric. 2004. "Does Illiquidity Alter Child Labour and Schooling Decisions? Evidence from Household Responses to Anticipated Cash Transfers in South Africa." Discussion paper, Dartmouth College and NBER.

——, Kristin Mammen, and Douglas Miller. 2003. "Rearranging the Family? Income Support and Elderly Living Arrangements in a Low Income Country." Discussion paper, Dartmouth College.

Ferreira, Monica. 1999. "The Generosity and Universality of South Africa's Pension System." *The UE Courier*, Vol. 176.

Jensen, Robert. 2003. "Do Private Transfers 'Displace' the Benefits of Public Transfers? Evidence from South Africa." *Journal of Public Economics* 88: 89–112.

Keswell, Malcolm. 2004a. "Education and Racial Inequality in Post-Apartheid South Africa." Working Paper No 2004-02-008, Santa Fe Institute, NM.

——. 2004b. "Social Networks, Extended Families, and Consumption Smoothing: Field Evidence from South Africa." Working Paper No 58, Centre for Social Science Research, University of Cape Town.

Kingdon, Geeta and John Knight. 2003. "Unemployment in South Africa: The Nature of the Beast." *World Development* 32(3): 391–408.

Klasen, Stephen and Ingrid Woolard. 2000. "Surviving Unemployment without State Support: Unemployment and Household Formation in South Africa." Discussion paper, Institute for the Study of Labor (IZA).

Lam, David and Murray Leibbrandt. 2003. "Family Support and Rapid Social Change in South Africa." Unpublished research proposal, University of Michigan, MI.

Legido-Quigley, Helena. 2003. "The South African Old Age Pension: Exploring the Role on Poverty Alleviation in Households Affected by HIV/AIDS." Discussion paper, IDPM, University of Manchester, UK.

Leibbrandt, Murray, Christopher Woolard, and Ingrid Woolard. 2000. "The Contribution of Income Components to South African Income Inequality: A Decomposable Gini Analysis." *Journal of African Economies* 9(1): 79–99.

Moller, Valerie and Ayanda Sotshongaye. 1996. " 'My Family Eats This Money Too': Pension Sharing and Self-Respect Among Zulu Grandmothers." *Southern African Journal of Gerontology* 5(2): 9–19.

Posel, Dori. 2001. "Intra-Family Transfers and Income-Pooling: A Study of Remittances in Kwazulu-Natal." *South African Journal of Economics* 69(3): 501–28.

——, James Fairburn, and Frances Lund. 2004. "Labour Migration and Households: A Reconsideration of the Effects of the Social Pension on Labour Supply in South Africa." Working paper, University of Kwazulu-Natal, June.

Sagner, Andreas. 2000. "Ageing and Social Policy in South Africa: Historical Perspectives with Particular Reference to the Eastern Cape." *Journal of Southern African Studies* 26(3): 523–53.

Schlemmer, Lawrence and Valerie Moller. 1997. "The Shape of South African Society and Its Challenges." *Social Indicators Research* 41(1–3): 15–50.

Van der Berg, Servaas. 1998. "Ageing, Public Finance and Social Security in South Africa." *Southern African Journal of Gerontology* 7(1): 3–9.

115

RACE, ETHNICITY, AND SOCIAL SECURITY RETIREMENT AGE IN THE US

Carole A. Green

INTRODUCTION

Due to improvements in healthcare, the development of new drugs to combat life-threatening conditions common among the elderly such as hypertension and high cholesterol, and perhaps because of increased knowledge of the importance of exercise and good nutrition, life expectancy in the United States, as in most other countries, is increasing. The number of Americans aged 65 and over is expected to double by the year 2030; projections indicate that by that time there will be only 2.7 people between the ages of 20 and 64 for everyone over 65.[1] Between 1970 and 2000, life expectancies at birth increased for both blacks and whites, by 6.9 and 4.5 years for white males and females, respectively, to 74.9 and 80.1 years. Corresponding increases for blacks were larger, 8.3 and 6.9 years, to 68.3 and 75.2 years, spans still significantly shorter than for whites.

When the US Social Security retirement system was instituted in 1937, one major objective was to provide incentives for older workers to retire so that more jobs would be available for younger workers. At that time, life expectancies were considerably lower, and there were far more working-age adults than elderly. Now, however, continuation of current benefit levels has been presented as a major funding problem.[2] In order to increase the ratio of workers who pay Social Security and Medicare taxes to the number of people receiving Social Security retirement income and Medicare benefits, or at least to reduce the rate of decline, public policy is turning toward encouraging people to delay retirement. Similar changes in attitude are apparent throughout the economy. In decades past, workers in the US were required by many employers to retire at a certain age, usually 65, and seldom later than 70. Today mandatory retirement ages are rare.

How does the Social Security retirement system in the US work?

All workers in the US are required to participate in the Social Security retirement program, regardless of citizenship. Currently, 6.2 percent of a worker's pay is withheld, up to a maximum that is adjusted annually.[3] An additional 1.45 percent (with no maximum) is withheld to support Medicare, making a total of 7.65 percent of earnings for most workers. The employer contributes the same amount. Self-employed workers must pay not only their own but also the employer's portion, a total of 15.3 percent up to the Social Security maximum for the year and then only the Medicare tax on any excess.

To receive benefits upon retirement, one must have received credit for working at least 40 quarters. Full benefits have long been available at age 65; reduced benefits are available at 62 years of age, with increased benefits for those who continue to work up to age 70. In order to help maintain the solvency of the system, the full retirement age (FRA) is gradually being increased to 67 years of age for those born in 1960 and later.[4] Reduced benefits are still available at 62 years of age but will be reduced proportionately more since they will eventually be available up to five years earlier than the FRA. The maximum age for earning increased benefits for delaying retirement will still be age 70.

Benefits that a retired worker receives depend on earnings in the thirty-five highest-earning years.[5] These benefits are calculated in such a way that the lowest-earning workers receive a relatively larger percentage of their total average earnings. The average received in 2002 was $814 per month ($9,768 annually), with a possible maximum of $1,660 ($19,920 annually). For purposes of comparison, for the same year the poverty line for an individual 65 years of age and older was set at $8,628 per year; median yearly income for all those 25 years and older was $31,356 in 2001.

Benefits are also available for spouses who have never worked for pay or who have not worked long enough to qualify, in the amount of one-half of the payment to the retired worker. Married persons who have earned benefits in their own right may receive payments based on their own contributions or an amount equal to one-half of the spouse's payments, whichever is larger. A widow or widower is entitled to 100 percent of the benefits the deceased spouse had received.

For workers who choose to receive Social Security benefits before reaching the FRA, benefits are reduced by $1 for every $2 of earnings above a set amount that increases annually based on changes in national earnings levels.[6] After reaching the FRA, there are no reductions no matter how much the person earns. Until 2000, this earnings test also applied to workers between 65 and 70. In that year, legislation abolishing the Social Security earnings test for all employed Americans 65 and over was passed, thus eliminating some of the disincentive to continue working for pay.

Retirement versus employment for the elderly

There is, of course, a large body of literature on retirement. Among recent studies of retirement in the US are Silvana Pozzebon and Olivia S. Mitchell (1989), Franco Peracchi and Finis Welch (1994), Cordelia Reimers and Marjorie Honig (1996), Dora Costa (1998), Michael Baker and Dwayne Benjamin (1999), Peter Diamond and Jonathan Gruber (1999), and Joseph F. Quinn (1999, 2000). These researchers have typically sampled populations between the ages of 50 and 65, using surveys such as the University of Michigan's Health and Retirement Study.

However, little research has been conducted on those who continue to work beyond the traditional retirement age, sometimes for many years.[7] Since this group is gaining in size we need to better understand the factors associated with the decisions these workers make about maintaining their attachment to the labor force (or, in some cases, beginning employment). Increased healthcare costs for the elderly, in particular the costs of prescription drugs not currently covered by Medicare, have undoubtedly been a factor for many who have decided to continue working for pay. Employer-provided health insurance generally pays for most prescription drugs, minus a modest co-payment. Recent erosion of the retirement savings of many Americans after a precipitous decrease in the US stock market during the first half of 2000 has also contributed to the reversal of the trend towards earlier retirement that reached a low in 1993. By 2003, the overall labor force participation rates for those 65 years of age and over had increased to 18.6 percent and 10.8 percent of men and women, respectively, from lows of 15.6 and 8.2 percent.

One important question that has yet to be answered satisfactorily is what impact having to work longer will have on the well-being of the oldest old. American policy-makers seem to assume that there will be little negative impact because the elderly are, in general, healthier, and are living longer.

119

Furthermore, little consideration has been given to the issue of whether the effects of the changes will differ by gender or race/ethnicity.

This study examines the impact of increasing the Social Security full retirement age and of increased economic pressures to delay retirement by modeling the labor force participation decisions of the elderly in the US. Conclusions drawn from this estimation will be used to show that, despite the greater financial need of elderly women and members of minority groups, there are significant differences in the ability and desire of these individuals to continue working for pay.

DATA

The sample used here comes from the US nation-wide AHEAD (Asset and Health Dynamics Among the Oldest Old) study conducted by the University of Michigan Institute for Social Research. For an overview of the AHEAD Survey, see Michael D. Hurd, Willard L. Rogers, Beth J. Soldo, and Robert B. Wallace (1994). The target population for the initial data collection in 1993-94 were people born in 1923 or before (i.e. aged 70 and older) living in households (i.e. not institutionalized) in the US.[8] Respondents were interviewed about income, assets, job history, and current job, if any. The inclusion of detailed questions about their health, limitations on activities performed in daily living (ADLs)[9] and cognitive status make this dataset a unique source of information about prospects for labor market participation by those in this age group. Although these individuals are older than the FRA, examining their decision-making provides useful insights.

LABOR FORCE PARTICIPATION BY AGE

Labor force participation (LFP) was determined by the answer to a question that simply asked whether the individual was currently working for pay.[10] Table 1 shows this information for all men and women in our sample by age, gender, and race/ethnicity.[11] The overall labor force participation rates were 6.7 percent for women and 12.6 percent for men. For the US population as a whole in 1993, the comparable figures for those 70 years of age and over were 4.7 and 10.3 percent. The slightly higher percentages in our sample reflect the inclusion of spouses between 65 and 70, an age group for which labor force participation rates are considerably higher. Although these rates are small compared to those of younger cohorts, with the projected increases in the size of the population over 65 years of age, the sheer number of workers (or potential workers) will become increasingly more important.

As would be expected, labor force participation rates decline with age. As Table 1 shows, among respondents 66 to 69 years old, 14.4 percent of

Table 1 Labor force participation rates by age, gender, race/ethnicity[a]

Age group	Women				Men			
	Whites	Blacks	Hispanics	Total	Whites	Blacks	Hispanics	Total
66–69[b]	15.2	14.3	6.1	**14.4**	31.1	22.2	16.7	**29.2**
70–74	11.5	12.0	5.3	**11.2**	19.2	15.5	8.8	**18.2**
75–79	5.1	4.7	1.5	**4.8**	12.2	7.5	5.3	**11.3**
80–84	2.1	2.9	2.0	**2.2**	7.2	7.7	0.0	**6.9**
85–89	0.5	1.4	0.0	**0.7**	2.8	0.0	0.0	**2.3**
90+	0.0	0.0	0.0	**0.0**	1.7	0.0	0.0	**1.3**
Totals	6.9	6.8	3.3	**6.7**	13.5	10.1	5.3	**12.6**
N	3,919	706	274	**4,899**	2,415	366	171	**2,952**

Notes: [a]This table includes information about those for whom labor force status was available. The column labeled "Whites" contains information about white non-Hispanics. The column labeled "Hispanics" shows information only for white Hispanics. Black Hispanics are included with non-Hispanic blacks.
[b]Any respondents in this age group were included only because they had spouses aged 70 and over. Thus, there are relatively few individuals in this age category and an even smaller percentage of men, since men tend to have younger spouses.

women and 29.2 percent of men were employed. In contrast, only 2.2 percent of women and 6.9 percent of men aged 80 to 84 reported working for pay.[12] This table reveals dramatic differences by race/ethnicity. Hispanic women have an overall labor force participation rate of only 3.3 percent versus 6.9 percent for white and 6.8 percent for black women. Black men have a labor force participation rate of only 10.1 percent versus 13.5 percent for white men; Hispanic males report an even lower rate, 5.3 percent. In the remainder of this paper we investigate the causes and implications of these differences.

DISPARATE IMPACTS ON MINORITY GROUPS

We now turn to more detailed examination of factors that would be expected to influence the likelihood of continuing to work for pay among individuals in this age group. Physical and mental ability to continue working, financial need, and the desire to continue to work for pay all exert strong influences on this decision. These differences are summarized in Table 2, which includes everyone in our sample. *t*-Tests for differences in means and proportions were performed to test for differences in characteristics between males and females of each group and between white and black and white and Hispanic males. Similar tests were performed for females. Results of these tests are indicated by superscripts. We note that white women are significantly less likely to work for pay than are white men and that both Hispanic men and women are significantly less likely to do so than their white counterparts.

Differences in the ability to continue working

It is well known that mortality rates differ by race.[13] In 2000 life expectancies at birth were 74.9 and 80.1 years for white men and women, respectively; for black non-Hispanics, comparable figures were 68.3 and 75.2 years. Although life expectancies for Hispanics nationwide have not previously been available, the US Census Bureau did publish life expectancies in 1999 that were considerably higher than those of whites, 77.2 and 83.7 years.[14] There is a body of related literature documenting the differences in health status and disability by race (see, for example, Pennifer Erickson, Ronald Wilson, and Ildy Shannon 1995; Elena M. Andresen and Ross C. Brownson 2000; and Arline T. Geronimus, John Bound, Timothy A. Waidmann, Cynthia G. Colen, and Dianne Steffick 2001).

The inclusion in the AHEAD dataset of a number of variables characterizing the respondents' physical and mental abilities allows us to examine several dimensions of disability and health. Despite the higher projected life expectancy for Hispanics, our results show that elderly Hispanics, as well as the elderly blacks in our sample, report faring disproportionately worse than whites with respect to health issues. Statistics reported in Table 2 show that for both men and women, half again as many blacks and Hispanics as whites are in poor or only fair health.[15] Among all three race/ethnic groups, a larger percentage of women than men suffer from cognitive impairment.[16] Over twice as large a percentage of blacks and Hispanics than whites are cognitively impaired to some extent.[17] Both black and white women need help with significantly more activities of daily living (ADLs) than do men. Black men report that they need assistance with 50 percent more ADLs than do white men; black women and Hispanics need help with over twice as many.[18] Roughly half as many blacks as whites, and only slightly more Hispanics, report being in excellent health.[19] Recall that all of the respondents in the AHEAD survey are still living in households. The differences in health and disability would doubtless be even greater if those confined to institutions were included. John Bound, Michael Schoenbaum and Timothy Waidmann (1996) found similar racial differences when investigating labor force attachment among considerably younger workers. The obvious conclusion that can be drawn is that far fewer elderly members of minority groups are *able* to continue working.

Differences in financial need

Mean nonlabor income for white males is highest, $26,921, followed by a significantly lower amount, $22,949, for white females; Hispanic women report the lowest, $15,124. For blacks and Hispanics, gender differences are not significant, but nonlabor incomes for men are significantly lower than

Table 2 Racial/ethnic and gender differences in variables influencing labor force participation

Variable	Whites		Blacks		Hispanics	
	Men	Women	Men	Women	Men	Women
Excellent health	0.12	0.11	0.08[a]	0.05[c]	0.06[a]	0.08[c]
Poor or fair health	0.33	0.33	0.50[a]	0.50[c]	0.49[a]	0.51[c]
Cognitive impairment	0.28	0.31[b]	0.71[a]	0.72[c]	0.59[a]	0.65[c]
Number of ADLs	0.51	0.67[b]	0.77[a]	1.07[bc]	1.05[a]	1.06[c]
Married	0.76	0.43[b]	0.56[a]	0.24[bc]	0.70	0.37[bc]
Age	76.86	77.06	77.15	77.35	77.54	76.07[bc]
	(5.68)	(6.50)	(5.86)	(6.38)	(6.98)	(6.15)
Years of education	11.56	11.45	7.72[a]	8.74[bc]	6.08[a]	6.00[c]
	(3.42)	(3.01)	(4.32)	(3.82)	(4.88)	(4.47)
Nonlabor income[d]	$26,921	$22,949[b]	$17,969[a]	$16,787[c]	$16,415[a]	$15,124[c]
	(24,361)	(24,343)	(16,257)	(22,525)	(14,234)	(14,369)
Social Security income	$8,805	$3,221[b]	$6,836[a]	$2,807[bc]	$5,700[a]	$2,173[bc]
	(3,832)	(3,824)	(4,104)	(3,452)	(3,723)	(3,211)
Percent of nonlabor income comprised of Social Security[e]	0.48	0.21[b]	0.53[a]	0.28[bc]	0.48	0.22[b]
N	2,417	3,926	367	708	171	275
LFP rate (percent)	13.5	6.9[b]	10.1	6.8	5.3[a]	3.3[c]

Notes: Not all variables are available for all respondents. Standard deviations are shown in parentheses where applicable.

[a]Indicates the mean or proportion differs from that of white males at a 5 per cent level of significance, using *t*-tests for differences in means and differences in proportions.

[b]Indicates the mean or proportion differs from that of males of the same race/ethnic group at a 5 percent level of significance.

[c]Indicates that the mean or proportion of women differs from that of white women.

[d]Social Security payments are included in this amount.

[e]Percentages were calculated only for those who had some nonlabor income.

123

Table 3 Occupational distribution: women[a]

Occupation	White	Black	Hispanic
Professional, technical workers	0.18	0.09**	0.06**
Managers, officials, or proprietors	0.09	0.03**	0.07
Clerical, kindred workers	0.33	0.06**	0.12**
Sales workers	0.09	0.02**	0.04**
Craft workers, foremen, kindred workers	0.03	0.02	0.03
Operatives, kindred workers	0.14	0.15	0.23*
Laborers	0.01	0.04**	0.23**
Service workers	0.14	0.58**	0.23*
Farm workers	0.002	0.00*	0.00*
N	2,527	527	137

Notes: [a]The occupation is the one in which the respondent reported working longest; this table includes only individuals who reported working at least ten years in one occupation.
** (*) = differs from the proportion of whites at a 1 percent (5 percent) level of significance.

Table 4 Occupational distribution: men

Occupation	White	Black	Hispanic
Professional, technical workers	0.14	0.04**	0.05**
Managers, officials or proprietors	0.21	0.04**	0.05**
Clerical, kindred workers	0.04	0.07*	0.06
Sales workers	0.06	0.01**	0.02**
Craft workers, foremen, kindred workers	0.27	0.19**	0.23
Operatives, kindred workers	0.16	0.34**	0.23
Laborers	0.03	0.18**	0.27**
Service workers	0.03	0.11**	0.06
Farm workers	0.04	0.02**	0.04
N	2,298	339	154

Notes: See the notes on Table 3.

those of white men; nonlabor incomes of black and Hispanic women are significantly lower than are those of white women. For all three groups of men, Social Security retirement income comprises approximately half of their nonlabor income. Social Security income is significantly lower for women than for men in all three groups, making up less than one-quarter of nonlabor income for white and Hispanic women and only a slightly larger percentage for black women. The average amounts vary from a high of $8,805 for white males to $2,173 for Hispanic females. Clearly, elderly blacks and Hispanics experience greater financial need. An additional consideration is economies of scale associated with being married. To the extent that a couple requires lower housing and other household expenses than do two unmarried individuals to achieve the same standard of living, the couple will be better off. As shown in Table 2, significantly fewer women than men in all three groups are married; significantly fewer black males than either white or Hispanic males are married. This difference probably offsets the difference in nonlabor income between black and Hispanic males, but it further increases the advantage of white males.

Differences in the desire to work for pay

Greater educational achievement is likely to lead to having a job that one would enjoy enough to want to keep late in life. Table 2 shows roughly 11.5 years of education, on average, for elderly whites; comparable figures are approximately 8.5 and 6.0 years for elderly blacks and Hispanics, respectively. For both males and females, the differences between members of the minority groups and whites are highly significant. However, only among blacks is there a gender difference: black women have one more year of education, on average, than do black men. Although in general this entire cohort is considerably less educated than younger Americans, doubtless reflecting less emphasis on education as a requirement for many career paths fifty or more years ago, these statistics indicate that the black and Hispanic elderly are in relatively worse positions. Their low levels of education suggest that they are far less likely to have held jobs that they would enjoy keeping as they age. Even those who may have enjoyed their work when they were younger were more likely to be performing physical work that is probably unsuitable for less physically able elderly workers.

More direct evidence as to whether elderly workers might be able to continue with their accustomed work can be seen by examining Tables 3 and 4. For all those who report having been employed for at least ten years, these tables show the occupations they reported having held the longest, broken down by gender and race/ethnicity. Table 3 shows the distribution for women, Table 4, for men.[20] Here we see reflections of the differences in educational levels discussed above, and most likely also the results of pre-market and labor market gender and racial/ethnic discrimination. Among black and Hispanic women, 77 and 69 percent, respectively, reported having been employed as service workers, operatives, or laborers, occupations that do not require much education but do involve manual labor. Only 29 percent of white women worked in those occupations. Among white women, the largest number reported having worked as professional, technical, or clerical workers. Not only might women be more likely to want to continue in the latter occupations because they are more interesting, but also the work is less taxing physically, therefore providing a better opportunity for employment as workers age.

Men were less concentrated in a few occupations. However, if we examine what percentages report having been employed in blue-collar occupations, those involving primarily physical labor, i.e., having been craft workers, operatives, laborers, service workers, and farm workers, we find 54 percent of white males, compared to 84 percent of blacks and 82 percent of Hispanics, differences that are highly significant.[21] The division is clear: for whatever reason, white- and pink-collar occupations were dominated by whites; most blacks and Hispanics worked at more physically demanding blue-collar jobs.

THE LABOR FORCE PARTICIPATION MODEL

Below we hypothesize the effects of demographics on labor force participation and consider how variables to be included in our model correspond to the three major factors discussed above.

Demographic variables

Aside from health considerations, there are cultural expectations in most economically advanced countries that people will eventually retire. We would expect that an increase in age, *ceteris paribus*, would decrease the probability that a person will be employed, as hypothesized by Alan A. Gustman and Thomas L. Steinmeier (1986): thus a negative sign would be expected on age.

Although in recent years labor force participation rates of black and white women have converged, historically black women of pre-retirement age have had higher rates of labor force participation than white women, whereas the opposite has been true for black males. If these same relationships hold for post-retirement-age black women and men, the dummy variable indicating that the respondent is black would be predicted to have a positive sign for women but a negative sign for men. For Hispanic respondents, a negative sign for women[22] and a positive sign for men would be consistent with recent statistics reporting that Hispanic women have lower and Hispanic men higher labor force participation rates than whites.[23] Clearly, however, differences by race/ethnicity may be more complex than can be accounted for by a simple dummy variable. Since sample sizes did not permit separate estimation of racial and ethnic groups, interaction terms between the two race/ethnicity dummy variables and all other variables were included wherever possible to capture differences in the coefficients as well as the intercepts.

Labor force decisions have been found to be so different for married than for unmarried women of pre-retirement age that they are generally modeled separately; in most studies of men, however, both married and unmarried men are included and are differentiated only by the inclusion of a dummy variable for marital status. Since we have relatively few who work for pay in this age group, we confine our analysis to two separate equations, one for men and one for women, with dummy variables to control for differences by marital status. Among non-elderly workers, married women are less likely to work for pay than are women who are not married, whereas married men are *more* likely to participate in the labor force. If these

126

tendencies are true for those in this age group as well, we would expect to see a negative sign on the marital-status dummy for women and a positive one for men. On the other hand, since loneliness is an issue among many of the elderly, unmarried individuals of both genders might be more likely to work for pay as a means of increasing social interaction.

Health variables

As would be expected, researchers have found health to be an important factor in determining the potential value of time spent working for pay and therefore to have a substantial effect on the labor force participation decision. Being in poor or only fair health, needing help with one or more activities of daily living (ADLs), or being cognitively impaired would tend to decrease the value of market time to the extent that these characteristics reduce one's ability to perform accustomed tasks and to learn new ones, or because they increase the effort required to do so. Thus we would expect negative signs on the dummy variables indicating these three conditions. On the other hand, being in excellent health would be associated with higher productivity for which one would presumably be rewarded with higher pay, thus providing increased financial incentive for working. Moreover, those with excellent health are more likely to find the effort of working less and the work itself more enjoyable. Consequently, a positive sign would be anticipated for this variable.

Financial need

Financial need is clearly an important factor in the decision to continue working for pay. If we assume that leisure time after retirement is a normal good, then it would be expected that those with the highest incomes would "consume" the most. Thus one would predict that, *ceteris paribus*, those with higher incomes from Social Security payments, pensions, investments, rental income, etc., would be less likely to work for pay. Accordingly, nonlabor household income, i.e., income unrelated to current work for pay, is included in the model.[24] A negative sign would be expected for this variable. It is quite possible that the relationship between income and labor force participation is not linear, but rather that the negative effect might be greatest at the lowest levels of income, exhibiting a weaker influence as income increases. To allow for this possibility, a squared term is also included: if the effects are nonlinear we should see a positive sign on this variable.

Desire to continue working

A strong relationship between the amount of education and labor force participation has generally been observed among non-elderly workers in

Table 5 Means of variables used in probit equation

Variable	Women	Men
Black[a]	0.14	0.12
Hispanic	0.06	0.06
Age[b]	76.97	76.83
	(6.44)	(5.71)
Married[c]	0.41	0.75
Self-rated health		
Excellent	0.10	0.11
Very good/good	0.53	0.54
Fair	0.24	0.22
Poor	0.13	0.13
Cognitive impairment[d]	0.39	0.35
Number of ADLs	0.75	0.56
Education		
Less than high school	0.43	0.45
High-school graduate	0.47	0.40
Graduate of four-year college	0.06	0.07
Graduate degree	0.04	0.08
Nonlabor income[e]	$22,530	$26,061
	(24,363)	(24,938)
N	4,753	2,835
Percentage employed	6.2	12.3

Note: Standard deviations, where applicable, are in parentheses.
[a]Since the AHEAD survey over-sampled African-Americans, these figures overestimate the percentage of blacks in this age group in the US population. This group includes black Hispanics.
[b]Only those over 65 were included in this study.
[c]Individuals who reported living with someone were considered married for purposes of this study.
[d]1 = cognitive impairment; 0 = little or no cognitive impairment.
[e]Previous year. This number includes a spouse's labor income.

part because more highly educated individuals are more likely to be able to choose careers that provide intrinsic satisfaction, work they might enjoy doing even if they were not paid for it. Moreover, these workers are likely to be performing mental labor that does not depend on physical strength or stamina. Although these jobs were probably higher paying and provided good pension plans that would allow workers to retire at relatively young ages, since we are controlling for nonlabor income we would expect higher levels of education to be associated with a greater tendency to remain in the labor force.

ESTIMATION OF THE MODEL

A probit regression is used to model the labor force participation decision. This procedure is a maximum-likelihood estimation method of fitting a set of explanatory variables to a dependent variable that can take on two possible responses. In this case, a value of 1 represents an individual who works for pay; a value of 0 indicates that he/she does not. Although the focus of this study is the maintenance of labor force attachment, we have included all individuals in our sample, regardless of previous work history, to allow for the possibility that economic hardship after the death of a spouse might force a widow with no previous labor market experience to work for pay. Table 5 shows the means of the variables for those respondents included in the regression equation. (Any respondent for whom one or more of the explanatory variables is missing has necessarily been excluded.) Means for males and females are similar in many respects. However, almost twice as large a percentage of men as women are married and women have considerably less nonlabor income. As discussed earlier, educational achievement is relatively low: 43 percent of women and 45 percent of men have less than a high school education, compared to only 16 and 15.8 percent of those 25 years of age and over in 2000. Men are less likely to have completed high school and are more likely to have acquired a graduate degree.

RESULTS OF THE PROBIT ANALYSIS

The results of the estimations using the probit models are shown in Table 6.[25] In the interest of brevity, the coefficients for some of the statistically insignificant interaction terms were omitted from Table 6. However, the following discussion includes some of these coefficients since in some cases the lack of significance may be attributable to the smaller sample sizes for blacks and Hispanics. Complete results may be obtained from the author on request.

Demographic variables

Not unexpectedly, age is a strong and highly significant predictor of labor force participation in both equations, although the magnitude is greater for women. None of the interaction terms were significant, but three of the four had negative signs, suggesting that aging alone may have a more negative impact on minority workers than on whites even after controlling for health conditions.

In neither equation is the coefficient on the dummy variable for Hispanic significant, but both have negative signs, suggesting a lower likelihood of working for pay. Cordelia Reimers (1985) found that, for married Hispanic women, cultural influences affect labor force participation through fertility, education, and language. We do not have information about proficiency in English in this dataset; and do not control for number of children in this model, since presumably any children born to these women will be grown. However, since, for women,

Table 6 Probit estimates of labor force participation

Variable	Women	Men
Black	− 0.114	0.114
	(0.307)	(0.440)
Hispanic	− 0.267	− 0.156
	(0.715)	(0.771)
Age[a]	− 0.086***	− 0.056***
	(0.009)	(0.008)
Age * Black	− 0.005	− 0.010
	(0.022)	(0.026)
Age * Hispanic	0.015	− 0.034
	(0.054)	(0.051)
Married	− 0.200**	0.291***
	(0.081)	(0.098)
Married * Black	− 0.114	− 0.617**
	(0.219)	(0.245)
Married * Hispanic	1.535**	0.022
	(0.609)	(0.591)
Self-rated health[b]		
Excellent	0.286***	0.226**
	(0.093)	(0.100)
Excellent * Black	0.355	− 0.767*
	(0.309)	(0.467)
Excellent * Hispanic	0.886	0.073
	(0.611)	(0.676)
Fair	− 0.353***	− 0.431***
	(0.105)	(0.106)
Poor	− 0.659***	− 0.572***
	(0.224)	(0.171)
Cognitive impairment[c]	− 0.273***	− 0.186*
	(0.101)	(0.096)
Number of ADLs	− 0.151**	− 0.167**
	(0.062)	(0.060)
Black * Number of ADLs	0.093	− 0.548*
	(0.097)	(0.326)
Hispanic * Number of ADLs	− 0.081	− 0.120
	(0.331)	(0.328)
Education[d]		
College graduate (four-year college)	0.133	0.258**
	(0.147)	(0.123)
Black * college graduate[e]	0.243	— —
	(0.389)	
Hispanic * college graduate	1.811**	1.798**
	(0.906)	(0.871)
Graduate degree	0.275*	0.708***
	(0.147)	(0.115)
Black * graduate degree[f]	— —	1.848**
		(0.700)
Nonlabor income ($10,000s)[g]	− 0.175***	− 0.186***
	(0.029)	(0.028)
Nonlabor income * Black	0.070	0.059
	(0.078)	(0.125)

(*continued*)

130

Table 6 (Continued)

Variable	Women	Men
Nonlabor income * Hispanic	− 1.499**	− 0.307
	(0.607)	(0.408)
(Nonlabor income)^2	0.0044***	0.0052***
	(0.0008)	(0.0010)
(Nonlabor income)^2 * Black	− 0.0019	0.0023
	(0.0023)	(0.0085)
(Nonlabor income)^2 * Hispanic	0.184***	0.060
	(0.071)	(0.059)
Constant	− 0.115	− 0.275**
	(0.118)	(0.137)
N	4,753	2,835
Number working	298	348
	1,851.48	1,769.29
− 2 x log likelihood ratio		
Significance level	0.0001	0.0001

Notes: Standard estimates are in parentheses. *** (**, *) = coefficient is significant at a 1 percent (5 percent, 10 percent level).
[a]In this regression "age" represents the number of years over 65.
[b]The omitted group is those rating themselves in good or very good health.
[c]1 = cognitive impairment; 0 = little or no cognitive impairment.
[d]The omitted group is those with less than a college education.
[e]The model could not be estimated for men with this interaction term since there are no employed black men with college degrees in the sample.
[f]The model could not be estimated for women with this interaction term since there are no employed black women with graduate degrees in the sample, nor are there any employed Hispanic respondents with graduate degrees.
[g]Previous year.

decisions about fertility and education are usually made simultaneously and are generally inversely related, it is likely that by controlling for education, fertility is also being taken into account. We have seen that Hispanic men have been employed disproportionately in unskilled work, which they may be less likely than other groups to be able to continue as they age, but this, too, is related to educational achievement (or lack thereof). Thus, although the negative signs on the dummy variables are not surprising, neither is the lack of significance.

Similarly, neither among men nor women is the dummy variable for black significant. Among younger workers, labor force participation rates for black males in the US are considerably lower than for white males. However, the differences lessen as men age, probably because fewer black men have sufficient resources to leave the labor force entirely. This finding is supported by reports from the US Bureau of Labor Statistics indicating that for 2003, labor force participation rates for men 70 and over were 12.4 percent for whites and a slightly lower 11.1 percent for blacks. This small difference is doubtless accounted for in our model by the health variables. Among black women we expected a positive sign,

131

since historically black women have had stronger labor force attachment than white women. However, as Francine Blau (1998) noted, the difference in labor force participation rates had disappeared by 1995 due to slower increases by black than by white women. In 2003, among women 70 and over, the US Bureau of Labor Statistics reports labor force participation rates of 6.5 and 5.7 percent for white and black women, respectively.

Among this age group, as among workers of pre-retirement ages in general, married women are less likely to work for pay than are unmarried women, especially black women. However, married Hispanic women are considerably *more* likely to be employed than are unmarried Hispanic women. This result is surprising since, among younger Hispanic women, married women are less likely to work for pay. However, since we saw in Table 4 that Hispanic men are more likely than men of the other two groups to report having been employed as laborers (and probably less likely to have pensions or large Social Security retirement incomes), they may be least likely to continue such work as they age; thus, when necessary, their wives take on more responsibility for making ends meet. Moreover, given cultural traditions of strong family ties, Hispanic widows may be likely to live with a child or other family member.

Married men are, as expected, more likely to work than single men, except among blacks, in which case married men are *less* likely to be employed, *ceteris paribus*. In the past, and to some extent today, black males have generally been subject to more labor market discrimination than have black women, which would put these elderly men at a relative wage and hiring disadvantage. Moreover, black women have traditionally been more strongly attached to the labor market than have white women. As a result, an elderly black couple may be better off than a couple of another race/ethnic group because both may be likely to have Social Security retirement income or other pension benefits, thus making it less necessary for the husband to seek employment.

Health variables

Turning to the health variables, we see that all ten plus two of the interaction terms are significant. As expected, being in poor or only fair health, suffering from cognitive impairment, and needing help with a greater number of ADLs all reduce the likelihood that an individual will work for pay. The negative effect associated with each ADL is considerably stronger for black males than for any of the other groups. Conversely, enjoying excellent health *increases* the probability that an individual will be employed, with the exception of black men: surprisingly, those in excellent health are *less* likely to work for pay than are those in good or very good health. For the most part these results among the "oldest old" echo the strong impact of poor health on retirement behavior found in the 51 to 61 age group (Robert L. Clark, Thomas Johnson, and Ann Archibald McDermed 1980; Giora Hanoch and Marjorie Honig 1983; Gary Burtless and Robert A. Moffitt 1985; Michael Hurd 1990; and Debra S. Dwyer and Olivia S. Mitchell 1999).

Financial variables

As expected, the coefficients of the linear nonlabor income variables are negative, those of the squared terms are positive, and all four are highly significant. The interaction terms were significant only for Hispanic women, suggesting a greater impact of nonlabor income for this group. To facilitate comparison, the coefficients were evaluated at the means, yielding the largest net values for Hispanics, -0.527 for men and -1.737 for women. Blacks had the smallest net coefficients, -0.191 and -0.161 for men and women, respectively; comparable values for whites were -0.440 and -0.368. This difference in magnitude suggests that, among the "oldest old," financial considerations have a larger impact on the labor market decisions of men than of women, except for Hispanics, where the opposite is true. These general results confirm earlier findings by researchers, such as Marjorie Honig (1996) who studied retirement decisions among a somewhat younger cohort. She concluded that men tend to be motivated primarily by economic incentives whereas women tend to be strongly influenced by other family considerations.[26]

Education variables

Education seems to be a more important factor in the labor force participation decision for men than for women among this age group.[27] For men, having a degree from a four-year college has a significant positive effect on the probability of participating in the labor force. The effect is particularly strong among Hispanic men and also among Hispanic women but is not important for either black or white women. Having a graduate degree has an even stronger impact, especially among black males.[28]

GENDER DIFFERENCES

This study follows the convention of modeling separately the labor market behavior of men and women. However, one could ask whether gender differences remain as important for this age group as they are assumed to be among those of pre-retirement ages. To answer this question, we ran a probit regression similar to the one described above, for all respondents, without the interaction terms for race/ethnicity but including both a dummy variable for gender and interaction terms between being male and all of the other variables. This procedure allows for differences in both the intercepts and the slopes of the variables and enables us to know where significant gender differences exist. The results showed that age has significantly less of a negative impact on labor force participation for men than for women; that married men are more likely to work for pay than unmarried men whereas married women are *less* likely to work for pay than are unmarried women; and that men with graduate degrees are considerably more likely to be employed than are women with comparable degrees. There were no significant differences in any of the other variables nor were the intercept terms significantly different.

Explanations for these gender differences may be that individuals in this age group are likely to have been strongly influenced by earlier cultural expectations that market work was an intrinsic part of the male (but not the female) identity and that married men would support their wives. Moreover, also due to societal influences of fifty or more years ago, few women planned on having careers and thus were far less likely to have acquired postgraduate education.

INTERPRETATION OF THE RESULTS

Since the coefficients from a probit equation are not partial derivatives as are those from an ordinary least squares regression equation, it is more difficult to assess the marginal effects of the variables. To better understand the impact of some of the key factors, probabilities of labor force participation have been estimated for hypothetical 72-year-old whites, blacks, and Hispanics with average characteristics for those in our sample 70–75 under a variety of scenarios.[29] The results are shown in Tables 7 and 8.

The first rows show probabilities of labor force participation for each group estimated from our model. Here we can see the net effects of the different probit regression coefficients for each gender and race/ethnic group combined with the differences in the means of the characteristics. The largest estimate is for white males, 0.16, with that of black males less than half as great, 0.07. The lowest estimates are for Hispanics, a probability of less than 0.01 for women and slightly over 0.03 for men. Convergence of the labor force participation rates of black and white women can be seen by the small difference in the estimates for black and white women in this age group, 0.09 versus 0.08 for blacks and whites, respectively.

Also shown in the first rows are probabilities estimated using the coefficients for each race/ethnic group, but means for white females (Table 7) or white males (Table 8). In general, the better health conditions and greater education levels of whites outweigh the negative impact on labor force participation of greater nonlabor income and result in larger probabilities than those estimates generated using their own means.

134

Table 7 Simulated probabilities of working for pay: females 72 years of age with average characteristics[a]

	White coefficients	Black coefficients		Hispanic coefficients	
	Own means	Own means	White means	Own means	White means
Probability of working estimated from probit model (base estimate)	0.0769	0.0918	0.0989	0.00049	0.00039
Difference (% difference)	—	+0.0149 (+19%)[b]	+0.0071 (+8%)[c]	−0.0764 (−99%)[b]	+0.0001 (+20%)[c]
Estimated probability with one additional year of age	0.0653	0.0777	—	0.00038	—
Change (% change)	−0.0116 (−15%)	−0.0141 (−15%)	—	−0.00011 (−22%)	—
Estimated probability for single woman	0.0934	0.1075	—	0.00001	—
Estimated probability for married woman	0.0642	0.0600	—	0.00792	—
Estimated probability with excellent health	0.1468	0.2855	—	0.02697	—
Estimated probability with good/very good health	0.0907	0.1136	—	0.00097	—
Change from excellent (% change)	−0.0561 (−38%)	−0.1719 (−60%)	—	−0.0260 (−96%)	—
Estimated probability with no ADLs	0.0859	0.0998	—	0.00090	—
Estimated probability with one ADL	0.0646	0.0900	—	0.00040	—
Change from 0 to 1 (% change)	−0.0213 (−25%)	−0.0098 (−10%)	—	−0.0005 (−56%)	—
Estimated probability without SS income[d]	0.0973	0.0944	—	0.01201	—
Change (% change)	+0.0204 (+27%)	+0.0027 (+3%)	—	+.01152 (+2351%)	—

Notes:
[a]Means used are for women in our sample ages 70–75.
[b]This difference is between probabilities estimated for white females and for this group of women.
[c]This difference is between the estimated probability calculated using the group's own means and the probability calculated using means of white women.
[d]The average amounts of nonlabor income for each group are reduced by $8,250, the average Social Security retirement income reported by all respondents in our sample ages 70–75. Differences are calculated between these probabilities and the base estimates shown in row 1.

135

Table 8 Simulated probabilities of working for pay: males 72 years of age with average characteristics[a]

	White coefficients		Black coefficients		Hispanic coefficients	
	Own means	White means	Own means	White means	Own means	White means
Probability of working estimated from probit model (base model)	0.1603		0.0698	0.1109	0.0345	0.0597
Difference (% difference)	—		-0.0905 (-56%)[b]	+0.0411 (+59%)[c]	-0.1258 (-78%)[b]	+0.0252 (+73%)[c]
Estimated probability with one additional year of age	0.1471		0.0614	—	0.0281	—
Change (% change)	-0.0132 (-8%)		-0.0084 (-12%)		-0.0064 (-19%)	
Estimated probability for single man	0.1088		0.0997		0.0199	
Estimated probability for married man	0.1730		0.0568		0.0406	
Estimated probability with excellent health	0.2497		0315		0.0848	
Estimated probability with good/very good health	0.1838		0.0939		0.0473	
Change from excellent (% change)	-0.0659 (-26%)		+0.0624 (+198%)		-0.0375 (-44%)	
Estimated probability with no ADLs	0.1730		0.1498		0.0586	
Estimated probability with one ADL	0.1337		0.0399		0.0319	
Change from 0 to 1 (% change)	-0.0393 (-23%)		-0.1099 (-73%)		-0.0267 (-46%)	
Estimated probability without SS income[d]	0.1946		0.0821		0.0604	
Change (% change)	+.0343 (21%)		+.0123 (18%)		+0.0259 (75%)	

Notes: [a]Means used are for men in our sample ages 70–75.
[b]This difference is between probabilities estimated for white males and for this group of men.
[c]This difference is between the estimated probability calculated using the group's own means and the probability calculated using means of white men.
[d]The average amounts of nonlabor income for each group are reduced by $8,250, the average Social Security retirement income reported by all respondents in our sample ages 70–75. Differences are calculated between these probabilities and the base estimates shown in row 1.

136

Increases vary from less than 0.01 (8 percent) among black women to over 0.04 (59 percent) among black men. The exception is among Hispanic women, for whom the additional nonlabor income has a sufficiently strong negative impact to outweigh the positive influences of better health and more education, causing the initially small probability to decrease still further.

Next shown in the tables are estimates for married and for single men and women of each group. In general, as we saw from the regression coefficients, probabilities are lower for married women than for single women, by 0.03 among white women and by nearly 0.04 for black women. The exception is among Hispanic women where we have a huge percentage increase for married women but less than 0.01 in absolute terms. In contrast to women, the marginal effect of being married is generally positive for men. Probabilities increase by 0.06 and 0.02 for white and Hispanic married men, respectively. The exception is black married men, who are over 0.04 *less likely* to be employed than are their single counterparts.

Other rows of the table show the effect of the change in estimated probabilities resulting from one additional year of age, i.e., going from age 72 to 73. In all cases the probabilities fall, by approximately 0.01, but differ considerably on a percentage basis. The marginal effect of one additional year results in an 8 percent decrease in labor force participation among white males, a 12 percent decrease for black males, and a 19 percent decrease among Hispanic males. The percentage declines for women are greater than for men of their respective race/ethnic groups – a 15 percent decline for both white and black women, and a larger decline, 22 percent, for Hispanic women.

Since the interaction terms with excellent health and number of ADLs were significant, we estimated additional probabilities for the groups to isolate marginal effects for these variables. To examine the marginal effects of one's health declining from "excellent" to "good or very good," probabilities were estimated using average characteristics for each group using 72 years of age, but first assuming excellent health and then assuming a decline to the next level. Changes were most dramatic among blacks: for women the estimated probability fell by 0.17, in this case a decline of 60 percent; for men, the probability *increased* by more than 0.06, to almost double the previous level. In a similar manner, probabilities were estimated for each group using a scenario first of no assistance needed for ADLs and then with assistance needed for one ADL. The largest decline was among black males, as we would expect from the regression results, of 0.11 or 73 percent. In contrast, the decline estimated among black females was only 0.01, or 10 percent from the previous level. The smallest decrease (but large in percentage terms) was again among Hispanic women.

Finally, we turn to the major focus of this study. If the full retirement age for Social Security were to be increased, the result would be a decrease in

137

nonlabor income for the elderly, presumably resulting in greater employment. To estimate the effect of such a change on the various groups, $8,250 (the mean amount of Social Security retirement income for those in our sample ages 70–75) was subtracted from the nonlabor income for each group, and probabilities of labor force participation were re-estimated. These results are shown at the bottom of Tables 7 and 8. We see the largest absolute increase among white males, whose estimates increase by more than 0.03 to 0.195, an increase of 21 percent. Among all of the other groups, the increases are smaller, varying from less than 0.01 among black women to 0.025 among Hispanic males. The largest percentage increase, but only 0.01 in magnitude, is among Hispanic females, those with the lowest estimated (and actual) labor force participation and the least amount of nonlabor income. Together, these simulations confirm suspicions that those most disadvantaged with respect to health, education, and nonlabor income will be least likely to respond to a loss of income by increased labor market activity.

Summary

Among individuals beyond the traditional retirement age, there are three critical issues involved in the labor force participation decision: the ability to work, financial need, and the desire to continue working. Analysis reveals significant differences by race and ethnicity in many of the key variables. Blacks and Hispanics have, on average, greater financial need than do whites. However, with respect to the ability to continue working, a larger percentage of blacks and Hispanics is in poor or only fair health, and a smaller percentage is in excellent health. Members of these groups are far more likely to suffer from cognitive impairment and to need help with a larger number of activities of daily living. Finally, the higher level of education of whites means that they are more likely to have done work that requires less physical effort and provides a greater level of intrinsic satisfaction.

Another way of looking at the second and third issues is by examining the occupations these individuals had when they were younger. Health considerations aside, and regardless of the person's desire to continue working, his or her ability to do so will be related to the physical requirements of the occupation itself. Again, this puts elderly blacks and Hispanics at a disadvantage.

The importance of these factors in the labor force participation decision is clearly established by the results of the probit equation. However, the dummy variables are not significant nor are the majority of the interaction terms. Thus, the probit analysis alone does not explain the differences in labor force participation between whites and minority groups. However, simulations using the net coefficients estimated for each group and actual means for those 70–75 show considerable differences in the impact of some of the key variables. They also reveal that blacks and Hispanics are less able to respond to a potential loss of Social Security retirement income than are whites and that, among all three race/ethnic groups, women are less able to do so than are men. Clearly, differences in well-being will result from any mandated increase in Social Security retirement age or other economic pressures to continue working for pay since the minority elderly and white women are less able to respond with increased labor market activity than are white males.

CONCLUSIONS

This research shows that, although elderly minority workers in the US have greater financial need than do elderly whites, they are less able to continue working. Apart from the greater incidence of disabilities, they are more likely to have been engaged in occupations requiring more physical strength and endurance than the occupations in which whites dominate. Clearly it would not be politically feasible to have the Social Security retirement age differ by race/ethnicity or by gender, although the differences in mortality rates discussed earlier mean considerably shorter lengths of time for elderly minority workers to collect full Social Security retirement benefits: among those surviving to age 40, in 2000 the average black male could expect to collect full benefits for only 5.3 years, compared to 10.1 years for a white male. Even if life expectancies continue to increase, the well-being of fragile elders should not be further threatened by additional increases in the FRA. As Baker and Weisbrot (1999) point out, there are other less-drastic ways to address any funding issues.

The most important issue that policy-makers face is to ensure that adequate provisions are made for the vulnerable elderly: those in poor health, those with cognitive and physical disabilities, and those who will effectively be disqualified due to declining physical strength. Unfortunately, blacks and Hispanics are over-represented among this group. One promising avenue is to expand the role of Social Security survivor and disability benefits by making their coverage broader and more generous.

While this particular study focuses on the US and its policies, many other countries are facing similar situations as life expectancies throughout much of the world increase. The type of analysis presented here should be performed in all countries that have heterogeneous populations to ensure that the full impact of such policies on minority groups can be predicted prior to making a change in the FRA.

Carole A. Green, Department of Economics, University of South Florida,
4202 East Fowler Avenue BSN 3403, Tampa, FL 33620-5500, USA
e-mail: cgreen@coba.usf.edu

ACKNOWLEDGMENTS

The author would like to thank Don Bellante, Marianne Ferber, Marjorie Honig, Gabriel Picone, and Jennifer Ward-Batts for helpful comments on earlier versions. The research reported here was supported by a grant from the University of South Florida Institute on Aging.

Notes

1 Estimates are from Bureau of the Census projections (Middle Series). There will, however, be a *greater* ratio of working adults to dependent children than has been true in the past, due to the declining birthrate. Because the labor force participation of women continues to rise, a larger proportion of the labor force will be comprised of women.

2 Whether this is actually the case is a matter of controversy. Dean Baker and Mark Weisbrot (1999) point out that those claiming that the Social Security system is in serious trouble base much of their argument on the increasing costs of Medicare. However, Medicare's looming funding difficulties arise from the inflation of healthcare costs for everyone, costs which they claim need to be dealt with by healthcare reform in the private sector. A comprehensive discussion of the funding issues is beyond the scope of this paper.

3 In 2003, the limit was $87,000.

4 The FRA began increasing in 2000; it is scheduled to reach 67 years of age by 2022.

5 Earnings are indexed according to increases in the average wage between the year in which they were received and the year of retirement.

6 The earnings limit was $11,520 in 2003.

7 The median retirement age in the US is now 62.

8 If an individual was married or living with a partner, the partner was also interviewed, regardless of age. Although some spouses as young as 39 were interviewed, for the present study only those over 65 years old were included.

9 The six "activities of daily living" with which an individual may have difficulty or need help are walking, dressing, bathing, eating, getting into or out of bed, and using the toilet.

10 Strictly speaking, these would be employment rather than labor force participation rates. However, since in the US unemployment rates among those 70 and over are only about half as large as those of the population in general, these numbers are a fairly close approximation. For example, in 2003, the labor force participation rate for those 70 and over was 8.8 percent. The employment rate, calculated by omitting those reported as unemployed, was 8.5 percent.

11 Information is provided separately for white and black Hispanics. For purposes of the analysis in this paper, black Hispanics were included with non-Hispanic blacks. Whites, on the other hand, include only non-Hispanic whites, and "Hispanics" refers only to white Hispanics.

12 The oldest employed woman, who reported working 56 hours per week during a typical week, was 89 years old at the time of the interview; the oldest man, who reported spending an average of 40 hours per week at work, was 90.

13 Studies have been conducted about returns to Social Security contributions that take into consideration these differences. For examples of fairly recent studies, see Michael D. Hurd and John B. Shoven (1985), Nancy Wolff (1987), and James E. Duggan, Robert Gillingham, and John S. Greenlees (1993), and Charles W. Meyer

and Nancy Wolff (1993). However, these types of studies do not address the issue of the abilities or the desires of these individuals to continue working late in life.

14 Source: National Projections Program, Population Division, US Census Bureau, Washington, DC 20233.

15 These figures are somewhat larger than those reported by Margaret E. Weigers and Susan K. Drilea (1996), whose source was the 1996 Medical Expenditure Panel Survey Household Component. They found that among those 65 and over, 25.3 percent of whites reported being in fair or poor health, 40.4 percent of blacks, and somewhat fewer Hispanics, 36.9 percent. However, since the ages of most of those in our sample are 70 and over, it is not surprising that we find larger percentages.

16 In cases where the respondent was unable to answer the questions posed by the interviewer due to illness or incapacity, a proxy answered the questions. Those with no apparent cognitive impairment and those with only a small amount were lumped together.

17 Weigers and Drilea (1996) found, among those 65 and over, a greater percentage of blacks than whites suffered from cognitive limitations, and still more Hispanics suffered from cognitive limitations.

18 In reporting their research, Weigers and Drilea (1996) did not separate out those over 65 needing help with ADLs from those needing help with IADLs (instrumental activities of daily living) such as shopping and paying bills, but found that almost twice as many blacks as whites needed such help. Hispanics fell between the two groups.

19 In 2002, over twice as many blacks and Hispanics fell below the poverty level, 22 percent and 21 percent, respectively, compared to 9 percent of whites. These lower average incomes generally mean less access to adequate medical care. Moreover, researchers have found that African Americans in the US tend to suffer more from high blood pressure and other stress-related diseases than do members of other demographic groups (Arline T. Geronimus 2000).

20 The well-known occupational segregation by gender dictates the necessity of examining the distributions separately.

21 Due to rounding these percentages differ slightly from the sum of the figures in Tables 3 and 4.

22 Cordelia Reimers (1985) found that Hispanic wives may actually be *more* likely to participate in the labor force than white wives after controlling for language, etc. However, since not all of the variables she used are available for this study, a simple dummy variable was used here.

23 However, we have little historical knowledge about trends in labor force participation rates of Hispanics in the US since these statistics were not reported separately until 1994.

24 In this model, any labor income of a spouse is counted as nonlabor income for the respondent.

25 Results from the same model run using only those with some employment history showed only small differences in the size or significance of the coefficients.

26 This is not to deny that the same types of financial incentives influence women, but rather to suggest that the widely accepted notion that women are primarily responsible for household work has tended to constrain their work behavior.

27 Preliminary versions of these regressions showed there to be no greater tendency to work among those with high-school diplomas than among high-school dropouts.

28 The model could not be estimated with all interaction terms since there were no employed black men with college degrees in our sample. Neither were there any employed Hispanic respondents with graduate degrees.

29 This age group, the youngest targeted by the AHEAD study, was chosen rather than an older group because these are the ones most likely to be affected by increases in

the full retirement age for Social Security. (Recall that those between the ages of 66 and 69 were only included in our sample if they were spouses of the primary respondents.)

REFERENCES

Andresen, Elena M. and Ross C. Brownson. 2000. "Disability and Health Status: Ethnic Differences among Women in the United States." *Journal of Epidemiology and Community Health* 54(3): 200–6.

Baker, Dean and Mark Weisbrot. 1999. *Social Security: The Phony Crisis.* Chicago: University of Chicago Press.

Baker, Michael and Dwayne Benjamin. 1999. "How Do Retirement Tests Affect the Labour Supply of Older Men?" *Journal of Public Economics* 71(1): 27–51.

Blau, Francine D. 1998. "Trends in the Well-Being of American Women, 1970–1995." *Journal of Economic Literature* 36(1): 112–65.

Bound, John, Michael Schoenbaum, and Timothy Waidmann. 1996. "Race Differences in Labor Force Attachment and Disability Status." *The Gerontologist* 36(3): 311–21.

Burtless, Gary and Robert A. Moffitt. 1985. "The Joint Choice of Retirement Age and Postretirement Hours of Work." *Journal of Labor Economics* 3: 209–36.

Clark, Robert L., Thomas Johnson, and Ann Archibald McDermed. 1980. "Allocation of Time and Resources by Married Couples Approaching Retirement." *Social Security Bulletin* 43: 3–16.

Costa, Dora L. 1998. *The Evolution of Retirement: An American Economic History 1880–1990.* Chicago: University of Chicago Press.

Diamond, Peter and Jonathan Gruber. 1999. "Social Security and Retirement in the US," in Jonathan Gruber and David A. Wise, eds. *Social Security Programs and Retirement around the World,* pp. 437–74. Chicago: University of Chicago Press.

Duggan, James E., Robert Gillingham, and John S. Greenlees. 1993. "Returns Paid to Early Social Security Cohorts." *Contemporary Policy Issues* 11(4): 1–13.

Dwyer, Debra S. and Olivia S. Mitchell. 1999. "Health Problems as Determinants of Retirement: Are Self-Rated Measures Endogenous?" *Journal of Health Economics* 18: 173–93.

Erickson, Pennifer, Ronald Wilson, and Ildy Shannon. 1995. "Years of Healthy Life." *Healthy People 2000 Statistical Notes* 7(2): 1–14.

Geronimus, Arline T. 2000. "To Mitigate, Resist, or Undo: Addressing Structural Influences on the Health of Urban Populations." *American Journal of Public Health* 90: 867–72.

——, John Bound, Timothy A. Waidmann, Cynthia G. Colen, and Dianne Steffick. 2001. "Inequality in Life Expectancy, Functional Status, and Active Life Expectancy across Selected Black and White Populations in the United States." *Demography* 38(2): 227–51.

Gustman, Alan A. and Thomas L. Steinmeier. 1986. "A Structural Retirement Model." *Econometrica* 54: 555–84.

Hanoch, Giora and Marjorie Honig. 1983. "Retirement, Wages, and Labor Supply of the Elderly." *Journal of Labor Economics* 1: 131–51.

Honig, Marjorie. 1996. "Retirement Expectations: Differences by Race, Ethnicity, and Gender." *The Gerontologist* 36: 373–82.

Hurd, Michael D. 1990. "The Joint Retirement Decision of Husbands and Wives," in David A. Wise, ed. *Issues in the Economics of Aging,* pp. 231–58. Chicago: University of Chicago Press.

—— and John B. Shoven. 1985. "The Distributional Impact of Social Security," in David A. Wise, ed. *Pensions, Labor and Individual Choice*, pp. 193–215. Chicago: University of Chicago Press.

——, Willard L. Rogers, Beth J. Soldo, and Robert B. Wallace. 1994. "Asset and Health Dynamics Among the Oldest Old: An Overview of the AHEAD Survey," *HRS/AHEAD Documentation Report*. Ann Arbor, MI: Institute for Social Research.

Meyer, Charles W. and Nancy Wolff. 1993. *Social Security and Individual Equity: Evolving Standards of Equity and Adequacy*. Westport, CT: Greenwood Press.

Peracchi, Franco and Finis Welch. 1994. "Trends in Labor Force Transitions of Older Men and Women." *Journal of Labor Economics* 12(2): 210–42.

Pozzebon, Silvana and Olivia S. Mitchell. 1989. "Married Women's Retirement Behavior." *Journal of Population Economics* 2: 39–53.

Quinn, Joseph F. 1999. *Retirement Patterns and Bridge Jobs in the 1990s*. Employee Benefit Research Institute Policy Brief No. 206. Washington, DC: EBRI.

——. 2000. "New Paths to Retirement," in Brett Hammond, Olivia Mitchell, and Anna Rappaport, eds. *Forecasting Retirement Needs and Retirement Wealth*, pp. 13–32. Philadelphia: University of Pennsylvania Press.

Reimers, Cordelia. 1985. "Cultural Differences in Labor Force Participation among Married Women." *American Economic Review* 75: 251–5.

—— and Marjorie Honig. 1996. "Responses to Social Security by Men and Women." *Journal of Human Resources* 31: 359–82.

Weigers, Margaret E. and Susan K. Drilea. 1996. "Health Status and Limitation: A Comparison of Hispanics, Blacks, and Whites, 1996." MEPS Research Findings No. 10. AHCPR Publication No. 00-0001. Rockville, MD: Agency for Health Care Policy and Research.

Wolff, Nancy. 1987. *Income Redistribution and the Social Security Program*. Ann Arbor, MI: UMI Research Press.

Linking Benefits to Marital Status: Race and Social Security in the US

Madonna Harrington Meyer, Douglas A. Wolf, and Christine L. Himes

INTRODUCTION

The Social Security system is the single largest social transfer program in the United States. Roughly 97 percent of all older persons receive monthly income through this nearly universal program. Most older people receive retired worker benefits, which are based on lifetime contributions. But most older women actually receive noncontributory Social Security spouse or widow benefits, which are equal to 50 percent or 100 percent of their spouses' benefit, respectively. Even though many are eligible for retired worker benefits, 64 percent of women aged 62 and older receive spouse or widow benefits because these benefits are greater than what they would receive based on their own work record (Social Security Administration 2002). This makes marital status more important than employment status in shaping old-age financial security for many older women. The frequency and length of marriages are down, however, particularly among African

Americans. In this paper, we explore the implications of linking benefits to marital status in the face of an unprecedented retreat from marriage.

MARRIAGE AND SOCIAL SECURITY BENEFITS

The welfare-state literature wrestles nonstop with the merits, or demerits, of linking benefits to citizenship, paid work, unpaid work, poverty, marital status, or parental status (Joan Acker 1988; Ann Orloff 1993; Jill Quadagno 1994; Madonna Harrington Meyer 1996; Walter Korpi and Joakim Palme 1998; Ailsa McKay 2001). In the case of Social Security, retired worker benefits are linked to employment history, but spouse and widow benefits are linked to marital history. Eligibility for spouse and widow benefits is determined by the recipient's history of marriage to a covered worker. The size of that benefit is determined by the retired worker's earnings history. Benefit formulas for retired workers redistribute resources and reduce inequality in old age (Martha Ozawa 1976; Richard Burkhauser and Jennifer Warlick 1981; Michael Walzer 1988). A high-wage earner receives benefits that replace 28 percent of pre-retirement income while a low-wage earner receives benefits that replace 78 percent (Century Foundation 1998; David Koitz 1998). While retired worker benefits redistribute from higher to lower lifetime earners, spouse and widow benefits do not. Because they disproportionately reward single-earner couples with lengthy marriages, these noncontributory benefits have features that are at odds with the otherwise redistributive impact of the program (Harrington Meyer 1996).

Initially only those who contributed to Social Security through their employment were eligible to receive benefits. But because early benefits were relatively small, and the retirement test was set at a very strict $15 per month, experts worried that married men, in particular, would have difficulty supporting a couple on such a meager monthly income (Harrington Meyer 1996; Edward Berkowitz 2002). Thus, the expansion of the program began even before the first benefits were distributed. By 1939, spouse and widow benefits were granted to women who were currently married and who were not eligible for an equal or larger benefit based on their own employment record. Therefore, the size of a spouse or widow benefit was, and continues to be, unrelated to the employment history of the recipient; rather, it is determined by the earnings history of the retired worker upon whom the benefit is based. Even though they had not contributed, wives received what was called a spousal allowance equal to 50 percent of the benefit the husband was receiving (Harrington Meyer 1996; Berkowitz 2002; Social Security Administration 2002). Widows received a benefit equal to 75 percent, later raised to 100 percent, of the benefit their husband received prior to his death.

As divorce became more common in the US, Congress created a requirement that divorcées must have been married for at least twenty years to claim a spouse or widow benefit. In 1950, Congress made the rules gender-neutral and men became eligible for both spouse and widower benefits. By 1977, the marriage requirement had been reduced to ten years (Social Security Administration 2002). Men rarely receive these benefits because their own retired worker benefits are almost always bigger. In 2000, 97 percent of spouse and widow beneficiaries were women (Social Security Administration 2002).

Table 1 shows the current eligibility guidelines. Retired workers become eligible by contributing to the system through the FICA tax, currently set at 5.6 percent for employees and an additional 5.6 percent for employers. The size of their benefit is linked to the size of their contributions over their lifetimes. Eligibility for spouse and widow benefits is based on marital status rather than contributions. Currently, married couples that apply for benefits face no length-of-marriage requirements. Those who are divorced, however, must have been married to a covered worker for at least ten years. If divorcées are remarried at the time of eligibility for benefits, they forfeit claims based on earlier spouses' earnings histories. For retired worker and spouse beneficiaries, eligibility for reduced benefits begins at age 62 and eligibility for full benefits begins between ages 65 and 67, depending on year of birth (US House Committee on Ways and Means 2002). Widows qualify for widow benefits after age 60 if they were married to a worker who was fully insured at the time of death. All spousal beneficiaries who outlive their spouses eventually become widow beneficiaries and, in the process, double their benefits (Harrington Meyer 1996). Even women with relatively high and stable earnings over the life course who are entitled to retired worker benefits larger than half the value of their husband's benefit are

Table 1 Eligibility for Social Security in the US

Retired worker benefits
40 quarters of covered employment
Benefits based on earnings over time

Spouse benefits
If married when applying, no length of marriage requirement
If divorced when applying, ten-year marriage requirement
If remarried, forfeit claims on earlier spouse
Benefit equal to 50 percent of spouse's covered worker benefit

Widow benefits
If married to an insured worker at time of his death, less than one-year marriage requirement
If divorced at time of his death, ten-year marriage requirement
If remarried, forfeit claims on earlier spouse, unless remarrying after age 60
Benefit equal to 100 percent of spouse's covered worker benefit

---

likely to prefer to receive widow benefits because the latter are generally greater.

Declining eligibility for spouse and widow benefits would not be troubling if other economic trends compensated for these losses. The elderly experienced a notable overall economic improvement in the second half of the twentieth century. Currently, poverty rates for the elderly are at an all-time low – just under 12 percent – and well below those for other age groups (Jill Quadagno 2001). Moreover, women's increasing labor force participation rates mean that more women will be eligible for larger retired worker benefits in their own right. But pockets of poverty among the elderly persist: older blacks, Hispanics, and unmarried persons all have poverty rates in excess of 20 percent. At the intersection of those variables, older single black women have poverty rates near 50 percent. Despite women's advances in the labor market, Social Security remains the leading source of income for older women (Madonna Harrington Meyer 1990; Lou Glasse, Carroll Estes, and Timothy Smeeding 1999). Women's increased employment and higher wages have helped to raise women's retired worker average monthly benefits, but it is unclear whether these increases will offset possible declines in access to spouse and widow benefits. The national average for women's wages in the US remains below 75 percent of men's, and average earnings for black and Hispanic women tend to be substantially lower than for white women (Nancy Hooyman and Judith Gonyea 1995; Irene Padavic and Barbara Reskin 2002).

Moreover, significant portions of women continue to take time away from paid work to care for young children or frail older relatives. Social Security benefits are based on indexed earnings over the forty years from age 22 to age 62. The Social Security Administration (2002) benefit calculator disregards the five lowest years of earnings, but those with more than five years out of the labor force will have zeros entered into their benefit formulas. The Social Security Administration estimates than even among women retiring in 2020, only 30 percent will have been employed for enough years to eliminate all of the zeros from their benefit formulas (Michael Boskin and Douglas Puffert 1987; Lois Shaw, Diana Zuckerman, and Heidi Hartmann 1998). The remaining 70 percent will continue to have at least some zeros, and their benefits will be smaller as a result. The impact of these zero- and low-earnings years may become more severe as fewer women rely on spouse and widow benefits. The Social Security Administration estimates that between 1990 and 2020, the proportion of women taking retired worker benefits will rise from one-third to one-half (Glasse, Estes, and Smeeding 1999). Single and divorced women are more likely to be in the labor force and to have higher earnings than married women, but they are not likely to have earnings records that match those of men.

The distribution of social benefits on the basis of marital status is based on the outdated traditional "breadwinner" model. When spouse and widow benefits were created in 1939, roughly 85 percent of married women were in single-earner marriages and marriage rates differed less dramatically by race (Berkowitz 2002). From the middle 1800s until the early 1960s, more than 90 percent of women in every birth cohort in the US married (Joshua Goldstein and Catherine Kenney 2001). But since the 1960s, a pronounced retreat from marriage has taken place. The percentage of women ever married dropped, age at first marriage rose, the tendency to divorce rose, and the tendency to remarry dropped (Teresa Castro Martin and Larry Bumpass 1989; Robert Schoen and Robin Weinick 1993; Joshua Goldstein 1999; Goldstein and Kenney 2001). Divorce rates rose steadily through the 1960s and 1970s, and then stabilized in the mid-1980s (Steven Ruggles 1997; Goldstein 1999). Since 1988, the average age at first marriage and first divorce have been less than ten years apart (Schoen and Weinick 1993). In fact, the tendency to divorce now peaks in the fourth year of both first marriages and remarriages (Goldstein 1999). Many demographers suggest that marriage will remain nearly universal, that perhaps 90 percent of American women will be married at some point in their lives (cf. Goldstein and Kenney 2001). Even if marriage remains common, marriages may not necessarily last the ten years needed to qualify for Social Security spouse and widow benefits. Moreover, the Social Security Administration does not acknowledge same-sex partnerships or cohabitation; thus, no matter how long those individuals live together, neither partner may make noncontributory spouse or widow claims.

Accordingly, the use of marital status as an eligibility requirement is problematic for two key reasons. First, marital rates are down. Table 2 reports US Census Data on the percent of women currently married by age group in 1970, 1980, 1990, and 2000. For example, among white women ages 45 to 54, 82 percent were married in 1970, compared to only 69 percent in 2000. One consequence of declining marital rates is that with each successive cohort we may expect fewer women to be eligible for spouse or widow benefits. As a result, more women may rely solely on retired worker benefits. This is problematic to the extent that women's Social Security benefits based on their own work records may be smaller than those they would have received as spouses or, more often, widows (Richard Burkhauser and Greg Duncan 1989). Thus, reduced reliance on spouse and widow benefits may lead to increased *gender inequality* in old-age income.

Second, a much more substantial retreat from marriage has taken place among black women than among white and Hispanic women (Schoen and Weinick 1993). For example, Goldstein and Kenney (2001) project that among women born between 1960 and 1964, 93 percent of whites, but only 64 percent of blacks, will ever marry. Table 2 shows that in 1998, black

149

Table 2 Percent of married women by age among whites and blacks, 1970, 1980, 1990, and 2000

				Age			
	Total	*15 to 24*	*25 to 34*	*35 to 44*	*45 to 54*	*55 to 64*	*65 and over*
1970[a]							
White	62	35	86	87	82	69	37
Black	53	29	74	76	71	57	32
Black as percent of white	85	83	86	87	87	84	87
1980[b]							
White	60	28	75	82	81	71	38
Black	44	17	56	66	64	56	31
Black as percent of white	73	61	75	80	79	79	82
1990[c]							
White	56	19	65	73	74	70	40
Black	31	9	34	42	45	42	25
Black as percent of white	55	47	52	58	61	60	63
2000[d]							
White	54	14	62	70	69	68	43
Black	29	5	31	41	40	39	25
Black as percent of white	54	36	50	59	58	57	58

Notes:
[a]US Bureau of the Census (1973a, Table 203, pp. 6543–643), married.
[b]US Bureau of the Census (1984a, Table 264, pp. 70–2), married.
[c]US Bureau of the Census (1992, Table 34, pp. 45–6), married except separated.
[d]US Bureau of the Census (2000, Marital Status of People 15 Years and Over, by Age, Sex, Personal Earnings, Race and Hispanic Origin/March 1, 2000; Table A1), married spouse present.
Source: Authors' calculations using Bureau of the Census data.

women aged 25 to 34 were only 52 percent as likely as whites of the same age to be married; similarly, black women aged 35 to 44 were only 54 percent as likely as whites of the same age to be married. One consequence of these decreasing marital rates is that with each successive cohort we may expect even fewer black women to be eligible for spouse or widow benefits. Thus, the safety net provided by noncontributory benefits may become increasingly irrelevant for older black women and may lead to increased race inequality in old-age income.

Past demographic research on trends in marriage, divorce, and remarriage has not addressed the issue of ten-year marriages, which are key to establishing eligibility for spouse and widow benefits. Thus we address the following questions:

- What proportion of women born in the 1920s and 1930s entered old age without being eligible for spouse and widow benefits?
- How is the picture changing for those born in the 1940s, 1950s, and 1960s?
- To what extent does declining eligibility for spouse and widow benefits vary by race?

DATA AND METHODOLOGY

Our analysis is based upon pooled data from the June 1985, 1990, and 1995 US Current Population Survey supplementary questions on marital history. Our sample included women 15–65 years old in each survey year. Sample sizes were 50,115 in 1985, 48,444 in 1990, and 44,944 in 1995. In each survey, women were asked a series of questions about their current marital status and previous marital history. They were asked to specify the month and year in which up to three marriages began and ended. The respondents' month and year of birth are also recorded. We determined the month and year (if any) in which a woman first reached the tenth anniversary of a marriage, then computed her age, in years, that month. We classified the women into five birth cohorts: 1920–29, 1930–39, 1940–49, 1950–59, and 1960–69. Then, using weighted data so that the sample is nationally representative, we plotted these trends. The cohort lines depict the cumulative percentage of women who have had a tenth anniversary at each age. The CPS provides self-reported race and ethnicity. We coded everyone who said they were Hispanic as Hispanic, regardless of what they indicated about race. Therefore, the white and black categories refer to non-Hispanic people.

In a series of figures, we show the cumulative percentage of each cohort that had at least one ten-year marriage by age and by race and ethnicity. What we chart is not the total number of women who are eligible for spouse and widow benefits in each cohort, but the moment at which they first become eligible on the basis of marital status. For the purposes of our analysis, we assume that all marriages are to a covered worker who will work the 40 quarters needed to qualify for Social Security. We under-report eligibility for Social Security benefits in two ways using this method. First, we chart the age at which women have a ten-year marriage. We do this because once a marriage lasts ten years, subsequent divorces do not alter eligibility. However, any women who reached age 52 without a ten-year marriage, who then married after age 52 and remained married until she began taking benefits, would not appear as eligible for Social Security spouse benefits in our charts. Second, widows are eligible at age 60 as long as they were married to a worker who was fully insured at the time of his death. Any women with less than ten years of marriage, but who were married briefly to fully qualified workers and then never remarried, would qualify as widows

151

for Social Security but would not appear as eligible for Social Security in our charts. Both groups who have been overlooked are relatively small. Moreover, we have no reason to believe that they have grown in recent cohorts, so this bias is likely to be consistent across the five cohorts we analyze.

RESULTS

Figure 1 shows the cumulative percentage of women with a ten-year marriage, by age, for each of the five birth cohorts. Between 80 and 90 percent of the women in the three oldest cohorts had a ten-year marriage by age 42. For those women born between 1950 and 1959, only 60 percent had a ten-year marriage by age 42. The youngest cohort, born between 1960 and 1969, can only be traced to age 32, so we can draw no firm conclusions about their chances of reaching old age without a qualifying marriage. However, the slope of their line is remarkably flatter than that for the preceding four cohorts, indicating an ongoing retreat from marriage.

The next five figures show the cumulative percentage of women with a ten-year marriage by race and ethnicity, for each cohort individually. Figure 2 depicts women born between 1920 and 1929 and shows very similar marital trajectories for white, Hispanic, and black women. By the time they reach age 62 and qualify for early Social Security benefits, 94 percent of the white, 90 percent of the black, and 80 percent of the Hispanic women had

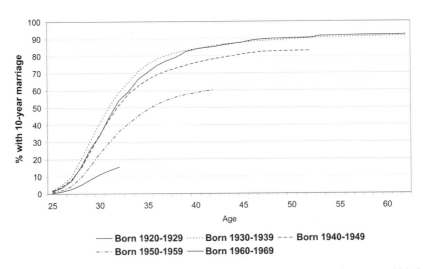

Figure 1 Cumulative percentage of women with ten-year marriage, by age and birth cohort

been married for at least ten years and would be qualified for Social Security spouse or widow benefits.

Figure 3 depicts women born between 1930 and 1939 and shows a pattern very similar to the earlier cohort. Much like those in the previous birth cohort, by the time they reach old age, 93 percent of white, 84 percent of black, and 87 percent of Hispanic women have had a ten-year marriage.

Figure 4 depicts women born between 1940 and 1949. The oldest of these women were only age 55 in the 1995 CPS, so we only chart their marital patterns through age 52. The marital trajectories are similar to those for the earlier two cohorts, but the curves flatten out earlier and the race gap is beginning to be apparent. By age 52, 85 percent of whites and 81 percent of Hispanics, compared to only 72 percent of blacks, had a ten-year marriage. (Looking back to those born between 1930 and 1939, by age 52, 92 percent of whites, 86 percent of Hispanics, and 84 percent of blacks had a ten-year marriage.) Thus, by the 1940–49 cohort, we see rising marital rates for Hispanics and declining rates for everyone else. The retreat from marriage is under way for whites and in full force for blacks.

Figure 5 depicts marital patterns for women born between 1950 and 1959, followed until age 42. In this figure, we see the race gap in marriage most clearly. Hispanics are marrying earliest and are most likely to remain married until at least their tenth anniversary, though whites catch up by age 42. The rate of marriage is slightly lower for Hispanics and dramatically lower for whites and African Americans when compared to the earlier cohorts. The slope of the lines flattens earlier and at a lower point for all

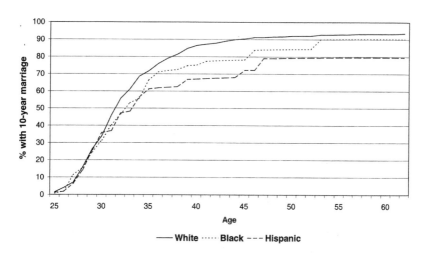

Figure 2 Cumulative percentage of women born 1920–1929 with ten-year marriage, by race

153

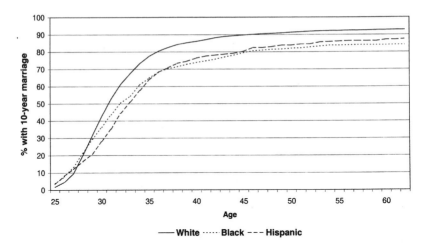

Figure 3 Cumulative percentage of women born 1930 – 1939 with ten-year marriage, by race

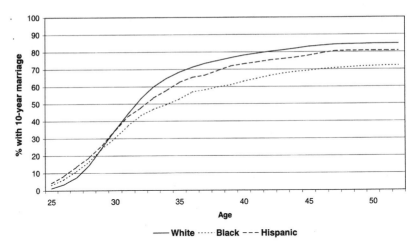

Figure 4 Cumulative percentage of women born 1940 – 1949 with ten-year marriage, by race

three race and ethnic groups. By age 42, 63 percent of whites and Hispanics, compared to 44 percent of blacks, have had a ten-year marriage. The most dramatic decline is among middle-aged black women: in a single decade, the proportion of black women who were qualified for Social Security spouse and widow benefits by age 42 dropped by nearly one-fourth, from 67 to 44 percent.

154

The proportion of women who are either currently married or have had at least a ten-year marriage at some point in their lives will surely be somewhat higher by the time this 1950s birth cohort reaches retirement age, but we find no reason to believe that the increases will be more than a few percent. If we look at past cohorts to see what percentage of women became eligible for spouse and widow benefits after the age of 42, we find that the figure is dropping rapidly. In the 1920s cohort, 13 percent of blacks became eligible between ages 42 and 62. In the 1930s cohort, only 8 percent of blacks became eligible between ages 42 and 62. In the 1940s birth cohort, less than 6 percent of black women became eligible between the ages of 42 and 52.

Finally, Figure 6 depicts women born between 1960 and 1969. The oldest of these women was only age 35 during the 1995 CPS; therefore, we can only chart their marital histories through age 32. Among women born between 1960 and 1969, 19 percent of Hispanic, 16 percent of white, and only 8 percent of black women had a ten-year marriage by age 32. Divorce rates have, however, stabilized (Goldstein 1999), and most people are marrying at some point in their lives. But for the purposes of gaining eligibility to Social Security spouse and widow benefits, a ten-year marriage is required. When this group of women reaches old age, the proportion qualified for spouse or widow benefits may well be lower than ever in the history of the program.

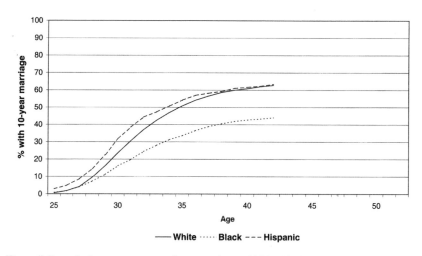

Figure 5 Cumulative percentage of women born 1950–1959 with ten-year marriage, by race

DISCUSSION AND POLICY IMPLICATIONS

Spouse and widow benefits have been subject to considerable criticism over the last two decades. First, the increase in women's labor force participation has led to an increase in dual eligibility (Harrington Meyer 1996). A growing share of women is qualified for retired worker and spouse benefits that are nearly identical. If the spouse benefit is the larger of the two, that means they have contributed to the Social Security system throughout their work lives but receive the same spouse or widow benefit they would have received had they not contributed at all. Second, the spouse benefit is criticized for rewarding single-earner families at rates higher than dual-earner families. Marilyn Flowers (1979) and Richard Burkhauser and Timothy Smeeding (1994) give examples of how the benefit formula is set so that single-earner couples often receive larger benefits than dual-earner families with identical household earnings. The explanation is simple: single-earner couples are receiving an additional noncontributory benefit, whereas dual-earner couples who split the earnings are each receiving their retired worker benefit. In the latter case, no one in the household is receiving a noncontributory benefit. Third, noncontributory benefits are more likely to go to white than black women. In an analysis of Social Security data from 1991, Harrington Meyer (1996) found that white and black women were equally likely to receive noncontributory widow benefits but that white women were nearly twice as likely as black women to receive

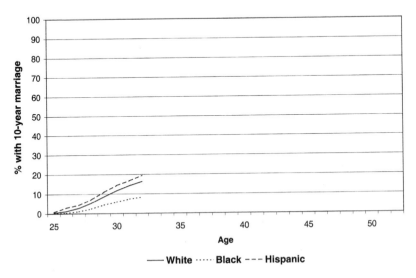

Figure 6 Cumulative percentage of women born 1960–1969 with ten-year marriage, by race

noncontributory spouse benefits. Moreover, the average monthly noncontributory benefit that white women received was more than 25 percent larger. Finally, all retired worker beneficiaries receive smaller benefits than they otherwise would to create a surplus that funds noncontributory benefits. In other words, unmarried men and women subsidize the unearned benefits of spouse and widow beneficiaries. Noncontributory benefits subsidize a traditional family form that is no longer typical (Harrington Meyer 1996).

Our paper adds a new concern about these noncontributory benefits. The previously documented retreat from marriage is pronounced, particularly for African American women. The implications of this trend for Social Security spouse and widow benefits are only beginning to be explored. In this paper, we show that a smaller percentage of each successive cohort will have a ten-year qualifying marriage. We also show that this trend is more pronounced among black women than whites and Hispanics, leading to a growing race gap in marriage and in eligibility for noncontributory benefits.

Despite this growing controversy, some policy analysts suggest that spouse and widow benefits could be regarded as a form of delayed or *de facto* wages for unpaid domestic labor performed by many women throughout their lives (Flowers 1979; Robert Myers 1982). However, current eligibility rules are unrelated to the performance of domestic labor. Women who perform unpaid care or domestic work within a marriage for nine but not ten years receive nothing. Those who perform it outside of a marriage receive nothing. Those who are married for ten years but hire others to perform domestic labor are as eligible as those who perform the unpaid work themselves. Those with children are as eligible as those without children. Women who are eligible for benefits based on the contributions of a previous husband forgo those claims if they are remarried at the time of application. In fact, spouse and widow benefits do not represent delayed domestic wages. They reward marital status rather than unpaid labor. Eligibility for these benefits is defined entirely by marital status, and the size of the benefit is determined by the size of the husband's wages (Karen Holden 1979; Harrington Meyer 1996). Women married to high earners receive a much larger benefit than women married to low earners, even though the quantity and difficulty of their unpaid labors may indeed be less.

The better justification for spouse and widow benefits is income adequacy. These benefits were added through the 1939 legislation precisely because program administrators recognized that two could not live as cheaply as one and were worried that single retired worker benefits would be inadequate. Those concerns remain legitimate, but such an argument begs the question: why would we be concerned about income adequacy only for married persons?

Many proposals to reform Social Security debate increasing the widow benefit or implementing earnings sharing (Richard Burkhauser and Karen

157

Holden 1982; Burkhauser and Smeeding 1994). Efforts to increase the widow benefit usually involve giving less money to a couple while the husband is alive and then more to the widow once he has died. Earnings sharing credits each spouse in a marriage with having earned one-half of the annual household income, regardless of who actually did earn the income. Such proposals are worth considering, but they are problematic precisely because they are aimed at increasing benefits to married women. What these proposals fail to take into account is the economic well-being of women without lengthy marriages. Such proposals further entrench marital status as an eligibility requirement, failing to take into account either the retreat from marriage or the growing race gap in marital rates.

Other analysts suggest that the US consider the European practice of implementing childcare or family care credits that either allow women to drop more zero years from their earnings history or actually insert a value in foregone wages into their earnings history (Burkhauser and Holden 1982; Glasse, Estes, and Smeeding 1999; Melissa Favreault, Frank Sammartino, and Eugene Steuerle 2002). The problem with proposals that link economic security to the provision of unpaid labor is that most bolster economic security only for women and men who are able to stay at home. For those without an alternative source of income, they are generally of little use. They would provide economic security for the growing share of women who balance unpaid and paid work simultaneously only if benefits accrue regardless of marital or work status.

The distributional effects of Social Security spouse and widow benefits are already in opposition to the efforts of the larger program to make the income distribution more equal. They will only become more so as more recent cohorts reach retirement age. Women with lengthy marriages, particularly if they are not employed, are disproportionately rewarded with noncontributory benefits, while those without lengthy marriages and those who were employed throughout all or most of their adult lives are not (Harrington Meyer 1996). Changing trends in marriage and employment are causing Social Security policy to exaggerate, rather than alleviate, inequality between different groups of older women. What was once an important safety net for lower income retirees has emerged as a marriage bonus with the greatest value for traditional – and disproportionately white – single breadwinner married couples in higher income brackets. Moreover, the decision to distribute noncontributory benefits on the basis of marital status means that gay and cohabiting relationships, as well as marriages lasting less than ten years, remain unrecognized and are not used to establish eligibility for these benefits.

One alternative mechanism for distributing benefits is to establish a fairly high minimum benefit. Throughout most of its history, Social Security had a minimum benefit, which ranged in value from $20 in 1940 to $110 in 1982. Congress eliminated the minimum benefit because of concerns that some beneficiaries were double- and triple-dipping. Some military and federal government employees retired from these venues with full pensions and then worked enough years under Social Security to receive the minimum pension. The elimination of the minimum, however, adversely affected many low-income women, blacks, and Hispanics who were neither military nor government employees (Harrington Meyer 1996). Although Social Security has a special minimum benefit at present, the eligibility requirements are so stringent that only a fraction of beneficiaries are eligible. Restoration of a minimum benefit that is broadly available would remove the links to marital status or the performance of unpaid domestic labor. Pam Herd (2002) and Paul Davies and Melissa Favreault (2004) show that even a modest minimum benefit is more effective than a childcare credit at reducing poverty and inequality among low-income beneficiaries. If the minimum were set equal to the federal old-age poverty line, it would be nearly equivalent to the maximum spouse benefit and thereby eliminate the need for such a benefit. The redistributive effect of a fairly generous minimum benefit would depend to a great extent on the mechanisms used to fund it. Such mechanisms are worth exploring by future researchers precisely because a minimum benefit approach would create an income floor that is independent of marital or employment history and reduce inequality in old age.

Madonna Harrington Meyer, Center for Policy Research, Syracuse University
426 Eggers Hall, Syracuse, NY 13244, USA
e-mail: mhm@maxwell.syr.edu

Douglas A. Wolf, Center for Policy Research, Syracuse University
426 Eggers Hall, Syracuse, NY 13244, USA
e-mail: dawolf@maxwell.syr.edu

Christine L. Himes, Center for Policy Research, Syracuse University 426 Eggers Hall,
Syracuse, NY 13244, USA e-mail: clhimes@maxwell.syr.edu

ACKNOWLEDGMENTS

We appreciate the very detailed data preparation performed by Pam Herd and the analysis run by both Herd and Caroline Cochran. We thank Martha Bonney for her word-processing assistance. The research reported herein was performed pursuant to a grant by the US Social Security Administration (SSA) to the Center for Retirement Research at Boston College, Grant No. 10-P-98357-1-05.

REFERENCES

Acker, Joan. 1988. "Class, Gender, and the Relations of Distribution." *Signs* 13(3): 473–97.

Berkowitz, Edward D. 2002. "Family Benefits in Social Security: A Historical Commentary," in Melissa Favreault, Frank Sammartino, and C. Eugene Steuerle, eds. *Social Security and the Family: Addressing Unmet Needs in an Underfunded System*, pp. 19–46. Washington, DC: Urban Institute Press.

Boskin, Michael J. and Douglas J. Puffert. 1987. "Social Security and the American Family," in Lawrence H. Summers, ed. *Tax Policy and the Economy*, Vol. 1, pp. 139–59. Cambridge, MA: MIT Press.

Burkhauser, Richard V. and Jennifer L. Warlick. 1981. "Disentangling the Annuity from the Redistributive Aspects of Social Security in the United States." *Review of Income and Wealth* 27(4): 401–21.

Burkhauser, Richard and Karen C. Holden, eds. 1982. *A Challenge to Social Security: The Changing Roles of Women and Men in American Society*. New York: Academic Press.

Burkhauser, Richard and Greg J. Duncan. 1989. "Economic Risks of Gender Roles: Income Loss and Life Events over the Life Course." *Social Science Quarterly* 70(1): 3–23.

Burkhauser, Richard and Timothy M. Smeeding. 1994. "Social Security Reform: A Budget Neutral Approach to Reducing Older Women's Disproportionate Risk of Poverty." Center for Policy Research: Policy Brief No. 2 Syracuse, NY: Syracuse University.

Castro Martin, Teresa and Larry L. Bumpass. 1989. "Recent Trends in Marital Disruption." *Demography* 26(1): 37–51.

Century Foundation. 1998. *The Basics: Social Security Reform*. New York: The Century Foundation.

Davies, Paul S. and Melissa M. Favreault. 2004. "Interactions between Social Security Reform and the Supplemental Security Income Program for the Aged." CRR Working Paper No. 2004-02. Center for Retirement Research, Boston College, Chestnut Hill, MA.

Favreault, Melissa M., Frank J. Sammartino, and C. Eugene Steuerle. 2002. "Social Security Benefits for Spouses and Survivors: Options for Change," in Melissa Favreault, Frank Sammartino, and C. Eugene Steuerle, eds. *Social Security and the Family: Addressing Unmet Needs in an Underfunded System*, pp. 177–228. Washington, DC: Urban Institute Press.

Flowers, Marilyn R. 1979. "Supplemental Benefits for Spouses under Social Security: A Public Choice Explanation of the Law." *Economic Inquiry* 17(1): 125–30.

Glasse, Lou, Carroll Estes, and Timothy Smeeding. 1999. "Social Security Reform and Older Women: How to Help the Most Vulnerable." Statement for the House Subcommittee on Social Security, Committee on Ways and Means. Washington, DC: Gerontological Society of America.

Goldstein, Joshua R. 1999. "The Leveling of Divorce in the United States." *Demography* 36(3): 409–14.

—— and Catherine T. Kenney. 2001. "Marriage Delayed or Marriage Forgone? New Cohort Forecasts of First Marriage for US Women." *American Sociological Review* 66(4): 509–19.

Harrington Meyer, Madonna. 1990. "Family Status and Poverty among Older Women: The Gendered Distribution of Retirement Income in the United States." *Social Problems* 37(4): 551–63.

——. 1996. "Making Claims as Workers or Wives: The Distribution of Social Security Benefits." *American Sociological Review* 61: 449–65.

Herd, Pam. 2002. "Crediting Care, Citizenship or Marriage? Gender, Race, Class, and Social Security Reform," PhD diss., Syracuse University.

Holden, Karen C. 1979. "The Inequitable Distribution of OASI Benefits among Homemakers." *The Gerontologist* 19(3): 250–6.

Hooyman, Nancy R. and Judith Gonyea. 1995. *Feminist Perspectives on Family Care: Policies for Gender Justice.* Thousand Oaks, CA: Sage.

Koitz, David Stuart. 1998. "The Entitlements Debate." 97-39 EPW (January 28, 1998) Washington, DC: Congressional Research Service, Library of Congress.

Korpi, Walter and Joakim Palme. 1998. "The Paradox of Distribution and Strategies of Equality: Welfare State Institutions, Inequality, and Poverty in the Western Nations." *American Sociological Review* 63(5): 661–87.

McKay, Ailsa. 2001. "Rethinking Work and Income Maintenance Policy: Promoting Gender Equality through a Citizen's Basic Income." *Feminist Economics* 7(1): 97–118.

Myers, Robert. 1982. "Incremental Change in Social Security Needed to Result in Equal and Fair Treatment of Men and Women," in Richard V. Burkhauser and Karen C. Holden, eds. *A Challenge to Social Security: The Changing Roles of Women and Men in American Society,* pp. 235–45. New York: Academic Press.

Orloff, Ann Shola. 1993. "Gender and the Social Rights of Citizenship: The Comparative Analysis of Gender Relations and Welfare States." *American Sociological Review* 58(3): 303–28.

Ozawa, Martha N. 1976. "Income Redistribution and Social Security." *Social Service Review* 50: 209–23.

Padavic, Irene and Barbara Reskin. 2002. *Women and Men at Work,* 2nd ed. Thousand Oaks, CA: Pine Forge Press.

Quadagno, Jill S. 1994. *The Color of Welfare: How Racism Undermined the War on Poverty.* New York: Oxford University Press.

——. 2001. *Aging and the Life Course: An Introduction to Social Gerontology,* 2nd ed. Burr Ridge, IL: McGraw Hill College.

Ruggles, Steven. 1997. "The Rise of Divorce and Separation in the United States, 1880–1990. " *Demography* 34(4): 455–66.

Schoen, Robert and Robin M. Weinick. 1993. "The Slowing Metabolism of Marriage: Figures from 1988 US Marital Status Life Tables." *Demography* 30(4) (November): 737–46.

Shaw, Lois, Diana Zuckerman, and Heidi Hartmann. 1998. *The Impact of Social Security Reform on Women.* Washington, DC: Institute for Women's Policy Research.

Social Security Administration. 2002. *Annual Statistical Supplement, 2002.* Washington, DC: Social Security Administration.

US Bureau of Census. 1973a. *Census of the Population: 1970.* Detailed Characteristics. United States Summary. Table 203: "Marital Status, Presence of Spouse, and Whether Married More Than Once, by Race, Sex, and Age: 1970," pp. 642–3. Washington, DC: US Government Printing Office.

——. 1973b. Census of the Population: 1970. Characteristics of the Population: United States Summary. Table 215: "Employment Status by Race, Sex, and Age: 1970," p. 680. Washington, DC: US Government Printing Office.

——. 1984a. *Census of Population: 1980.* Detailed Characteristics.United States Summary. Table 264: "Marital Status, Presence of Spouse, and Marital History for Persons 15 Years and Over, by Race, Spanish Origin, Sex, and Age: 1980," pp. 70–2. Washington, DC: US Government Printing Office.

——. 1984b. *Census of Population: 1980.* Characteristics of the Population. United States Summary. Table 272: "Labor Force Status by Age, Race, Spanish Origin, and Sex: 1980," pp. 119–20. Washington, DC: US Government Printing Office.

——. 1992. *Census of Population: 1990*. General Population Characteristics. United States. Table 34: "Persons 15 Years and Over by Marital Status, Age, Sex, Race, and Hispanic Origin," pp. 45–6. Washington, DC: US Government Printing Office.

——. 1993. *Census of Population: 1990*. Social and Economic Characteristics Table 44: "Labor Force Characteristics by Race and Hispanic Origin: 1990," p. 44 Washington, DC: US Government Printing Office.

——. 2000. Marital Status of People 15 Years and Over, by Age, Sex, Personal Earnings, Race and Hispanic Origin/March 1, 2000. Table A1. Washington, DC: US Government Printing Office.

US House Committee on Ways and Means. 2002. "Green Book: Background Material and Data on Programs within the Jurisdiction of the Committee on Ways and Means," *Committee Report WMCP*, pp. 106–14. Washington, DC: Government Printing Office.

Walzer, Michael. 1988. "Socializing the Welfare State," in Amy Gutmann, ed. *Democracy and the Welfare State*, pp. 13–25. Princeton, NJ: Princeton University Press.

EXPLORATIONS
GENDER AND AGING: CROSS-NATIONAL CONTRASTS

Guest Editors: Agneta Stark, Nancy Folbre, and Lois B. Shaw
Contributors: Timothy M. Smeeding, Susanna Sandström,
Lois B. Shaw, Sunhwa Lee, and Kyunghee Chung

I. POVERTY AND INCOME MAINTENANCE IN OLD AGE: A CROSS-NATIONAL VIEW OF LOW-INCOME OLDER WOMEN

Timothy M. Smeeding and Susanna Sandström

Great strides have been made in reducing poverty amongst individuals ages 65 and older in most rich countries over the past forty years. But pensioner poverty has not been eradicated, especially in the English-speaking nations; and women's poverty status in old age is a concern in all rich societies. In fact, due to demographic and other policy changes, pensioner poverty may rise again in the coming decades. This paper looks at elder poverty using the Luxembourg Income Study (LIS) database.

Poverty among younger pensioners is no longer a major policy problem in most rich nations, but older women remain vulnerable. Poverty rates amongst older women are more directly related to changes in living arrangements than to age. We find that poverty is especially a problem amongst women 75 or older who are living alone. The solutions to this problem lie in establishing a safety net, which helps keep the poorest out of poverty regardless of alternative income sources or policy changes that affect the younger and more affluent elderly.

Methodology, measurement, and data issues

Differing national experiences in social transfer and anti-poverty programs provide a rich source of information for evaluating the effectiveness of alternative social policies amongst the elderly. Policy-makers in the industrialized countries share common concerns about social problems such as poverty and social exclusion. Poverty measurement is an exercise that is particularly popular in the English-speaking countries. Few northern European and Scandinavian countries calculate low income or poverty rates, because their social programs already ensure a low poverty rate under any reasonable set of measurement standards (Anders Björklund and Richard Freeman 1997). Instead they concentrate their efforts on measures of social exclusion, mobility, and inequality (e.g., Anthony Atkinson, Bea Cantillon, Eric Marlier, and Brian Nolan 2002; Robert Erikson and John H. Goldthorpe 2002).

While there is no international consensus on guidelines for measuring poverty, groups such as the United Nations Children's Fund (UNICEF), the United Nations Human Development Report (UNHDR), the Organization for Economic Cooperation and Development (OECD), the European Statistical Office (Eurostat), the International Labor Office (ILO) and the Luxembourg Income Study (LIS) have published several cross-national studies of the incidence of poverty in recent years. As a result, there is considerable agreement on the appropriate measurement of poverty in a cross-national context and on the calculation of the anti-poverty effect of transfers. Most of the available studies share the following similarities that help guide our research strategy:

- For purposes of international comparisons, poverty is almost always a relative concept. A majority of cross-national studies define the poverty threshold as one-half of national median income. In this study, we use the 50 percent of median income to establish our national poverty lines. We also use the 40 percent of national median income as our relative poverty threshold because it is closest to the ratio of the official United States poverty line to median United States household (pre-tax) cash income (42 percent in 1998 and 2002).

164

Alternatively, the United Kingdom and the European Union have selected a poverty rate of 60 percent of the median income (Atkinson *et al.* 2002; Jonathan Bradshaw 2003). We use only the 40 and 50 percent standards here.

- Poverty and income measurement is based on the broadest income definition that still preserves comparability across nations. The best current definition is disposable cash and near-cash income (DPI) which includes all types of money income, minus direct income and payroll taxes and including all cash and near-cash transfers, such as food stamps and cash housing allowances and refundable tax credits such as the earned income tax credit (EITC). We do not include healthcare benefits in kind, even though they are large (Irwin Garfinkel, Lee Rainwater, and Timothy Smeeding 2004).

- In determining the anti-poverty effects of social transfers and tax policy, we also use a measure of "before tax and transfer" market income (MI), which includes earnings, income from investments, and private transfers. To this measure we can add private and occupational pensions. In tracing the effects of income transfer policy from MI to DPI poverty, we determine the effects of two additional bundles of government programs: Social Insurance and Taxes (including all forms of universal and social insurance benefits, minus income and payroll taxes) and Social Assistance (which includes all forms of income- and asset-tested benefits targeted at poor people). Again, in making these comparisons for all persons and for groups, we use one set poverty line, half of median DPI, throughout. However, in this case we base our analysis on households (with a head aged 65 and over) not persons.

The data we use for this analysis are from the Luxembourg Income Study (LIS) database, which now contains more than 140 household income data files for thirty nations covering the period 1967 to 2001 (http://www.lisproject.org). We can therefore analyze patterns of poverty and low incomes across a wide range of nations. In this paper we focus on seven nations, each with a recent 1998–2000 LIS database. These include the United States; two other English-speaking nations (Canada and the United Kingdom); two central European nations (Italy and Germany, including the eastern states of the former German Democratic Republic); and two Nordic nations (Finland and Sweden). These were chosen to typify the broad range of variation available within LIS and to simplify our analysis.

Poverty and demography

Despite major progress over the past forty years, significant pockets of poverty remain among the elderly, especially among elderly women living alone. The relatively precarious economic position of the elderly in the United States, as detailed in the next report by Lois Shaw and Sunhwa Lee, is even more evident when we look at comparative data. Table 1 shows "relative poverty" rates – that is, poverty measured relative to median income in the country – for eight rich countries using two alternative thresholds: 40 and 50 percent of median income. In Table 1, the United States and the United Kingdom have relatively higher poverty rates for all groupings; Italy and Germany are in the middle range poverty rate range (especially using the half median international poverty line); and Canada, Finland, and Sweden have generally lower overall elder poverty levels. The United States, the United Kingdom, and Italy also stand out with the highest overall elder poverty rate especially at the higher standard, suggesting that they all have a large near-poor population, with incomes between the 40 and 50 percent lines. The United States and United Kingdom stand out especially at the 40 percent of median line as no other nation has an elder poverty rate higher than 5.6 percent (Table 1, Panel A).

These patterns are even more striking if we focus on poverty among older women. Older women in general (Table 1, Panel B), women living alone (Panel C), and the oldest (aged 75 and over) women living alone (Panel D), do progressively worse on average and in almost every country. While there is surprisingly little difference between 65- and 75-year-old women living alone, in some places the differences are very large. The general pattern is that poverty rates rise within countries as one moves down the table and to the right, suggesting that gender, living arrangements, and to a lesser extent, age, all tend to increase poverty status. Not only does the average fraction of women who are poor increase as we move down the table, but the difference between the percent poor at the 40 and 50 percent poverty standards also widens.

In some nations – e.g., Sweden, Finland, and Canada – older women generally do better than in others. And in all nations (even including these three), poverty rates for the older women living alone at the one-half median poverty standard are 27 percent or more. The United States, with 45–48 percent of older women living alone in poverty at the higher standard, is only close to the United Kingdom at 41 percent poor. At the 40 percent of median income standard, the poverty of older women is also highest in the United States (followed closely by the United Kingdom) where rates are between 25 and 30 percent for 65- and 75-year-olds. In other nations, older women's poverty is 11 percent or less. In four nations, it is 7 percent or less.

Because of differences in life expectancy, older women make up the majority of the elderly population in every rich country. The fraction of the elderly poor who are women in general and women living alone in particular is very high. While 55 percent of all persons aged 65 and over are elderly women, 70 percent of the elderly poor are women (unpublished

166

Table 1 Poverty[a] rates among the aged[b]: being old and being female, percent of population with income less than given percent of adjusted national median disposable income

Country	Year	40 percent	50 percent
A. Elderly			
United States	2000	15.0	24.7
United Kingdom	1999	10.2	20.9
Germany	2000	3.9	10.1
Canada	1998	1.7	7.8
Sweden	2000	2.1	7.7
Italy	2000	5.6	13.7
Finland	2000	1.1	8.5
Average		**5.7**	**13.3**
B. Elderly women			
(65 +)			
United States	2000	17.7	28.6
United Kingdom	1999	14.4	26.2
Germany	2000	4.8	13.0
Canada	1998	1.5	9.6
Sweden	2000	2.5	10.3
Italy	2000	6.8	16.2
Finland	2000	1.8	11.8
Average		**7.1**	**16.5**
C. Elderly women			
(65 +) living alone			
United States	2000	29.6	45.5
United Kingdom	1999	25.3	40.7
Germany	2000	7.1	19.6
Canada	1998	1.2	17.7
Sweden	2000	3.6	16.5
Italy	2000	11.0	28.7
Finland	2000	2.8	21.2
Average		**11.5**	**27.1**
D. Elderly women			
(75 +) living alone			
United States	2000	30.4	48.3
United Kingdom	1999	26.7	41.3
Germany	2000	6.8	17.7
Canada	1998	0.8	19.8
Sweden	2000	4.3	19.6
Italy	2000	10.5	28.3
Finland	2000	4.2	26.4
Average		**12.0**	**28.8**

Notes:
[a]Poverty is defined as percentage of elderly living in households with adjusted disposable income less than given percent of median adjusted disposable income for all persons. Incomes are adjusted by $E = 0.05$ where adjusted DPI = actual DPI divided by household size (S) to the power E: adjusted $DPI = DPI/S^E$.
[b]Aged are all persons at least aged 65 and older. Person-level and household-level files were matched and income data weighted by the person sample weight from the person-level file.
Source: Authors' calculations from Luxembourg Income Study.

tabulations). Older women living alone average about 29 percent of all persons 65 and over but are nearly one-half (49 percent) of all poor persons in these nations. At still older ages (75 and over), where needs are greatest, 75 percent of the poor are women and 59 percent are women living alone (Timothy M. Smeeding 2001a: Table 3). Thus, the poverty problem in old age in all of these rich nations is concentrated among the oldest women, particularly single older women who live alone. But some nations cope with this problem better than others.

Most current Social Security reform proposals, both in the United States and other nations, are not well attuned to meet the needs of the most vulnerable elders, those 75 or over, especially older women living alone (Timothy M. Smeeding 1999; Eugene Steuerle 2001). Indeed, the economic vulnerability of the elderly is likely to be increased if the United States moves toward partial privatization, because such a system would likely be less redistributive toward retirees with low lifetime earnings than the current system (Gary Engelhardt and Jonathan Gruber 2004). Seniors would probably also be exposed to increased administrative costs and greater risks regarding the value and variation in their retirement savings accounts and annuity prices when they retire under such a system (Peter Diamond 2004). Finally, most of the Social Security reform proposals that do address these issues only partially address them, for instance, by only considering benefit changes for elderly widows and survivors (e.g., David A. Weaver 2001) and by not including other groups of at-risk elders such as divorcees or the never married (Smeeding 1999, 2001a).

Income maintenance and anti-poverty effects

Every nation fights poverty among the old by assembling some combination of three programmatic income maintenance strategies:

- citizenship retirement (universal pensions);
- social retirement (social insurance);
- social safety net (social assistance).

The first strategy usually consists of a universal (or nearly universal), pay-as-you-go, flat-rate benefit, sometimes phased out for those with higher incomes. The second strategy, social insurance, generally ties benefits more closely to earnings histories, although many social insurance pension systems also provide a modicum of benefit adequacy to all of their participants by tilting benefits toward those with lower lifetime earnings histories.

Countries like the United Kingdom and Canada combine universal and earnings-related social insurance pensions: a lower tier provides a higher

Table 2 Elderly poverty rates by income maintenance source[a] and income definition and 50 percent needs standard

	(A) Market Income (MI)	(B) A + Occupational Pensions	(C) B+ Universal and Social Income Transfers – Taxes	(D) C + Social Safety Net Transfers (DPI)[b]	(E) Social Insurance B to C	(F) Safety Net C to D	(G) Total System Effect E + F
A. Poverty rate for all elders household by income definition							
United States	71.9	60.5	24.9	24.7	35.6	0.2	35.8
United Kingdom	85.9	70.4	31.0	20.9	39.4	10.1	49.5
Germany	88.4	78.5	10.3	10.1	68.3	0.2	68.5
Canada	78.8	59.1	14.3	7.8	44.8	6.5	51.3
Sweden	88.7	82.0	19.5	7.7	62.5	11.8	74.3
Italy	73.8	65.1	17.4	13.7	47.7	3.7	51.4
Finland	87.8	37.9	11.1	8.5	26.8	2.6	29.4
Average	**82.2**	**64.8**	**18.4**	**13.3**	**46.4**	**5.0**	**51.5**
B. Poverty rate for female headed households by income definition							
United States	80.0	71.9	39.7	39.6	32.2	0.1	32.3
United Kingdom	91.0	84.7	56.3	36.7	28.4	19.6	48.0
Germany	94.0	85.3	19.1	18.9	66.2	0.2	66.4
Canada	84.9	70.5	25.7	15.4	44.7	10.3	55.1
Sweden	96.7	93.3	45.5	16.6	47.8	29.0	76.7
Italy	81.9	72.5	25.2	23.4	47.3	1.7	49.1
Finland	94.8	56.9	25.5	19.8	31.4	5.7	37.1
Average	**89.0**	**76.4**	**33.9**	**24.3**	**42.6**	**9.5**	**52.1**

Notes:
[a]Poverty measured as percent of households with incomes below 50 percent of median adjusted household disposable income, where $E=.5$ and $ADI=DI/S^E$.
[b]Column D presents disposable income household poverty rates.
Source: Authors' calculations from Luxembourg Income Study.

169

replacement rate for lower lifetime earners, coupled with an upper tier that is more closely related to contributions up to an earnings ceiling. Social retirement schemes are usually based on individual earnings, supplemented by a spousal benefit package (including survivor's benefits) for those who spent less career time in the paid labor force. In most European and Scandinavian countries, the citizen pension is relatively high while the social insurance tier is smaller (Weaver 2001).

In most societies, these citizenship and/or social retirement schemes are the major source of income of the aged (Engelhardt and Gruber 2004; see also Shaw and Lee report). Many nations, however, also couple these programs with some form of social assistance or safety-net benefit targeted at the low-income population.[1]

The effects of both types of benefits on household poverty rates (measured at the 50 percent level) are clearly laid out in Table 2, where we progress from market income (MI) poverty rates (in column [A]) to disposable income (DI) poverty rates (in column [D]), factoring in all three types of social spending outlined above. We also include the effects of occupational pensions that are contributory old-age income schemes, related to either private or public employment, and almost always directly related to previous earnings. We include two separate panels: one for all households, the other for female-headed households, and both measured at the 50 percent needs standard. The poverty rates in Table 2 are for households, not persons, so they do not directly correspond to the poverty rates in Table 1. Moving from left to right, we can identify the sequential impact of each type of old-age income support. As expected, poverty rates are highest based on market income alone. Most elderly households do not have sufficient earnings and property income (interest, rent, dividends) to eliminate poverty by themselves. This is particularly true for older female-headed units (Panel B). Countries that have higher labor force participation rates or larger accumulated financial wealth stocks at older ages have lower market income (MI) poverty rates (e.g., United States, Italy) excluding occupational pensions than do other nations.

The second column (B) adds in occupational pensions (and other private transfers). In nations that rely more heavily on such schemes, poverty rates are lower. For instance, elder poverty, including occupational pension benefits, is 38 percent in Finland where employment-related pensions have replaced a great deal of public pension spending[2] and in the 59 to 65 percent range in the United States, Canada, and Italy. Poverty for older women, including occupational pensions, is 57 percent in Finland, and in the 70 to 73 percent range for older women in these same three nations (United States, Canada, Italy). It is much higher in societies that have much lower (or fewer) occupational pensions, e.g., Sweden and Germany. Since women's labor force participation rates have increased over recent decades, women (Panel B) will look increasingly more like

170

those in all other households (Panel A) as the baby-boom generation ages into retirement.

Counting these several sources of income sets the stage for measuring the impact of the income maintenance system. Column (C) shows the impact of universal and social insurance programs and taxes. Column (D) shows the impact of the social assistance "safety net" programs. The largest effect on old-age poverty in every nation comes from the citizenship/social retirement systems in both panels. In general, the larger and more inclusive the social insurance system and the higher the first-tier benefit for lower wage earners, the larger the anti-poverty effect (column [E]). Thus, Sweden and Germany have the largest effects on poverty with 63 to 68 percentage point reductions for the elderly in general and a 60 percentage point decline for older women in Germany.

In lower-spending nations like the United Kingdom and the United States, the effect on poverty is also less, with social retirement reducing elder poverty by only 36 to 39 percentage points overall. For older women, the effects of social retirement on poverty run from 28 to 32 percent reductions in the United States and the United Kingdom. Canada does much better for a low-spending nation, with a 45 percent reduction for all households and also for reduction for older women.

Because elder women are liable to have less in terms of occupational pensions, earnings, and wealth, they are more likely to be dependent on social insurance and social assistance (safety net) programs to keep them from poverty. This is true in all of these nations, the United States included (Timothy M. Smeeding, Carroll L. Estes, and Lou Glasse 1999). Universal and social insurance pensions can also be very expensive and blunt instruments, spending quite a large amount of public funds to achieve a low poverty result (Timothy M. Smeeding and James Smith 1998; Jonathan Gruber and David Wise 2001; Timothy M. Smeeding 2004).

These benefits set the scene for the final stage impacts of the social assistance or "safety net" programs (in column [F]). Here skillfully targeted supplements with high participation rates may produce large marginal anti-poverty effects. Take-up rates and other features of the systems also affect the results. In the United Kingdom, Sweden, and Canada, the safety net impacts are largest. In the other countries (e.g., Germany and Finland) the effects are small with most of the "heavy lifting" of the elderly from poverty being already accomplished by their social retirement system. In other nations, especially in the United States, the effects are weak, owing to the less than full integration of Supplemental Security Income (SSI) with social retirement, as evidenced by low take-up rates in SSI, the relatively low SSI benefit guarantee, relatively low Food Stamp take-up rates among the elderly, and the stringent liquid asset tests in both programs (Mary Daly and Richard Burkhauser 2003; Janet Currie 2004; Paul Davies and Melissa Favreault 2004; US Congress 2004).

The effects for older women show much the same cross-national pattern but with larger safety net impacts, again largest in Canada, Sweden, and the United Kingdom. In the United States, the safety net effects have a below 1 percent overall reduction in poverty and an almost zero impact for older women. Thus, while the SSI program and Food Stamps provide some help to low-income older Americans, the benefits do not seem to be sufficient to lift them out of poverty.

The net effects of these systems (column [G]) are to produce widely varying poverty outcomes depending on the mix and strength of each component of the system. Those systems that spend more, especially on social insurance (e.g., Sweden and Germany) end up with lower poverty rates. Those whose spending is modest, but with well-targeted, high participation rate social assistance benefits also seem to do well (e.g., Canada), while those who do not spend as much or whose systems are not well targeted, do worse (e.g., Italy, the United Kingdom, and especially the United States). Finland has a relatively effective overall set of programs, with all types of support contributing to their low overall poverty rates.

In sum, countries that do best in the fight against elder poverty are those with high minimum "first-tier" traditional (defined benefit type) social retirement plans for all elderly, as in Germany and Italy. But population aging in coming decades will increase pressure on these governments to reduce these benefits and to turn their systems more toward defined contribution-type pension plans. Targeted income-tested benefit strategies such as those implemented by Canada (especially), Sweden, and the United Kingdom are also relatively successful in reducing elderly female poverty, at a much lower overall budgetary cost.

Benefit levels: au Canada?

However it is structured, the minimum old-age benefit for a single person from the combined social retirement/social safety net package is also an important determinant of vulnerability to poverty. If a nation has a low minimum benefit package, poverty rates will be higher than if it has a higher level of minimum benefit generosity. The level of the safety net benefit varies considerably across countries. The United States has the least generous minimum benefit level of all the nations studied here, far below the next nearest country, the United Kingdom (Timothy M. Smeeding 2003; US Congress 2004).

The integration of safety net and social insurance systems as well as rules restricting eligibility to those with liquid assets below a certain level make a big difference for the overall anti-poverty effectiveness of social spending on the aged. Canada and the United Kingdom, for example, offer a basic quasi-universal pension topped up by an income-tested pension received by over 30 percent of all pensioners.

Minimum pension guarantees vary substantially across countries in their transparency, as well as their generosity. The most notable difference is whether the minimum guarantee is embedded in a universal or earnings-related program or takes the form of a separate program that disproportionately rewards the first dollars of earnings in calculating benefit replacement rates, providing additional benefits to those working at low wages. The United States does not have a specific income guarantee within Social Security, but instead a higher replacement rate for long-time low-wage earners. Moreover, it only has a special minimum benefit, far below the 40 percent poverty line, for those who work for many years at low wages.

In contrast, the United States SSI program does offer a minimum guarantee (about 80 percent of the poverty line once combined with Food Stamps), but it serves only about one-twenty-fifth as many aged persons as Social Security, and it suffers from both low take-up rates and strict liquid asset tests. The take-up rates in SSI among the elderly are only in the 55 to 65 percent range (Currie 2004), while many are not eligible because of the stringent liquid asset tests of $2,000 for a single person ($3,000 for a couple). Benefit levels (but not asset levels) are annually adjusted for changes in the consumer price index (CPI). Low take-up issues also plague the United Kingdom system (Stephen Pudney, Ruth Hancock, and Holly Sutherland 2004).

The Canadian case is particularly instructive in each of these comparisons. Canada has managed to achieve much greater poverty reduction among seniors while spending much less on social retirement programs than most other rich countries (but slightly more than the United States). The reason is that Canada spends its public pension money differently, prioritizing its near-universal Old Age Security and linking it seamlessly to the income-tested Guaranteed Income Supplement (GIS) program. This program has no asset test and a relatively simple annual application process, which permits an income test integrated with income tax filing so as to avoid stigma and encourage take-up. In effect, the GIS "tops up" the Canadian Pension Plan – the social insurance component of the Canadian system, at source. Over 90 percent of the eligible Canadian elderly participate in GIS (Ken Battle 1997), compared to about 60 percent of eligible elder participation in SSI in the United States (Paul S. Davies *et al.*, 2000; Kathleen McGarry 2000; US Congress 2004; Weaver 2001). Canada allocates close to 9 percent of its total tax and transfer retirement income spending on GIS, while the United States allocates less than 2 percent of government retirement income spending on the SSI program. SSI benefits accrue to about 10 percent of the United States aged; GIS benefits reach 33 percent of Canadian elders (Battle 1997; Timothy M. Smeeding 2001b). By 1999, the Canadians spent C$5.1 billion (or 0.83 percent of gross domestic product [GDP] – about US$3.5 billion) on GIS benefits for the elderly.[3] In contrast, and with almost ten times the number

173

of elderly, the United States spent only US$3.9 billion (0.031 percent of GDP) on SSI for the elderly in 1999 (US Congress 2004; Smeeding 2001b).

Future differences

Older women in the next two decades will look very different from older women today as a result of changing earnings histories (Alicia Munnell 2004) and different demographic characteristics (Madonna Harrington Meyer, Douglas Wolf and Christine L. Himes 2005). Many will have good occupational pensions and partners who have similar benefits. But not all women of the baby-boom cohort will benefit equally from their labor market experience. Poverty rates among older women are highest amongst divorced, widowed, and never-married women, groups whose prevalence within the elder population will rise significantly over the next decades (Smeeding 1999). For instance, in the United States, divorced and never-married women who were 10 percent of all older women in the 1990s will comprise over 25 percent of all aged in the 2020s. And these groups have poverty rates more than double overall elder poverty rates, despite the high average labor force participation rates and pension benefits of their cohorts.

The current and future challenge will be to encourage self-funded occupational and savings-related contributory pension systems (such as investment retirement accounts or IRAs and 410[K] plans) which encourage individual responsibility, but at the same time provide retirement benefits that guarantee minimum standards of living for very elderly women, especially those who have never been married or are widows or divorcees. Cutting Social Security benefits will raise older women's poverty (Engelhardt and Gruber 2004). Once taken up, these benefits are unlikely to increase in real terms in future years. Integrating an income-tested benefit for those at older ages who have nothing else to rely on is crucial to protecting older women against poverty. A famous book on Canadian social policy is entitled *Small Differences that Matter* (David Card and Richard Freeman 1993). Policy-makers in the United States should recognize that our neighbors to the north offer a blueprint for a cost-effective system that protects older women without stigmatizing benefit receipt.

II. GROWING OLD IN THE US:
GENDER AND INCOME ADEQUACY

Lois B. Shaw and Sunhwa Lee

As the preceding report by Smeeding and Sandström shows, poverty rates for the elderly are higher in the US than in most European countries, and

174

the risk of poverty is greater for women than for men. The greater risk of poverty for older women is closely associated with marital status. Because of longer life expectancy for women than men, women are more likely to experience the loss of their spouses and live alone in old age. In this report, we describe the major sources of income of the US elderly by gender, marital status, and living arrangement and highlight the precarious situation of those who live alone, especially women. Although we do not present differences by race and ethnicity in this report, it is important to note that on almost every measure African Americans and Hispanics are considerably worse off than the white population, with Asians generally occupying an intermediate position.

Our analyses are based on data from the 1999–2001 March Current Population Survey (CPS) collected by the US Census Bureau. The March CPS is the primary source of detailed information on annual income in the US as it gathers detailed information on earnings, Social Security payments, pensions, income from assets (interest, dividends, and rent), and other government cash and noncash benefits. We combine three years of data to secure a sufficient number of observations for analysis of different subgroups. The merged data also provide more stable estimates that balance out short-term fluctuations.

Data from the CPS have one important limitation when considering the welfare of the elderly population: they do not include people living in institutions, who among the elderly are primarily those in nursing homes. Data from the 2000 Census of the population show that about 4.5 percent of those aged 65 and older live in nursing homes; the percentage increases from only 1 percent at ages 65–74 to over 8 percent at ages 75 and over (Lisa Hetzel and Annetta Smith 2001: 7). Because of their longer lives and lower level of resources, women are more likely than men to spend their last years in this way. In 2000, about 74 percent of the residents in nursing homes were women (US Census Bureau 2001). Many nursing home residents quickly exhaust their savings, so their expenses are partly paid for by Medicaid, a means-tested government benefit (Joshua Wiener, Catherine Sullivan, and Jason Skaggs 1996).

Marital status and living arrangements

As in other countries, women in the US tend to marry men who are older than them and to live longer than men. As a result, there are marked differences in marital status and living arrangements between women and men as they enter into the retirement years. As Table 3 shows, the great majority of older men are married: at ages 65–74 over three-quarters are married and even at age 75 and older over two-thirds are married. In contrast, the proportion of women aged 65–74 who are married is slightly

175

more than half, and it declines dramatically to less than one-third for women 75 years and older.

Nearly 80 percent of unmarried women aged 65 and older are widows compared with approximately 55 percent of unmarried men. Correspondingly, fewer women than men are divorced or never married.[4] The majority of unmarried elderly in the US live alone. Living with relatives or unrelated people is often not possible and may not be the preferred arrangement. Since so many elderly men are married, women are much more likely than men to live alone. In the oldest age group – 75 years and older – nearly half of all women are unmarried and living alone, compared with only 20 percent of men. These differences in marital status and living arrangement are closely associated with the economic well-being of older women and men.

Overview of income in the retirement years

In the years of the survey, median personal income of the elderly was $13,580 compared with approximately $25,000 for the population aged 25–64. Median personal income of elderly women was 56 percent of elderly men's ($10,730 compared with $18,990).

As Figure 1 shows, personal income is unequally distributed among both elderly women and men. At the upper end of the distribution, about 18 percent of men but only 6 percent of women had personal incomes of $40,000 or more. At the lower end of the distribution, 45 percent of women compared with about 20 percent of men had personal incomes of $10,000 or less. Of course, many women and men who have little personal income receive support from other family members; yet, family incomes are also very unequally distributed. It is, therefore, important to keep in mind the great diversity in economic circumstances among the elderly population in the US. This issue is discussed further when we present poverty rates based on official poverty thresholds that vary by family size.

The major sources of income for people aged 65 and older are Social Security (the social insurance system for the elderly),[5] employer-provided

Table 3 Marital status and living arrangements among older women and men by age

	Women (percent)		Men (percent)	
	Age 65 – 74	Age 75 +	Age 65 – 74	Age 75 +
Married	54.8	30.1	78.2	68.7
Unmarried living alone	29.3	49.2	13.5	20.2
Unmarried living with others	15.9	20.7	8.4	11.1
Total	100.0	100.0	100.0	100.0

Source: Authors' calculations based on the March Current Population Surveys, 1999–2001.

pensions, income from assets (interest, dividends, and rent), and earnings. Figure 2 shows the percentage of elderly women and men receiving income from each of these sources. A small number of the elderly also receive some form of means-tested public assistance. Social Security is by far the most common source of income, received by approximately 90 percent of those 65 and older. Income from assets is the next most common source, received by over 60 percent. Nearly half of elderly men receive employer-provided

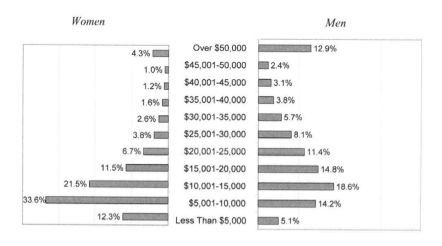

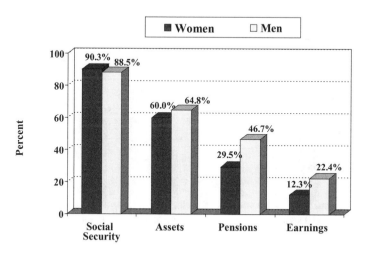

Source: Authors' calculations based on the March Current Population Surveys, 1999-2001. (Data are for calendar years 1998-2000.)

Figure 2 Percent of women and men aged 65 and older receiving income from each source

pensions, but only 30 percent of women do. Even fewer of the elderly have any earnings (12 percent of women and 22 percent of men).

Figure 3 compares median annual income from each of these sources among those who received any income from that source. Median earnings for both women and men exceed median Social Security benefits, but earnings are received by relatively few elderly people. Social Security benefits, therefore, represent the largest commonly received source of income for people 65 and older. Median income from pensions is fairly large for men, but it is only about half as large for women. Although relatively widespread, median income from assets is quite small for both women and men. We next consider each of these sources in greater detail.

Social Security

Among countries of the developed world, the US is unusual in that Social Security is not universal. Eligibility for worker benefits requires a record of at least ten years of employment in jobs covered by Social Security (about 96 percent of all jobs).[6] Spouses and in some cases divorced spouses of retired workers are eligible for a dependent benefit of 50 percent of the retired worker's benefit, and surviving widows/widowers are entitled to 100 percent of the deceased worker's benefit. In the event that the spouse or survivor has also been employed and paying into the system, she/he

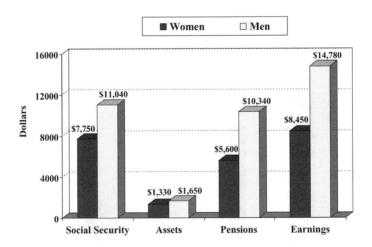

Source: Authors' calculations based on the March Current Population Surveys, 1999-2001.
(Data are for calendar years 1998-2000 in 2000 constant dollars.)
Note: Median annual income for each source is calculated only among those receiving income from each source, excluding zero values.

Figure 3 Median annual income received from each source among women and men aged 65 and older

178

receives either the worker benefit or dependent benefit, whichever is larger. Thus women who have considerable paid employment may receive no more than those who have paid little or nothing into the system. (See Madonna Harrington Meyer, Douglas Wolf, and Christine Himes 2005 for a more extended critique of this issue.)

On the positive side, some features of the US Social Security system are especially beneficial for women. The benefit formula is progressive, offering a higher percentage of earnings replacement to low earners than to high earners, which is important for all low earners, and especially for single women and those not married long enough to receive divorced spouse benefits. Of special importance to women because of their longer life expectancies is the annual increase in benefits based on consumer price increases. These increases assure that those who live many years after retirement will not see their benefits eroded by inflation.

Table 4 shows the percentage of total personal income provided by Social Security benefits. As can be seen here, about two-thirds of all women and half of all men aged 65 and older depend on Social Security for at least half of their income. In fact, Social Security is the only source of income for over 20 percent of women and about 15 percent of men 65 and older.

Table 5 shows receipt of Social Security among women and men by marital status and living arrangement. Median benefits for married women are only slightly more than 50 percent of married men's benefits, reflecting the fact that many women are receiving the wife's benefit. Among unmarried women, benefits are higher and much closer to those of men; in fact, unmarried women have benefits that are about 90 percent of those of unmarried men. These figures reflect the prevalence of widow's benefits that are 100 percent of deceased spouse benefits for most of these women.

Employer-provided pensions

Employer-provided pensions in the US are basically of two types (for further description, see Patrick Purcell 2001). In defined *benefit* plans, employers usually pay pensions as an annuity, using a set formula based on an employee's years of employment and earnings. In defined *contribution* plans, employees make pre-tax contributions to their retirement plans, often matched by contributions from employers. The amount available at retirement depends on these contributions plus accrued interest, dividends, and capital gains (or losses). Most defined contribution plans offer a lump-sum distribution of the proceeds and less than one-third offer a life annuity option (Olivia Mitchell and Sylvester Schieber 1998). Plans that offer annuities must include a joint and survivor benefit for spouses unless both spouses opt out in writing. Defined benefit plans were the most common kind of pension during the working lives of most current retirees, but defined contribution plans are now becoming predominant.

179

Table 4 Share of Social Security in total personal income among women and men 65 and older

	Women	Men
Social Security accounts for		
100% of total personal income	22.8%	14.9%
50–99%	43.3	37.4
1–49%	24.3	36.3
None	9.7	11.5

Source: Authors' calculations based on the March Current Population Surveys, 1999–2001. (Data are for calendar years 1998–2000).

Table 5 Receipt of Social Security among women and men 65 and older

	Women	Men
Percent Receiving Social Security		
Married	89.9%	88.9%
Unmarried living alone	93.8	91.0
Unmarried living with others	83.8	81.3
Total	90.3	88.5
Median Annual Benefits		
Married	$6,150	$11,350
Unmarried living alone	$9,430	$10,440
Unmarried living with others	$8,660	$9,660
Total	$7,750	$11,040

Notes: Median annual benefits are for calendar years 1998–2000 (2000 constant dollars). Median Social Security benefit is calculated only among those who received any income from Social Security, excluding zero values in the calculation.
Source: Authors' calculations based on the March Current Population Surveys, 1999–2001.

While Social Security now covers about 96 percent of all jobs, supplementary employer-provided pensions are very unevenly distributed. Most government jobs offer pensions, but only about two-thirds of full-time year-round workers in the private sector work for employers who offer pension plans.[7] However, not every worker participates in these pension plans; about 58 percent of full-time private-sector workers (ages 25–64) were participating in pension plans in 2000 (Purcell 2001). Eligibility is often limited to full-time employees and those who have worked for the firm for a given number of years. In general, jobs that are well paid carry pensions, and low-paid jobs do not.

Not all pension plan participants will actually receive regular pension income in retirement (Sunhwa Lee and Lois Shaw, forthcoming). Some will leave their jobs too soon to be fully qualified for pension benefits. Pensions that would be quite small if paid on an annuity basis are often cashed out at retirement, as will be many defined contribution plans that offer no annuity option. Among current retirees, fewer than one-third of women (30 percent) and half of men (47 percent) aged 65 and over receive income from either their own or their spouses' pension (see Table 6). Women who live alone are the most likely to receive a pension: about 40 percent of unmarried women living alone receive pension income compared with 27 percent of unmarried women living with others and 21 percent of married women. This is in part due to many widows who are receiving survivor benefits from their husbands' pensions. About 15 percent of unmarried women living alone and 10 percent of those living with others receive these survivor pensions. But unmarried women who live alone are also more likely than other women to have a pension based on their own employment.

The median pension income for men 65 and older ($10,340) comes close to their median Social Security benefit ($11,040), but about half of men do not have any pension income. For women, pension income is only slightly more than half of men's ($5,600) and substantially less important, because far fewer women than men receive it. These differences reflect the fact that women have, on average, worked fewer years than men and had lower earnings in the years they worked.

Employment and earnings

In the years leading up to retirement, the majority of both women and men in the US are employed: 70 percent of women and over 80 percent of men in the 50–61 age group reported working at paid employment at some time in the previous year (see Figure 4).[8] At age 62 when eligibility for receiving Social Security retired worker benefits begins (albeit at actuarially reduced amounts), employment decreases dramatically. Yet, slightly over 40 percent of women and nearly 60 percent of men remain employed at ages 62–64. A further decrease in employment occurs at age 65 when full Social Security benefits become available.[9] At ages 65–74, nearly 20 percent of women and about 30 percent of men are still employed, but by age 75 and over, only 5 percent of women and 11 percent of men are continuing to work for even part of the year.

Reasons for continuing to work are varied. Some workers have jobs they enjoy and may prefer not to retire early. Many people continue to work until age 65 in order to keep their health insurance.[10] Before age 65 most people depend on employer-provided health insurance, since the only government-sponsored insurance requires either long-term disability or stringent means and asset tests. Some women workers especially are still working in order to become eligible for a pension or to increase its size (Courtney Coile, Peter Diamond, Jonathan Gruber, and Alain Jousten 1999).

Table 6 Receipt of pension income and median annual pension income[a] among women and men 65 and older

	Women	*Men*
Percent Receiving Pension Income		
Married	21.1%	48.1%
Unmarried living alone	40.0	46.4
Unmarried living with others	27.0	36.0
Total	29.5	46.7
Median Annual Pension Income		
Married	$5,690	$10,800
Unmarried living alone	$5,700	$9,600
Unmarried living with others	$5,400	$8,070
Total	$5,600	$10,340

Notes: Median pension incomes are for calendar years 1998–2000 (2000 constant dollars). Median pension income is calculated only among those who received any type of pensions, excluding zero values in the calculation.
[a]The March Current Population Survey provides information on the receipt of general retirement income (other than Social Security) that includes income from company or union pension plans, government pensions, regular payments from IRAs or Keogh accounts, and regular payments from annuities or paid insurance policies. For our analysis, veterans' pensions and survivor's pensions are also included as part of general pension income.
Source: Authors' calculations based on the March Current Population Surveys, 1999–2001.

Most commonly, employment after age 65 is part-time, and it is often a way of supplementing inadequate retirement income. In fact, working at older ages is a way to avoid poverty for those who do not have pensions or have small or non-existent Social Security benefits. Research with long-itudinal data has shown that some Social Security beneficiaries who were working after beginning to receive benefits became poor or near-poor when they stopped working, usually in their 70s (Lois Shaw and Hsiao-Ye Yi 1997).

At older ages, women's earnings diverge from men's even more than at younger ages. At age 65 and over, women working full-time year-round earn only two-thirds as much as men. Part-time earnings of about $5,500 for women and $7,800 for men are more nearly equal (table not shown), but are obviously adequate only as supplements to other income.

Income from assets

After Social Security, the most common source of retirement income for people 65 and older comes from assets (interest, dividends, and rent). About 60 percent of women and 65 percent of men receive income from these sources (see Figure 2).[11] Married men and women are most likely to have income from assets, followed by unmarried women living alone. Less than 40 percent of unmarried women and men living with others have any asset income (table not shown).

182

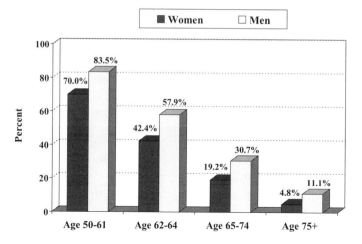

Source: Authors' calculations based on the March Current Population Surveys, 1999-2001. (Data are for calendar years 1998-2000.)

Figure 4 Employment status in the previous year among women and men 50 and older

Even though the majority of the elderly receive some income from assets, the median amount is only $1,330 for women and $1,650 for men (see Figure 3). Of those who receive any income from these sources, only 30 percent of men and 27 percent of women receive as much as $5,000 per year. Also reflecting the uneven distribution of asset income is the fact that the median is considerably lower than the mean asset income of $3,440 for women and $4,770 for men, indicating that a small number of retirees tend to hold a large proportion of assets while the majority of retirees receives either none or a very small amount of income from assets.

Means-tested benefits and other income sources

When Social Security and other sources of income are very low, Supplemental Security Income (SSI) provides a means-tested safety net for women and men aged 65 and older, as well as for the disabled at any age. However, SSI is not very effective in preventing poverty because its income and asset limits are so low.[12] Unmarried people 65 and older are more likely than married people to receive support from SSI, and unmarried women are somewhat more likely than unmarried men to do so. While only 2 percent of married couples receive SSI, 6 percent of unmarried women living alone and 9 percent of unmarried women living with others receive SSI, as do about 5 percent of unmarried men regardless of living arrangement (see Table 7). The receipt of Food Stamps, another means-tested government program, follows similar patterns.

Income assistance from family members is important in many countries (see the subsequent report by Kyunghee Chung). This is not a major source in the US: less than 1 percent of elderly women and men report receiving any income from family members or others living outside the household. These figures undoubtedly understate assistance from children and other relatives who may pay bills or provide food or clothing rather than giving money directly. In addition, some of the elderly living with other family members are undoubtedly receiving material support in this way.

Poverty among the elderly

The poverty rates we present are based on comparing total family income with current US official poverty thresholds for families of different sizes.[13] Our data show poverty rates that are quite low for married couples at ages 65 and over (Figure 5). In contrast, among unmarried women who live alone, more than 20 percent are poor, nearly four times greater than the rate among married people. The poverty rate is high among unmarried women living alone, despite the fact that these women, compared with married women, tend to receive pensions and Social Security at higher rates and receive relatively greater median benefits from Social Security. Unmarried men living alone also have poverty rates (approximately 15 percent) that are much higher than those of married men.

Unmarried people living with others show a lower poverty rate than those living alone, because poverty rates are estimated based on total family income. Nevertheless, unmarried women and men who live with others at older ages are less likely than either the unmarried living alone or married people in their age group to have any of the kinds of retirement income considered: income from Social Security, pensions, or assets. This lack of retirement income may be an important reason underlying their

Table 7 Percent of women and men 65 and older receiving Supplemental Security Income (SSI) by marital status

	Women	*Men*
Married	1.9%	1.7%
Unmarried living alone	6.0	4.6
Unmarried living with others	9.1	5.1
Total	4.8	2.5

Source: Authors' calculations based on the March Current Population Surveys, 1999–2001. (Data are for calendar years 1998–2000.)

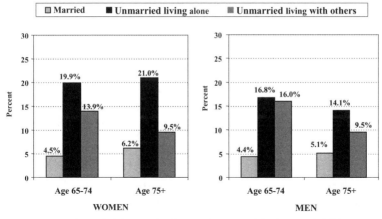

Source: Authors' calculations based on the March Current Population Surveys, 1999-2001.

Figure 5 Poverty rates among older women and men by age

arrangement to live with relatives or others. Their economic security will then depend on the stability of this living arrangement.

The poverty statistics presented here are conservative in that they are lower than commonly used poverty rates based on the percentage of households with income (adjusted for family size) less than 40 or 50 percent of the median. For example, the preceding report by Smeeding and Sandström shows poverty rates for women living alone of nearly 30 percent and over 40 percent respectively, using these alternative measures.

Poverty rates are also undoubtedly underestimated for married couples, as they are based on economies of scale that are unlikely to be realized today when medical expenses consume an increasing fraction of family income, especially among the elderly. (For a comprehensive critique of both the income measures used and the thresholds themselves, see Constance F. Citro and Robert Michael 1995.) However, research using recommended revisions to the US poverty measures also shows the highest poverty rates among unmarried women, especially those living alone (Kelly Olsen 1999; David Johnson and Timothy Smeeding 2000).

Changes in income adequacy in the future

As people retire from the workforce and earnings decrease with age, income from Social Security, pensions, savings, and investments become crucial for the financial security of older women and men. As at earlier ages, however, women's income from all sources lags behind men's during retirement. With less income of all kinds, older women are at greater risk of poverty than men.

Changes in both Social Security and employer-provided pension systems pose significant risks for older women. Women's organizations, as well as many researchers, have advocated changes in Social Security that would make the system more equitable. Suggested changes include rewarding caregiving specifically rather than through dependent-spouse benefits, modifying survivor's benefits to recognize both spouses' contributions, and instituting an adequate minimum benefit for low earners (Heidi Hartmann and Catherine Hill with Linda Witter 2000; Melissa Favreault, Frank Sammartino, and C. Eugene Steuerle 2001). The present political climate focuses on partial privatization of the system. Privatization, unfortunately, would jeopardize the positive features of the current system for women such as inflation-adjusted guaranteed benefits and a progressive benefit structure, while adding the risks of stock market investing. Furthermore, current privatization proposals include large reduction in future benefits to pay for the transition to a partially-privatized system.

Employer-provided pensions are also changing away from plans that offer defined benefits in the form of annuities toward defined contribution plans that depend on the vagaries of stock and bond markets. At present, plans that offer annuities must offer survivor benefits to spouses unless the spouse opts out of this benefit. Many widows have benefited from this provision. If no annuity is offered, there is no guarantee that any income from her husband's pension will be left for the widow.

As future generations reach retirement, women will have more labor market experience than those who are now retired. A recent study predicts much reduced poverty rates overall with rising earnings that would benefit both women and men (Barbara Butrica, Karen Smith, and Eric Toder 2002). Yet, women continue to have lower earnings and face a greater likelihood of working part-time or taking time out of the labor force because of caregiving responsibilities. Other research predicts that gains in women's earnings and retirement income may be offset by declining rates of marriage and rising rates of divorce which place women at greater risk of living alone (Smeeding, Estes, and Glasse 1999). These differences are likely to mean a continuing gap in economic well-being between women and men at older ages.

III. GENDER AND AGING IN SOUTH KOREA

Kyunghee Chung

Over the past thirty years birth rates have declined rapidly in South Korea. Between 1970 and 1990 the average number of lifetime births per woman (total fertility rate) fell from 4.5 to 1.6 with a further decrease to 1.4

projected for 2004. At the same time, life expectancy has increased markedly: female life expectancy at birth in South Korea (80 years) is now as high as that in many industrialized countries. Male life expectancy at birth has also increased rapidly to 72.8 years (see Table 8). The seven-year difference between males and females is similar to gender differences noted in other advanced countries.

Due to the rapid decrease in the fertility rate and the sustained increase in life expectancy, the number and proportion of the elderly population has substantially increased. Between 1970 and 2004, the percentage of the population aged 65 and over increased from 3.1 percent to 8.7 percent and is expected to increase further to 14.4 percent in 2019.

Gender differences in age, marital status, living arrangements, and education

As their longer life expectancy suggests, the proportion of the population aged 80 and over was higher among women than among men, while men were more likely than women to be in the 65–69 age group (see Table 9). There were also large gender differences in marital status: over 85 percent of older men were currently married, compared with only 32 percent of older women. These differences again reflect the longer life expectancies of women who are likely to outlive their spouses and become widows. As in other countries, women in the Republic of Korea are also likely to marry men older than themselves.

In terms of living arrangements, the differences between older women and men are again striking, reflecting in part the large differences in marital status. Nearly half of older men, but only 18 percent of older women, lived with their spouses only. Older women were much more likely to be living with their children, whereas this arrangement was much less

Table 8 Population characteristics of the Republic of Korea, 1970–2019

	1970	*1980*	*1990*	*2004*	*2019*
Elderly population (age 65 +)					
As percent of the total	3.1	3.8	5.1	8.7	14.4
Number	991,000	1,456,000	195,000	171,000	7,314,000
Life expectancy					
Female	66.1	70.5	75.9	80.0	—
Male	59.0	62.3	67.7	72.8	—
Total	62.3	66.2	71.7	76.5	—
Total fertility rate	4.5	2.7	1.6	1.4	—

Sources: Economic Planning Board 1970, 1980. *Population and Housing Census Report*; National Statistical Office (NSO) 1990, 1995; *Population and Housing Census*; NSO 2001. *Population Projection*; NSO 2002. Life Table.

Table 9 Characteristics of older people by gender, 2001[a] (Percentage Distributions)

Characteristics	Female	Male	Total
Age			
65–69	37.3	45.8	40.5
70–74	27.3	26.6	27.1
75–79	18.6	17.3	18.3
80+	16.6	10.3	14.2
Marital status			
Currently married	31.7	86.3	52.4
Unmarried, divorced, or widowed	68.3	13.7	47.6
Living arrangement			
Older person living alone	23.5	5.9	16.8
Older person living w/ spouse only	18.0	47.5	29.2
Older person living w/ married children	42.7	24.3	35.7
Others	15.8	22.3	18.3
Educational attainment			
Illiterate	29.7	4.4	20.2
No formal education but literate	28.8	14.9	23.6
Primary school graduate	31.3	39.7	34.5
Middle/high school graduate	8.5	27.9	15.8
College graduate or higher	1.7	13.0	6.0
Employment status			
Unemployed	76.4	63.7	71.6
Employed	23.6	36.3	28.4

Notes:
[a]Duk Sunwoo *et al.* (2001).
[b]For living arrangement, statistics include households where both the husband and wife or where just one person in the couple is 65 years or over.
Source: Korea National Statistical Office (2001).

common for men. Nearly a quarter of older women lived alone compared with only 6 percent of older men. It should be noted that some elderly married couples as well as widows or widowers live with their children, who may be married or unmarried.

The educational attainment of older women (age 65 and older) was very low: nearly 30 percent were illiterate, while nearly as many were literate but had no formal schooling. In contrast, only 4 percent of men were illiterate and another 15 percent were literate without formal schooling. High school or college graduation was unusual among older women with about 9 percent having graduated from high school and less than 2 percent from college. Men were much more likely than women to have advanced schooling: nearly 28 percent of men were high school graduates and 13 percent college graduates. These differences can be explained in part by the fact that the women, being older on average, would have been growing up when education was less available to either gender, but in part is also undoubtedly due to greater efforts to educate boys than girls.

Gender differences in health status

Chronic conditions and self-reported health status

The great majority of older people had at least one chronic disease. The most commonly mentioned conditions among older women were arthritis, a lame back, high blood pressure, ulcers, and cataracts (Table 10). Men also mentioned these conditions, though less commonly than women, but men were more likely than women to have chronic bronchitis. Nearly 11 percent of elderly women were suffering from dementia compared with only 2.4 percent of men.

Women tended to evaluate their health status more unfavorably than men (Table 10). About 63 percent of older women and 46 percent of older men felt that their overall health condition was poor or very poor, whereas about 19 percent of older women but 30 percent of older men described their health status as good or very good.

Dependency levels among older persons by gender

In the Long-Term Care Survey conducted in 2001, dependency level of older persons is measured in terms of restricted activities of daily living (ADLs) and instrumental activities of daily living (IADLs).[14] For the purpose of understanding dependency levels among older persons, the ADL category is the best indicator of higher levels of dependency, while the IADL category functions as a useful indicator of lower levels of dependency. According to the survey, over 40 percent of older women had a mild activity limitation as measured by having IADLs only, and an estimated 12.5 percent reported having one or more severe activity limitations (ADLs; see Table 11). Comparable figures for men were approximately 14 percent and 10.5 percent respectively. About 46 percent of women reported no functional limitation compared with over three-quarters of men.

Care for older persons

As the aged population increases, the number of frail or disabled elderly the Republic of Koreans who need assistance in normal daily life will also increase. In South Korea, family members have traditionally provided most physical care for elderly persons. Though the concept of family care is prevalent, the role of the family in providing this care is no longer taken for granted. The changing values of family life, the nuclearization of the family, the decrease in family size, and women's increasing participation in the workforce and social activities have made it more difficult to care for frail elderly persons in the family.

189

Table 10 Health status of older persons by gender

	Female	Male	Total
Self-reported health status			
Very good	2.8	5.6	3.9
Good	15.8	24.1	19.5
Fair	17.8	24.4	20.3
Poor	33.9	24.9	30.5
Very poor	28.7	21.0	25.8
Prevalence of chronic conditions[a]			
Arthritis	53.3	26.6	43.4
Lame back	37.1	15.9	29.2
Disk	5.6	4.9	5.4
Gastric ulcer	18.3	11.7	15.9
Diabetes mellitus	9.2	8.6	9.0
Hypertensive diseases	27.0	17.5	23.5
Angina pectoris	5.3	4.7	5.1
Chronic bronchitis	4.7	9.1	6.3
Asthma	4.5	6.0	10.6
Cataracts	13.4	6.0	10.6
Sequela of bone fracture	4.7	6.6	5.4
Dementia[b]	10.8	2.4	7.6

Notes: More than one condition may be mentioned by respondents.[a]Sunwoo *et al.* (2001).[b]Kyunghee Chung *et al* (1998).

The consequences of these changes are more serious for elderly women than for men, because older men are able to rely on their wives for care as they grow frail. However, older women, after having first cared for an aging parent or parent-in-law or aging husband, are themselves often left without a spouse to provide the care that they need as they age. Table 12 shows the gender asymmetry in care arrangements. Among older persons with activity restrictions, about two-thirds of men received care from family members compared with only 46 percent of women. Women were much more likely than men to receive care from nonfamily members or to receive no care at all. Wives are the main caregivers for the majority of men. On the other hand, few women receive care from their husbands; daughters-in-law or daughters are the main caregivers for the majority of older women who receive care from their families.

Gender differences in sources of income

When asked about how they view their economic situation compared with other people their age, about one-quarter of older women said they were much worse off while only about 16 percent of older men gave the same response. At the other end of the scale, approximately 10 percent of women and 14 percent of men said they were somewhat or much better off than their peers (Kyunghee Chung *et al.* 1998).

Table 11 Dependency levels among older persons by gender (percent)

	Female	Male	Total
No limitations	46.3	75.8	57.5
Limitation only in IADLs	41.2	13.8	30.8
With restrictions in 1–6 ADLs	11.2	9.3	10.5
With restrictions in all ADLs	1.3	1.2	1.3
Total (N)	(3,147)	(1,911)	(5,058)

Source: Sunwoo *et al.* (2001).

Table 12 Caregiving source among people with activity limitations by gender, 2001 (percent)

Caregiving source	Female	Male	Total
By family members	46.3	67.1	50.9
By nonfamily members	25.5	14.9	23.1
No caregiving	28.3	18.0	26.0
Total	100.0	100.0	100.0
N	(1,783)	(504)	(2,287)

Source: Chung *et al.* (2001).

Older people's perceptions of economic status may be related to the sources of income they depend on. In contrast to the older industrialized countries, the elderly in South Korea still rely largely on financial support from their children. Table 13 shows that two-thirds of older people receive financial support from their children (or spouses of their children) who are not residing with them, and nearly one-quarter of older people receive support from children they live with. (Support may be received from either or both sources.) Support from co-resident children is much higher for older women (28 percent) than for older men (16 percent) because older women are more likely to reside with their children.

The next most common source of income in old age is from employment: nearly one-quarter of older women and nearly half of older men rely at least in part on their own earnings from employment. Property rentals also provide income to a small minority of the older population. In 1988 South Korea introduced a public pension system contributed to by working people ages 18–60. The Old-Age Pension for low-income elderly people was instituted in 1991 for people age 70 or over who met low-income and asset limits and other conditions. Given that South Korea's pension systems have been instituted only recently, very few women and men in the current

Table 13 Sources of income of older persons by gender, 1998 (percent)

Sources of Income	Female	Male	Total
Employment	25.2	48.2	33.7
Real estate/rental	11.0	13.6	12.0
Savings	4.3	8.1	5.7
Social pension	1.5	5.1	2.8
Retirement annuities	0.4	1.7	0.9
Private pension	0.3	0.2	0.2
Support from non-coresident children	68.6	62.4	66.3
Support from coresident children	27.5	16.3	23.3
Support from other relatives	1.5	0.7	1.2
Public assistance	9.5	6.8	8.5
Support from organizations	0.7	0.6	0.7

Source: Chung *et al.* (1998).

elderly generation receive income from pension or other retirement sources.

Conclusion

In South Korea, older women have few economic resources, many health problems and functional limitations, and less access to care when they need it. Improving women's status in all stages of the life course will be necessary if their situation in old age is to be improved. Policy measures to guarantee equal access to social welfare and health services and to increase women's participation in the labor force should be an important part of the discussion on how to enhance elderly women's well-being. Strengthening preventive health policies and paying special attention to diseases such as arthritis and osteoporosis, which are more prevalent for women, can lead to better health in old age.

In addition, governments should assume a greater share of the responsibility for protecting and caring for older persons. Governments should share the responsibility of caring for older persons with individual families by strengthening social care services for older persons, such as home-help services, adult daycare centers, and short-term care centers. Older women, who have more difficulties in ADLs and chronic diseases and suffer longer, would especially benefit from the expansion of social care services.

Finally, policy measures are required to relieve the risk of poverty among the elderly, especially women. Strengthening the Old-Age Pension would benefit older women currently. For the economic security of older women in the future, improvement in the opportunity for women's labor force participation, reduction of wage gaps between males and females, and

192

social recognition of unpaid caring work carried out by women could be the ways to reduce their economic insecurity.

Timothy M. Smeeding, Center for Policy Research and Luxembourg Income Study 426 Eggers Hall, Syracuse University, Syracuse, NY 13244-1020, USA e-mail: tmsmeed@maxwell.syr.edu

Susanna Sandström, World Institute for Development Economic Research, Katajanokanlaituri 6 B, 00160 Helsinki, Finland e-mail: sandstrom@wider.unu.edu

Lois B. Shaw, Institute for Women's Policy Research, 403 Russell Ave. #804, Gaithersburg, MD 20877, USA e-mail: lbshaw@his.com

Sunhwa Lee, Institute for Women's Policy Research, 1707 L. Street, NW, Suite 750, Washington, DC 20036, USA e-mail: lee@iwpr.org

Kyunghee Chung, Elderly Welfare Research Team, Korea Institute for Health and Social Affairs, San 42-14 Bulgwangdong Eunpyeonggu, Seoul, Korea 122-705 e-mail: khlc@kihasa.re.kr

ACKNOWLEDGMENTS

The research reported in Timothy Smeeding and Susanna Sandström's "Poverty and Income Maintenance in Old Age: A Cross-National View of Low-Income Older Women" was supported in part by the Center for Retirement Research at Boston pursuant to a grant from the US Social Security Administrator as well as by the LIS member countries. The opinions and conclusions are solely those of the authors and should not be construed as representing the opinions or policy of the Social Security Administration or any agency of the federal government or the Center for Retirement Research at Boston College. Timothy Smeeding and Susanna Sandström thank Nancy Folbre and Gary Burtless for comments on an earlier draft, and Kim Desmond, Mary Santy, and Kati Foley for manuscript preparation. Lois Shaw and Sunhwa Lee thank the Institute for Women's Policy Research and its director, Heidi Hartmann, for support in producing this report. Funding for analysis of the Census data was provided by the Retirement Research Foundation, the Open Society Institute, and the AARP. The conclusions are those of the authors.

NOTES

1 Even if the benefits in principle are divided into the three categories mentioned, it is sometimes very difficult in practice to divide the original variables correctly into the LIS variables. In many cases, different pensions are combined, or they are hard to split correctly due to insufficient information. Additional information was needed, for instance, to separate the effects of the Canadian safety net from the Canadian social retirement program.

2 The Finnish case is a very hard one to classify, because the most important pensions are not only occupational, but are also insured by the Social Insurance System. These schemes are compulsory occupational schemes, providing an earnings-related amount to all workers and self-employed persons, organized by sector and covering almost all Finnish workers and insured by the Finnish Social Security System. These insurances are stronger than the ones made by the Pension Benefit Guarantee Corporation (PBGC) in the United States. But, as they are contributory pensions, they are best classified as occupational pension.

3 Ken Battle provided this data in an e-mail message to the author on April 20, 2001.

4 About 80 percent of unmarried women aged 65 and older are widows, 14 percent are separated or divorced, and 6 percent are never married. The figures for men are 56 percent, 29 percent, and 16 percent, respectively.

5 Outside of the US the term "social security" is commonly used to describe all of a government's income security programs. In the US, Social Security refers to the Old-Age and Survivors Insurance (OASI) program. Long-term disability insurance was later added and is also administered by the Social Security Administration, but it is much smaller, and some people are probably not even aware of their disability insurance unless they or friends have made use of it.

6 Still not included are some state and local government workers covered by other pensions and household workers who earn less than $1,000 per year from any one employer or whose employer (illegally) fails to deduct the required payroll tax.

7 Estimates of the percentage of the employed population offered pensions and the percentage actually participating vary considerably. Much research on pensions covers only employees in the private sector. Self-employed workers can participate through special plans (Keogh) but are usually not included. Government employees are usually covered but seldom studied because participation is required and thus not subject to a choice of whether to participate.

8 Ages in the CPS refer to the person's age on the interview date, while the interview question referred to employment during the past twelve months. Thus, small numbers of individuals in each age group may have stopped working before they attained the lowest age in each group: 50, 62, 65, or 75.

9 The age for full retirement benefits is being raised gradually from age 65 to age 67, with the first incremental increase affecting workers who reached age 62 in 2000.

10 At age 65, everyone covered by Social Security is also covered by Medicare, the government health insurance program for the elderly and long-term disabled.

11 Interest income is the most common source received by nearly all of those receiving any income from assets. Among women, about 58 percent receive interest income, 25 percent receive income from dividends, and 9 percent have rental income. Somewhat higher percentages of men receive income from each of these sources.

12 In order to receive SSI, a person must be age 65 or older or have a disability that prevents work. In addition, he/she may have not more than $2,000 in assets apart from a home ($3,000 for a couple) and small life insurance or burial insurance policies. Full benefits in 2000 were $513 per month for a single person and $769 for a couple and, except for the first $20 per month, the benefits were reduced dollar for dollar on unearned income including Social Security benefits. For example, a person

who had no income except $400 from a Social Security benefit would have received an SSI benefit of $133 per month.

13 The US Census Bureau calculates official "poverty thresholds" each year for families of different sizes and ages, updated from the previous year by the increase in the consumer price index. In 2000, the poverty threshold was $8,259 for a person 65 or older living alone and $10,419 for a two-person household with the householder aged 65 or older.

14 The ADL category includes dressing, washing, bathing, eating, moving, toilet use, and bladder function. The instrumental category includes grooming, housework, food preparing, cleaning, laundry, walking outside, use of public transportation, shopping, financial management, telephone use, and medication use.

REFERENCES

Atkinson, Anthony, Bea Cantillon, Eric Marlier, and Brian Nolan. 2002. *Social Indicators: The EU and Social Inclusion.* Oxford: Oxford University Press.

Battle, Ken. 1997. "A New Old Age Pension," in Kalman Banting and R. Boadway, eds. *Reform of Retirement Income Policy,* School of Policy Studies, pp. 135–89. Kingston, ON, Canada: Queens University.

Björklund, Anders and Richard Freeman. 1997. "Generating Equality and Eliminating Poverty – The Swedish Way," in Richard B. Freeman, Robert Topel and Birgitta Swedenborg, eds. *The Welfare State in Transition: Reforming the Swedish Model.* Chicago: University of Chicago Press.

Bradshaw, Jonathan. 2003. "Using Indicators at the National Level: Child Poverty in the United Kingdom." Unpublished manuscript. Social Policy Research Unit, University of York, UK.

Butrica, Barbara, Karen Smith, and Eric Toder. 2002. "Projecting Poverty Rates in 2020 for the 62 and Older Population: What Changes Can We Expect and Why?" Presented at the 4th Annual Retirement Research Consortium.

Card, David and Richard Freeman, eds. 1993. *Small Differences That Matter: Labor Markets and Income Maintenance in Canada and the United States.* Chicago: University of Chicago Press.

Chung, Kyunghee, AeJeo Cho, YoungHee Oh, and Duk Sunwoo. 2001. *2001 Survey of Care-Giving Status and Welfare Needs of Older Persons in Korea.* Seoul: Korea Institute for Health and Social Affairs.

Chung, Kyunghee, AeJeo Cho, Young Hee Oh, JaeKwan Byun, Youngchan Byun, and HyunSang Moon. 1998. *Living Profiles and Welfare Service Needs of Older Persons in Korea.* Seoul: Korea Institute for Health and Social Affairs.

Citro, Constance F. and Robert T. Michael. 1995. *Measuring Poverty.* Washington, DC: National Academy Press.

Coile, Courtney, Peter Diamond, Jonathan Gruber, and Alain Jousten. 1999. "Delays in Claiming Social Security Benefits." National Bureau of Economic Research Working Paper W7318, Cambridge, MA.

Currie, Janet. 2004. "The Take Up of Social Benefits." National Bureau of Economic Research (NBER) Working Paper 10488, Cambridge, MA.

Daly, Mary C. and Richard V. Burkhauser. 2003. "Left Behind: SSI in the Era of Welfare Reform." Federal Reserve Bank of San Francisco Working Paper 2003-12.

Davies, Paul S. and Melissa M. Favreault. 2004. "Interactions between Social Security Reform and the Supplemental Security Income Program for the Aged." Center for Retirement Research Working Paper 2004-02, Boston College, Chestnut Hill, MA.

Davies, Paul S., Kalman Rupp, and Alexander Strand. 2001. "The Potential of the Supplemental Security Income Program to Reduce Poverty among the Elderly." Social Security Administration, Office of Research, Evaluation, and Statistics, Washington, DC.

Davies, Paul S., Huynh Minh, Chad Newcomb, Paul K. O'Leary, Kalman Rupp, and James Sears. 2000. "Modeling SSI Financial Eligibility and Simulating the Effect of Policy Options." Paper presented at the Annual Meeting of the Southern Economic Association.

Diamond, Peter. 2004. "Social Security." *American Economic Review* 94(1): 1–24.

Economic Planning Board. 1970, 1980. *Population and Housing Census Report.* Seoul: EPB.

Engelhardt, Gary V. and Jonathan Gruber. 2004. "Social Security and the Evolution of Elderly Poverty." Working Paper 10466, Cambridge, MA.

Erikson, Robert and John H. Goldthorpe. 2002. "Intergenerational Inequality: A Sociological Perspective." *Journal of Economic Perspectives* 16(3): 31–44.

Favreault, Melissa M., Frank Sammartino, and C. Eugene Steuerle. 2001. "Social Security Benefits for Spouses and Survivors: Options for Change," in Melissa Favreault, Frank J. Sammartino, and C. Eugene Steuerle, eds. *Social Security and the Family*, pp. 177–227. Washington, DC: Urban Institute Press.

Garfinkel, Irwin, Lee Rainwater, and Timothy M. Smeeding. 2004. "Welfare State Expenditures and the Distribution of Child Opportunities." http://www-cpr .maxwell.syr.edu/faculty/smeeding/selectedpapers.htm (accessed May 31, 2005).

Gruber, Jonathan and David Wise. 2001. "An International Perspective in Policies for an Aging Society." NBER Working Paper 8103, Cambridge, MA.

Harrington Meyer, Madonna, Douglas A. Wolf, and Christine L. Himes. 2005. "Linking Benefits to Marital Status: Race and Social Security in the US." *Feminist Economics*, this issue.

Hartmann, Heidi and Catherine Hill with Lisa Witter. 2000. *Strengthening Social Security for Women.* Washington, DC: Institute for Women's Policy Research and the National Council of Women's Organizations' Task Force on Women and Social Security.

Hetzel, Lisa and Annetta Smith. 2001. *The 65 Years and Over Population: 2000*, Census 2000 Brief, C2KBR/01-10 Washington, DC: US Census Bureau.

Johnson, David S. and Timothy M. Smeeding. 2000. "Who are the Poor Elderly? An Examination Using Alternative Poverty Measures." US Census Working Papers, Washington, DC.

Lee, Sunhwa and Lois Shaw. Forthcoming. *Women and Pension Loss: Tracking Women Workers' Pensions into the Retirement Years.* Washington, DC: Public Policy Institute of AARP.

McGarry, Kathleen. 2000. "Guaranteed Income: SSI and the Well-Being of the Elderly Poor." NBER Working Paper 7574, Cambridge, MA.

Mitchell, Olivia S. and Sylvester J. Schieber. 1998. *Living with Defined Contribution Pensions: Remaking Responsibility for Retirement* Philadelphia: University of Pennsylvania Press.

Munnell, Alicia H. 2004. "Why Are So Many Older Women Poor?" *Just the Facts on Retirement Issues.* Center for Retirement Research at Boston College, Chestnut Hill, MA.

National Statistical Office. 1990, 1995. *Population and Housing Census.* Seoul: NSO.

——. 2001. *2000 Census Report.* Seoul: NSO.

——. 2001. *Population Projection.* Seoul: NSO.

——. 2002. *Life Table* Seoul: NSO.

Olsen, Kelly A. 1999. "Application of Experimental Poverty Measures to the Aged." *Social Security Bulletin* 62(3): 3–19.

Pudney, Stephen, Ruth Hancock, and Holly Sutherland. 2004. "Simulating the Reform of Means-Tested Benefits with Endogenous Take-Up and Claim Costs." Institute for Social and Economic Research (ISER) Working Paper 2004-04, University of Essex, UK.

Purcell, Patrick. 2001. "Pension Sponsorship and Participation: Summary of Recent Trends." Congressional Research Service Report for Congress, Library of Congress, Washington, DC.

Shaw, Lois and Hsiao-Ye Yi. 1997. "How Elderly Women Become Poor: Findings from the New Beneficiary Data System." *Social Security Bulletin* 60(4): 46–50.

Smeeding, Timothy M. 1999. "Social Security Reform: Improving Benefit Adequacy and Economic Security for Women." Center for Policy Research Policy Brief Series 16, The Maxwell School, Syracuse University, New York.

——. 2001a. "Income Maintenance in Old Age: What Can Be Learned from Cross-National Comparisons." Presented at "Making Hard Choices About Retirement," the Third Annual Joint Conference for the Retirement Research Consortium Washington, DC.

——. 2001b. "SSI: Time for a Change?" Working Paper, Center for Policy Research, Maxwell School, Syracuse University, New York.

——. 2003. "Income Maintenance in Old Age: Current Status and Future Prospects for Rich Countries." *Genus* 59(1): 51–83.

——. 2004. "Government Programs and Social Outcomes: The United States in Comparative Perspective." Presented at the Smolensky Conference "Poverty, the Distribution of Income and Public Policy," University of California-Berkeley.

——and James P. Smith. 1998. "The Economic Status of the Elderly on the Eve of Social Security Reform." http://www.ppionline.org/ppi_cl.cfm?knlgAreaID=125&subsecID=165&contentID=1990 (accessed May 31, 2005).

——, Carol L. Estes, and Lou Glasse. 1999. "Social Security Reform and Older Women: Improving the System." http://www-cpr.maxwell.syr.edu/incomsec/pdf/inc22.pdf.

Steuerle, C. Eugene. 2001. "Social Security: The Broader Issues." Urban Institute Working Paper Series, The Urban Institute, Washington, DC.

Sunwoo, Duk, Kyunghee Chung, YoungHee Oh, AeJeo Cho, and JaeEun Seok. 2001. *2001 Survey of Long-Term Care Service Needs of Older Persons in Korea.* Seoul: Korea Institute for Health and Social Affairs.

US Census Bureau. 1999–2001. "March Current Population Survey (CPS)."

——. 2001. "Census 2000 Summary File 1 (Table P38): Group Quarters Population by Sex, by Age Group, by Quarters Type." http://www.census.gov/Press-Release/www/2001/sumfile1.html

US Congress House Committee on Ways and Means. 2004. "2004 Green Book: Background Material and Data on the Programs within the Jurisdiction of the Committee on Ways and Means." WMCP:108–6 (108th Congress, 2nd session). Washington, DC: Government Printing Office, March. http://waysandmeans.house.gov/Documents.asp?section=813.

Weaver, David A. 2001. "The Widow(er)'s Limit Provision of Social Security." ORES Working Paper 92, Social Security Administration, Office of Research, Evaluation, and Statistics, Washington, DC.

Wiener, Joshua M., Catherine M. Sullivan, and Jason Skaggs. 1996. *Spending Down to Medicaid: New Data on the Role of Medicaid in Paying for Nursing Home Care.* Public Policy Institute of AARP, Washington DC.

197

NOTES ON CONTRIBUTORS

Justine Burns is Senior Lecturer in the School of Economics at the University of Cape Town. She has a PhD in Economics from the University of Massachusetts Amherst and teaches courses in microeconomics, computational political economy, and behavioral economics. Her primary research has employed experimental economics to study the impact of racial identity on social exchange. In addition, her work has also investigated the role of family background and neighborhood effects on schooling outcomes.

Kyunghee Chung, PhD is a research fellow of Korea Institute for Health and Social Affairs. She received her BA at Yonsei University of Korea and her MA and PhD from the University of North Carolina at Chapel Hill. She directed 1998 and 2004 Surveys on Living Profile and Welfare Service Needs of the Elderly in Korea. Her publications include *Development of Long-term Care System in Korea* (2005) and *Development of Korean Elderly Welfare Indicators* (2002), as well as other papers in the areas of aging. Her research interests are intergenerational relationships, older women's issues, and long-term care services.

Susan Eaton was Assistant Professor of Public Policy at the John F. Kennedy School of Government at Harvard University. She spent twelve years working for the Service Employees International Union as an international representative, organizer, negotiator, researcher, and eventually a senior manager. Her article "Beyond Unloving Care: Linking Nursing Home Quality and Working Conditions" was a co-winner of the 1996 Margaret Clark award of the Institute of Gerontology. Susan Eaton died in December 2003, and her contribution to this issue of *Feminist Economics* was prepared for publication under the supervision of Nancy Folbre. Please see the tribute at the beginning of this volume.

Marianne A. Ferber is Professor of Economics and Women's Studies Emerita at the University of Illinois, Urbana-Champaign. She was born in Czechoslovakia in 1923, obtained her BA from McMaster University in 1944, and her PhD at the University of Chicago in 1954. She has co-authored or co-edited several books and numerous articles. She was Distinguished Visiting Professor at Radcliffe. In 2002, she received the Carolyn Shaw Bell Award from the Committee on the Status of Women in the Economics Profession, and an honorary doctorate from Eastern Illinois

University. She is past president of the Midwest Economic Association and of IAFFE.

Nancy Folbre is Professor of Economics at the University of Massachusetts Amherst and an Associate Editor of *Feminist Economics*. Her research focuses on nonmarket and care work. Her most recent book, co-edited with Michael Bittman, is entitled *Family Time: The Social Organization of Care* (Routledge, 2004). Her current projects include a book on the economics of childrearing in the US. For more information see her personal website, http://people.umass.edu/folbre/folbre.

Carole A. Green is Associate Professor of Economics at the University of South Florida in Tampa. She earned her PhD from the University of Illinois at Urbana-Champaign after spending ten years working as a computer programmer on mainframe computers. Most of her research has been in the areas of labor economics and discrimination. Her current affiliations include the AEA, MEA, SEA, CSWEP, and IAFFE. She is married and has two grown children. Carole and her husband own a house in the mountains of North Carolina to which they retreat whenever they can get away.

Madonna Harrington Meyer is Director of the Gerontology Center, Professor of Sociology, and Senior Research Associate at the Center for Policy Research at Syracuse University. She is editor of *Care Work: Gender, Labor and the Welfare State* (Routledge 2000), and author, with Pam Herd, of the forthcoming manuscript, *Retrenching Welfare, Entrenching Inequality* (Russell Sage).

Christine L. Himes is Professor of Sociology and Senior Research Associate, Center for Policy Research, at Syracuse University. Her research interests include the impact of increasing obesity on later life, health, and economic security and projections of active life expectancy.

Therese Jefferson is Research Associate in the Women's Economic Policy Analysis Unit (WEPAU) at Curtin University of Technology. She has a BCom from the University of New South Wales and a MEc from La Trobe University. Her MEc thesis examined some implications of the increasing commodification of household production. She is currently researching in the area of women's retirement incomes as part of her PhD candidacy.

Malcolm Keswell is Senior Lecturer in the School of Economics at the University of Cape Town. He has a PhD in Economics from the University of Massachusetts Amherst and teaches graduate econometrics, microeconomis, and computational political economy. His research focuses on education and racial inequality, unemployment and social networks, and more generally the role of education in post-apartheid South Africa.

Kilolo Kijakazi is Program Officer for the Ford Foundation. She has also been a senior policy analyst for the Center on Budget and Policy Priorities; a program analyst for the US Department of Agriculture, Food and Nutrition Service; a policy analyst at the National Urban League; and a research fellow at the George Washington University Institute for Policy Education and Research. Kilolo received a PhD in public policy from George Washington University, and her dissertation was published in 1997 as a book titled *African-American Economic Development and Small Business Ownership*. She also holds an MSW from Howard University.

Sunhwa Lee is Study Director at the Institute for Women's Policy Research in Washington, DC. She conducts research on a variety of older women's economic issues including Social Security preservation and privatization proposals, access to pensions, employment, and poverty issues. Her recent projects examined women's potential loss of pension income over time and poverty dynamics over women's lifecourse, both of which are based on a longitudinal survey of women in the US. She received a PhD in sociology from the University of Chicago.

Murray Leibbrandt is Professor of Economics in the School of Economics and Director of the Southern African Labour Development Research Unit (SALDRU) at the University of Cape Town. He obtained his PhD at the University of Notre Dame and teaches courses in labor economics and the analysis of survey data. His research focuses primarily on labor markets, inequality, and demography, and he was appointed by Nelson Mandela to serve on the Presidential Labour Market Commission, which completed its work in 1996.

Jennifer C. Olmsted is Associate Professor of Economics at Drew University. Having grown up in Beirut, Lebanon, she has a long-standing interest in Arab economies and the intersections between gender, economics, and conflict. She has written about the Palestinian, Egyptian, and US economies, and has also examined the impact orientalist thought has had on the discipline of economics. For over six years she served as the editor of the *Middle East Women's Studies Review*, and she is currently on the board of the Palestinian American Research Council.

Alison Preston is Associate Professor at Curtin University where she teaches economics and industrial relations. She holds a PhD from The University of Western Australia and has published widely on wage determination, pay equity, and labor market structures. Her recent research includes nurse labor markets, career formation, and pension policy. She is co-editor of the *Australian Journal of Labour Economics*, co-Director of the Women's Economic Policy Analysis Unit (WEPAU) at Curtin University, and a government appointee to the Western Australian Women's Advisory Council.

Susanna Sandström is a research associate at the United Nations University – World Institute for Development Economics Research, in Helsinki, Finland. She used to work at the Luxembourg Income Study as a microdata expert.

Lois B. Shaw is Senior Consulting Economist at the Institute for Women's Policy Research in Washington, DC, where she advises on social insurance, pensions, and other issues of concern to women. Previously she was senior economist at the US General Accounting Office. She has written numerous journal articles, monographs, and chapters in books on women's employment, retirement, and poverty.

Timothy Smeeding is Maxwell Professor of Public Policy, Professor of Economics and Public Administration, Director of the Center for Policy Research, and Director of the Luxembourg Income Study.

Agneta Stark has been President of Dalarna University in Sweden since 2004, when she left a position as Guest Professor in Gender and Economic Change at Linkoping University. Her research interests focus on the concept of work and international comparisons of paid and unpaid work. She has lectured in many European countries and is a feminist activist with extensive publications on gender issues in Sweden. She is an Associate Editor of *Feminist Economics*.

Monica Townson is an independent economic consultant working in the field of social policy. She is the author of five books and many studies and reports on pensions and retirement as well as the economic situation of women. She is currently working on a book about changing views of retirement.

Douglas A. Wolf is Gerald B. Cramer Professor of Aging Studies at Syracuse University. His areas of research include the measurement and modeling of disability and active life expectancy among the older population, informal care and its consequences, and migration and the spatial distribution of families.

INDEX

Index notes: Tables and illustrations are denoted by page numbers in italics and bold respectively